P9-DNE-970

GLUTEN-FREE BAKING

More Than 125 Recipes for Delectable Sweet and Savory Baked Goods, Including Cakes, Pies, Quick Breads, Muffins, Cookies, and Other Delights

Rebecca Reilly

Photographs by Romulo Yanes

Simon & Schuster Paperbacks

NEW YORK LONDON TORONTO SYDNEY

SIMON & SCHUSTER PAPERBACKS
Rockefeller Center
1230 Avenue of the Americas
New York, NY 10020

First Simon & Schuster paperback edition 2007

SIMON & SCHUSTER PAPERBACKS and colophon are registered trademarks of Simon & Schuster, Inc.

For information about special discounts for bulk purchases, please contact Simon & Schuster Special Sales:
1-800-456-6798 or business@simonandschuster.com

Designed by Ellen R. Sasahara

Manufactured in the United States of America

10 9 8 7 6 5 4 3 2

The Library of Congress has cataloged the hardcover edition as follows:

Reilly, Rebecca.
Gluten-free baking: more than 125 recipes for delectable sweet and savory baked goods, including cakes, pies, quick breads, muffins, cookies, and other delights / Rebecca Reilly; photographs by Romulo Yanes.
p. cm.
1. Gluten-free diet—Recipes. 2. Baking. I. Title.

RM237.86 .R449 2002
641.5'638—dc21 2001049667

ISBN-13: 978-0-684-87252-0
ISBN-10: 0-684-87252-8
ISBN-13: 978-1-4165-3599-7 (Pbk)
ISBN-10: 1-4165-3599-3 (Pbk)

To my celiac angel Leon Berkowitz

and

To my children, Portia and Reilly

ACKNOWLEDGMENTS

TO MY MOTHER, GRANDMOTHER, AND GRANDFATHER for raising me with an awareness of the relationship between health and food. And especially to my mother for her commitment to learning how to bake gluten-free so that she could make treats for her grandchildren.

To my father and my sister, Penelope, for so graciously and kindly sampling the many baked goods and never scolding me for the extra calories I was asking them to consume. My father also took a red pen to correct my work, looking for consistency, punctuation, and spelling.

To my children, Portia and Reilly, who were the force behind creating recipe after recipe of gluten-free goodies that they would be thrilled to share with their friends. They were willing tasters every time.

To Becky Quinlan, who kept me on schedule, helped format the chapters, and knew my voice. Her love of my food and her faith in this book kept me going when I would get stuck. She is very much a part of this book. I can't imagine how I would have written it without her help and input.

To Ethel Goralnick for her unconditional love and never-ending help and faith. For hounding me until I finally got hooked up to the Internet and e-mail, which facilitated sharing recipes and getting answers to cooking problems. For all her baking expertise, which she has been so generous in passing on to me. For teaching me about kosher foods. For the hours we have shared catering, giggling, developing recipes and menus, and commiserating together.

To Madeleine Kamman for the strong culinary foundation on which I have built my career. Without this I would never have had so much fun or success with my gluten-free baking.

To Bette Hagman, Beth Hillson, and Steve Rice, who were always ready to answer questions about ingredients and sources and many times just to "talk gluten-free" with me.

To my editor, Sydny Miner, who listened and understood from the beginning. I didn't have to sell my idea to her. It was as if she already knew. She gave me lots of space and always had just the right words to say to me. And she made my book happen.

To my agent, Doe Coover, who made me feel special when she "took me on."

To Marianne Sauvion for her expertise in baking and her kindness toward me. Her ability to read a recipe and see any changes that could improve the final product is a gift that I was fortunate she shared.

To many others who have been longtime fans, who have believed in me and, when the "cookie crumbled," were there: Rachel Armstrong, John Bubier, Mimi Clegg, Kerry Courtice, Ramsey Fifield, Judith Friedlaender, Audrey Himelhock, Eileen Kindle, Shirley and David Lake, Jan Nicols, Susan and Bob Nielsen, Robert Morrill, Winter and Michael Robinson, Becki Smith, Leslie Vlachos, and John Yates.

To Judith Friedlaender, Ramsey Fifield, and Becky Quinlan for constantly encouraging me to publish my recipes and for leading me to the people who have made this possible.

To Leon Berkowitz, whose phone call started me on this journey and changed everything for me and my family. I have so enjoyed making gluten-free tiramisu, peach pie, sour cream coffee cake, and biscotti, along with many pasta dishes and paellas, for him over the years. I am so grateful for that phone call he made to me.

To Kris Saunders, Nancy Calson, Elaine Godsoe, Anne Vatakin, Susan LaVerriere, and Molly Brown. As I began my gluten-free baking, they were there to push me to test my talents and patience.

To the members of the celiac support groups in the Portland, Maine, area and those who traveled from far away to attend my cooking classes and "feed" me with their enthusiasm and appetites.

To the many testers who struggled through my beginning attempts and were honest and helpful with their critiquing.

To Carol Field for sharing her experience in the cookbook world and guiding me to Doe Coover.

To Dr. Kathleen Norris for her knowledge about food and healing.

CONTENTS

INTRODUCTION

Ever since I can remember, food has been an important part of my life. It started at the big house in Cooperstown, New York, where my grandparents lived. I was a little girl in love with what seemed like endless joyful family summers. French-born Gran-mère raised flowers around the house, which sat in the middle of the woods. My Pennsylvania Dutch grandfather had cleared space for his gardens, where he raised many types of vegetables and grew fruit trees farther up the hill. We used to eat organic currants, flageolets, carrots, tomatoes, and leeks right from the garden. The taste of wild berries takes me back, even now, to those sunny days when we had picnics and family celebrations centered around the table. Tante Edmée, my godmother, would bring her vegetable *tian,* a Mediterranean-inspired dish of sliced eggplants, garlic, peppers, tomatoes, and olive oil arranged in concentric circles and baked. Gran-mère would create her baked fish with a creamy white sauce that had even the kids asking for seconds. My mother produced wonderful islands of poached meringues created from farm-fresh eggs, floating on top of a rich vanilla egg cream. We celebrated family, food, and life.

During those summers, I learned that it is special to share meals together but even more special to create food for those you love. Gran-mère taught me how to carefully measure the flour for my favorite shortbread cookies. I was barely able to see over the counter, but she'd pull up a chair so that I could roll the dough into round cakes and cut them in the traditional triangle shape and mark them with a fork. She taught me how food should be economical as well as nutritious. As a French World War I bride, she had learned frugality well during the war, when she had to coax sumptuous soups out of vegetable peels.

My mother learned well from Gran-mère. She, too, always had a garden at home. She raised tomatoes, eggplants, string beans, carrots, radishes, lettuce, and fresh herbs (tarragon was my favorite) in neat rows in our backyard next to the swing set. What she did not raise herself, she bought from the nearby farmers' markets every Saturday in town. I remember riding with her in the early morning to get things when they were at their freshest. We bought chickens and Black Angus beef from the Ambrose Clark Farm in Cooperstown, New York; eggs from Mrs. Merrit, a farmer's wife with an ample bosom sporting an apron and a funny hat; and colorful gladiolas from Mr. Fitch in nearby Fly Creek. The best cookies ever came from Cobleskill, New York, and we waited with anticipation for my uncle to arrive with the large oatmeal ones that were our favorite when he visited from his home on Long Island.

We ate with the seasons; a constant variety of fresh vegetables and fruits appeared on our table in the form of delicious compotes, baked apples, ratatouille, white bean and tomato salad, cucumbers and sour cream, and green bean vinaigrette. And every fall Mother would "put by" some of the produce from her garden: her own tomato juice, jams and jellies from the fruit trees, and pickles that put a pucker on our faces all winter long. My sister and I were responsible for peeling pounds of onions for the pickles—weeping all the while. She made her own whole wheat bread every Friday morning, and we ate rice and barley as well as potatoes. From her I learned that a varied diet could be interesting.

Every night when my father came home, we sat around the table, eating and sharing and taking the time to be together. We told lots of jokes and riddles and were encouraged to share the day's events. And manners were stressed. When my parents entertained, it was in that spirit—with guests sitting around the dinner table, not standing around balancing a drink and a plate of hors d'oeuvres. There was always laughter and conversation, but the best part was when my sisters and I would sneak downstairs and enjoy the leftovers still on the sideboard in the kitchen.

From the beginning, good food had a deep meaning for me—it became my passion and my career. My passion led me to Paris, where I studied classic French cuisine at the Cordon Bleu. After graduation, I continued to live in France and enrolled in the leading pastry school, Le Nôtre Pâtissier, which offered master classes for professionals. It was located outside Paris, so I hitched a ride on a 6 A.M. delivery truck every day to go to class. What an experience! Every day I was, literally, up to my elbows in wonderful ingredients—white chocolate, dark chocolate, and genoise batter. As I turned the ingredients into delicious cakes and pastries, I realized the importance of baking with the finest and freshest ingredients possible.

In the early seventies I came back from the Cordon Bleu to visit my family. My plan was to return to pastry school and stay in Paris. During a last-minute shopping spree in Newton Center, a Boston suburb, a sign on a storefront space caught my eye: "Future

Home of Madeleine Kamman's Modern Gourmet Cooking School." Kamman, whose first book was written in 1971, was a noted pioneering chef who took French cooking techniques and applied them to American ingredients in a style that came to be called "nouvelle cuisine." I went onto the construction site and met Madeleine, and at her urging, I returned to Newton when I finished pastry school. My apprenticeship with Kamman was hard work; we put in 12- to 14-hour days. But those two years working as her assistant—and even living in her attic—shaped me. Without that intensive experience, I believe that I would have fumbled as a professional chef. I had earned my chef's diploma, but from Kamman I learned so much more about food—its history and heritage, as well as cooking basics—particularly the chemistry of food.

Kamman was the kind of teacher who motivated students through discipline. We did anything we could not to make a mistake, and while she was not forthcoming with praise, when she did compliment us, it was worth all the effort it took to receive the accolade. I was both surprised and honored to be included in the dedication of her book *The Making of a Cook: The Art, Techniques and Science of Good Cooking,* acknowledging my role as one of her assistants.

Years later I would again return to Europe, but this time to live in Florence, Italy, with my husband and 11-month-old baby. It gave me a chance not only to be a full-time mom but also to live and cook the way Italians do: loose and casual. Each day, like all the other women in Florence, I walked my daughter, Portia, to the market to select from among the fresh produce. Soon I became a familiar fixture, and with Portia as the conversational catalyst, I talked cooking with the *nonnas,* who shared their secrets for simple and delicious northern Italian cuisine. From them I learned the importance of beautiful presentation of wonderful foods.

My restaurant and café in Portland, Maine, gave me yet another opportunity to feed people well. The café was popular, and we employed a number of very creative women in the kitchen, who were encouraged to try new recipes for our guests. We all became close, stirring the memories of my childhood and the bonds that form among people through food and cooking. Years later, as a cooking teacher, I rediscovered that the presentation of food to an appreciative audience was a part of eating well, and I taught my cooking classes to enjoy cooking food as a social experience. And, furthermore, as a media chef, I found that television enabled me to emphasize values that are essential to successful members of the culinary arts.

One day a man came to my catering business looking for gluten-free foods because he was just coming home from the hospital and would be bedridden and unable to cook. Besides having kidney problems, he had celiac disease. I learned from him that people with this disease must eliminate gluten, which is found in most breads and baked goods, from their diet. He was craving a bagel and wanted my help. Although I had no idea how to create baked goods without gluten, the critical element that makes muffins fluffy, cakes tender, and pie dough hold together, I viewed it as a great challenge. It was exactly the opposite of everything I had learned at Le Nôtre Pâtissier and Madeleine Kamman's school. Those early days starting my trip into the gluten-free baking world, I felt the way Alice must have from behind the looking glass. But most good cooks like challenges—at least, I do—and so I made bagels. Some came out better than others, but I learned to improve them by drawing on my classic cooking background, which taught me about food's underlying chemistry and the techniques—the "how to's"—that make it work. All of that knowledge still applied even if the list of ingredients was a little different. Of course, trial and error was a big part of my learning curve as well.

Cooking gluten-free became almost a challenging game. I expanded my repertoire for my special clientele. From bagels, I moved on to muffins, pasta, and cookies and even perfected a flaky pie crust.

At about this time, my son, Reilly, was not doing well. He was wheezy; he was skinny, cranky, and difficult. I was so involved with gluten-free cooking by then that I decided to try it out on him. My child healed. It was a remarkable recovery. That is when I resolved that, for Reilly, eating would be done in a spirit of celebration, not only of food and eating but also of good health. Despite his multiple food allergies, Reilly would know the joy of food that I had learned as a child. He would heal in spirit as well as in body.

After a while, dealing with celiac disease becomes easier. And as I watch my son and daughter thriving each and every day, I know that it is worth it. You don't have to be a victim. You are not your disease. If there are foods that you never again can safely eat, face that and move past it. There are always foods that can be adapted using special ingredients. You can have breads, pasta, muffins, and bagels. You can have fried cream puffs if that is your pleasure. Above all, you can have a joy-filled life with friends gathered around your table. You and your family can be happy and thriving. This book is a guide for your journey.

Eating well is living well.
Feeding well is loving.
Be well!

Rebecca Reilly

WORKING WITH GLUTEN-FREE BAKING INGREDIENTS

AS A CHEF AND COOKING TEACHER, I have applied my culinary sensibilities to the gluten-free kitchen. My aim here is not to write a health book; you are already well acquainted with the nutritional issues relating to gluten. Nor will I revisit the basic recipes of a gluten-free kitchen that have appeared in earlier books, such as the pioneering work by Bette Hagman. Rather, my hope is that, even though you need to eat gluten-free, this book can help you be a part of the everyday events, special occasions, and holidays that are celebrated with food.

It seems that everyone's journey on the gluten-free path evolves. Initially, we avoid gluten products altogether. Then we timidly venture toward replacing the products we miss in our lives with manufactured mixes. We try out a few recipes, and that's where we often get stuck. My goal is to urge you to create gluten-free baked goods that are "beyond the basics." I want to revive your interest in baking, recharge your comfort level in the kitchen, and most of all renew your appreciation of sophisticated flavors and high-quality foods in your diet.

Baking is more precise and scientific than any other kind of cooking—it is a complex interaction of ingredients that makes baked goods rise, keeps them moist, and creates a delicious taste. Do not be intimidated. Practice is the key.

A SHORT SCIENCE LESSON

Take the proteins in flour—gliadins and glutenins—add liquid and a mechanical action (such as stirring or kneading), and you get the elastic property we call gluten in classic baking. The right amount of gluten gives baked goods texture and structure. Too much and the texture can be rubbery or hard. Too little and there won't be enough structure—breads will collapse and cookies will crumble. Heat precipitates the development of the structure of gluten; cold retards it. Acids such as vinegar, buttermilk, or lemon juice will inhibit its development. Even sugar and salt act as inhibitors.

Because gluten-free flours do not have the capacity to develop the elasticity needed to create structure, the baker needs to add other ingredients, such as egg, pectin powder, grated apple, banana, xanthan gum, guar gum, and gelatin, to do the job. The addition of tapioca starch and sweet rice flour helps to give structure, as does the use of warm liquids. The techniques used in classic baking also give air and lightness to baked goods.

IN SEARCH OF THE HOLY GRAIL: THE MIX

Throughout this book, many recipes call for a brown rice flour mix. I developed this mixture to replace white rice flour and to add more fiber and nutrition to baked goods. The mixture has a deep, rich flavor that enhances the taste of most recipes. Rather than mix it up each time I want to bake, I make a large quantity at a time and keep it in a canister—so I can dip into my brown rice flour mix just as I would dip into a bag of flour. If you choose, you can replace the brown rice flour mix with Bette Hagman's gluten-free mix for most recipes.

BASIC GLUTEN-FREE MIX *Makes about 3 cups*

Mix 2 cups brown rice flour or chickpea flour, ⅔ cup potato starch, and ⅓ cup tapioca starch. Or mix 1 cup chickpea or Garfava flour, 1 cup brown rice flour, ⅔ cup potato starch, and ⅓ cup tapioca starch. Store in an airtight container in the refrigerator.

You can substitute any of the following for each cup of all-purpose wheat flour:

- 1 cup Basic Gluten-Free Mix or Bette Hagman's Gluten-Free flour mix
- ⅞ cup rice flour
- 9 tablespoons potato starch
- 1 cup corn flour
- 1 scant cup cornmeal
- ¾ cup cornstarch
- 1 cup minus 1 tablespoon chickpea flour or Garfava flour
- ½ cup each soy flour and potato starch
- ½ cup nut flour (see technique, page 30)
- 1 cup tapioca starch

ABOUT THE FLOURS

Welcome to the wacky world of flours! Before I started baking gluten-free, I admit that I was pretty much a wheat flour/white flour kind of baker. Okay, every once in a while I experimented with rye but then went back to the safety of what I knew. When I began gluten-free baking, however, I was in free fall. But I have very much enjoyed experimenting with and varying the flours—and therefore the taste—in recipes.

Arrowroot is a flour that thickens sauces that do not require high heat. Like cornstarch, it gives a glossy finish to the sauce.

Bean Flour is another name for chickpea flour or Garfava flour.

Brown Rice Flour has the same properties as rice flour but improves the nutritional value of baked goods. Keep it refrigerated.

Chickpea Flour is made from ground chickpeas (garbanzo beans). It is very high in protein and has a distinct nutty, slightly bitter flavor. Combine it with other flours. To mask its flavor, use chickpea flour in recipes calling for fruit purees, chocolate, or spices.

Corn flour is flour milled from corn. Use it for muffins, breads, cakes, and pancakes.

Cornmeal is ground corn. Use it for muffins, breads, and cakes.

Cornstarch is derived from corn and used in combination with other flours. When used as a thickener, it gives a clear finish to a sauce. Arrowroot can be substituted in equal amounts if you are allergic to corn.

Garfava is a bean flour developed by Authentic Foods. A combination of garbanzo (chickpea) and fava beans, it is much milder than chickpea flour and can be used in recipes for cookies, breads, and cakes. Bean flours have a great texture, but many people are put off by some of the side effects of the beans, which may cause gastrointestinal distress.

Potato Flour is much heavier than potato starch and has a distinct potato flavor. I suggest that you reserve its use to bread making and recipes that may call for mashed potatoes.

Potato Starch must be used in combination with other flours. It tends to lump easily, so blend well. You will find it readily available during Passover in the spring, but it can also be purchased at natural food stores and supermarkets and by mail order.

Quinoa Flour, though high in protein, has a somewhat bitter taste. When blended with other flours, it is excellent for pancakes, breads, cookies, cakes, and biscuits.

Rice Flour is the most common flour used in gluten-free baking. Combine it with other flours by using two-thirds of the total flour called for in the recipe. Rice flour can be purchased at natural food stores, supermarkets, and Asian markets or by mail order. The best rice flours are found in Asian markets or grocery stores. Rice flours are not all alike, and some require more liquid, but as always in gluten-free baking, add the liquid slowly.

Soy Flour is a yellowish tan flour that boosts nutritional value. Be certain to refrigerate it to keep it from getting rancid.

Sweet Rice Flour has a sticky quality that is useful in gluten-free baking. Working in combination with other flours, it keeps baked goods moist. It can be purchased at natural food stores, supermarkets, and Asian markets and by mail order.

Tapioca Starch, also known as cassava or manioc, is great combined with other flours for baking. It can be purchased at natural food stores, supermarkets, and Asian markets and by mail order.

Xanthan Gum, derived from the bacteria in corn sugar, is used in gluten-free baking to replace the gluten found in wheat. It makes up for the structure lost by omitting gluten. Without it, baked goods tend to lack texture and structure and will crumble. Add ¼ teaspoon per cup of flour for cakes and ¼ to ½ teaspoon per cup of flour for cookies, quick breads, and muffins. For baked goods that require kneading, add 1 to 2 teaspoons of the xanthan gum per cup of flour. **Guar gum,** a plant derivative, can be used to replace xanthan gum.

ABOUT OTHER INGREDIENTS

Egg Replacer is a white powder consisting of a blend of starches and a little leavening agent. It is used along with an egg to enhance the finished product or as a replacement for eggs. It can be found in the baking aisle in natural food stores. Ener-G Foods makes it.

Cinnamon Sugar adds taste and sparkle as a topping on quick breads and muffins. To make it, combine 1 cup white sugar with 1 to 2 teaspoons ground cinnamon.

Brown Sugar is white sugar with molasses. Keep it stored in an airtight container. If it gets hard, add a piece of gluten-free bread or an apple to the bag to soften it up. The microwave will also soften it. Always firmly pack brown sugar when measuring. Use it when you want soft cookies.

Table Salt should be used in baking. It has a finer texture and mixes better into the dry ingredients than kosher or sea salt. Use less of it than coarse salt. Remember, many table salts contain dextrose, which is a sugar.

Kosher Salt is used for flavoring foods and is too coarse for baking.

Sea Salt is too coarse for baking.

White Pepper is milder than black pepper. Freshly ground peppercorns taste much better than already ground pepper.

Nuts and Dried Fruits should be rolled in a little of the flour mixture before they are added to any batter. This helps keep them separated and suspended in the batter. Freeze nuts to prevent them from getting rancid.

Herbs and Spices can be purchased whole or ground. Herbs are the leaves and stems of plants, while spices are the dried seeds, stems, roots, and berries. Buy small amounts of herbs and spices and store them in an airtight container in a cool, dry place away from sunlight. Do not keep them more than six months. Try drying your own herbs by hanging fresh leaves in a cool, dry place. You can also use a dehydrator or the microwave. Use 1 tablespoon of chopped fresh herbs for 1 teaspoon of dried. Grind whole spices in your coffee grinder for a fresh taste.

Keep the following three blends on hand at all times.

CURRY POWDER *Makes about ½ cup*

Do not make a big batch, or the flavors will fade or become acrid.

3 tablespoons coriander seeds
2 teaspoons fenugreek seeds
2 teaspoons cumin seeds
2 teaspoons black mustard seeds
1 teaspoon cardamom seeds
2 inches cinnamon stick
1 tablespoon turmeric
¼ teaspoon ground mace
¼ teaspoon freshly grated nutmeg
⅛ teaspoon ground cloves
Pinch of cayenne, or more to taste

Preheat the oven to 225°F. On a small jelly roll pan, toss together the coriander, fenugreek, cumin, mustard, and cardamom seeds and the cinnamon. Bake for 15 minutes, shaking the pan several times. Cool.

Put the toasted seeds and cinnamon stick into a spice mill along with the remaining spices. Grind to a powder. Store in an airtight container.

QUATRE EPICES *Makes about ⅓ cup*

2 tablespoons ground ginger
2 tablespoons freshly grated nutmeg
1½ tablespoons each freshly ground white and black pepper
2 teaspoons ground cloves

Blend the spices together. Store in an airtight container.

HERBS OF PROVENCE BLEND *Makes about 1 cup*

¼ cup each dried thyme, marjoram, and tarragon
3 tablespoons dried chervil or ¼ cup dried parsley
3 bay leaves
1 heaping tablespoon dried oregano
1 tablespoon each dried rosemary and mint

Mix all the herbs together. Store in an airtight container.

SUBSTITUTIONS

- Potato starch and cornstarch can be exchanged one for one.
- 1 cup minus 1 tablespoon tapioca starch can replace 1 cup sweet rice flour.
- Instead of 1 teaspoon baking powder, use ½ teaspoon cream of tartar plus ¼ teaspoon baking soda.
- Instead of 1 cup sugar, use 1 cup packed brown sugar.
- Instead of 1 cup sour cream, use 1 cup yogurt.
- Instead of 1 cup buttermilk, use 1 tablespoon lemon juice plus 1 cup whole milk and let sit 5 minutes, or use 1 cup yogurt.
- Instead of 1 ounce semisweet chocolate, use 1 square (1 ounce) unsweetened chocolate plus 1 tablespoon sugar.
- Instead of 1 ounce unsweetened chocolate, mix 3 tablespoons unsweetened cocoa powder with 1 tablespoon oil.
- Oil can be substituted for melted unsalted butter.

STOCKING THE GLUTEN-FREE KITCHEN

WHILE I DON'T WANT TO SOUND like your middle school home ec teacher, I must urge you to think about planning and organizing your kitchen, paying particular attention to avoiding cross-contamination. If you continue to use standard flours, try to isolate them. Use wipes or paper towels, not sponges, to clean up after you use gluten flour—and wash your hands often and dry them on a clean paper towel. Wash cutting boards, knives, and other utensils with hot soapy water or run them through the dishwasher. Use 1 tablespoon of bleach per gallon of water to sterilize cutting boards and work surfaces. Change your apron frequently.

Many people who live gluten-free keep everything separate to make cooking easier. They label everything. They maintain gluten-free cupboards. They purchase separate bowls and measuring utensils and color-code them.

Raw eggs may contain a harmful bacteria that should be killed by cooking eggs thoroughly. Use a thermometer for the safest way to check, but make certain that egg yolks and egg whites are fresh. If a recipe calls for raw egg yolks or egg whites and you are not confident that your eggs are of the freshest quality, temper them (see technique, page 31) or use powdered egg whites. Once you crack open an egg, you can determine how old it is by examining the size of the air pocket between the thin white skin and the shell at the large end of the egg. The larger the air pocket, the older the egg.

Refrigerate leftovers immediately, once they have cooled. Don't leave food out for more than 1 to 2 hours. If food is still hot, cool it quickly over ice—never put hot food directly into the refrigerator. Your refrigerator should remain between 33° and 40°F. Date all leftovers, and if there is any doubt about whether the food is safe to eat, throw it away. Keep foods in tightly sealed containers so they do not pick up the odors of other foods.

Do not overload your freezer, and keep the temperature at 0°F. Use heavy-duty wrap when freezing foods. Defrost foods in the refrigerator—bacteria can develop rapidly in food thawed at room temperature. Once a food has been thawed, prepare it as soon as possible.

THE KEY TO GLUTEN-FREE BAKING

When it comes to gluten-free baking, do as the Boy Scouts do: "Be prepared." A well-stocked pantry and a collection of high-quality equipment make the job much easier and more enjoyable.

DRY GOODS PANTRY

Arrowroot
Baking powder: gluten-free
Baking soda
Canned goods: beans, fruits, gluten-free broths
Chocolate: milk, semisweet, unsweetened, and white
Cocoa powder: unsweetened
Coconut: shredded
Coffee: instant, gluten-free
Condensed milk
Cooking spray: gluten-free
Cornflakes: gluten-free
Corn flour
Cornmeal
Cornstarch
Corn syrup: light Karo
Crisp rice cereal: gluten-free
Egg Replacer
Egg whites: powdered
Evaporated milk
Flax meal
Garfava or chickpea flour
Garlic
Gelatin powder
Herbs and spices
Honey
Jams and marmalades
Maple syrup
Molasses
Nuts: unsalted
Oils: canola, olive, corn, safflower
Oils: assorted nut/seed—almond, walnut, pistachio, grape seed, pumpkin, dark sesame (purchase in small amounts and keep refrigerated)
Pasta: gluten-free
Peanut butter or almond butter
Potato starch
Rice flour: brown, white, and sweet
Salt: kosher or sea salt and table salt
Soy flour
Soy sauce: wheat-free
Sugar: granulated, brown, and confectioners'
Tahini
Tapioca: instant
Tapioca starch
Vanilla and other gluten-free extracts
Vanilla pudding: Jell-O instant
Vinegars: cider, red wine, and balsamic
Xanthan gum

HIDDEN GLUTEN: READ THE LABELS

Watch out for: hydrolyzed vegetable or plant proteins; textured vegetable protein; extracts and flavorings; processed meats and fish; modified food starches; pastas; barley malt; and distilled vinegar. These foods probably contain gluten.

PERISHABLE GOODS PANTRY

Cheeses: assorted gluten-free
Cream: light and heavy
Eggs: large
Flax meal (refrigerate after opening)
Fruits and vegetables: assorted fresh
Ginger root
Lemon juice: frozen
Lemons
Milk: cow's, rice, almond, or soy
Onions: do not store in refrigerator or with potatoes
Parsley: fresh
Potatoes: do not store in refrigerator or with onions
Ricotta cheese: gluten-free
Sour cream: gluten-free
Tofu
Yeast
Yogurt: gluten-free

SMALL APPLIANCES

Blender
Coffee grinder for making nut flours
Food processor
Heavy-duty stand mixer with extra bowls
Microwave oven

MEASURING TOOLS

Dry measuring cups
Glass or clear plastic liquid measuring cups: 1-, 2-, and 4-cup
Measuring spoons

KNIVES

Chopping knife: 8- or 9-inch chef's
Paring knives (2)
Serrated bread knife
Slicing knife
Steel to sharpen knives

USEFUL UTENSILS

Biscuit cutters (2 or 3): 4-inch, plain and fluted
Cake spatulas: long-handled
Candy thermometer
Cheese grater
Cherry pitter
Cookie cutters
Dough scraper
Ice cream scoops
Meat thermometer: instant-read
Melon baller
Mortar and pestle for grinding spices (optional)

Pastry bags: various sizes
Pastry brushes: natural bristle
Pastry nozzles: 5-point star or fluted, basket-weave, petal, leaf, plain
Ravioli cutter
Spatulas: 6- and 9-inch flat plastic, 4- and 7-inch metal
Strawberry huller
Thermometers: oven, refrigerator, and freezer
Timer
Vegetable peeler
Whisks: assorted
Zester

BAKING PANS

Bundt pan or ring mold: 10-cup
Cake pans: 8- or 9-inch round (2), 8-inch square, and 13 × 9-inch rectangular
Cardboard cake rounds of varying sizes
Cookie sheets (2 to 4): heavy nonstick
Cooling racks
Jelly roll pan: heavy aluminum 11 × 17 inches, 11 × 7 inches, or 12 × 18 inches
Loaf pans: nonstick 8½ × 3½ × 2½ inches, 9 × 5 × 3 inches, and mini
Muffin pans: assorted nonstick
Pie or quiche pan: ovenproof 8- or 9-inch ceramic or glass
Springform pans: 8-, 9-, and 10-inch, 3 inches deep
Tart pans with removable bottom: round, rectangular, square (large and small)

COOKING POTS AND PANS

Crêpe pan
Double boiler
Saucepans
Skillets, nonstick
Tin- or stainless-lined copper, or stainless aluminum-core pots and pans

MISCELLANEOUS

Chopping boards: plastic and wooden
Confectioners' sugar sifter
Flour sifter
Liners and baking mats, such as Cook/eze or Silpat
Mixing bowls, assorted
Oven mitts and pot holders
Parchment paper
Rolling pin: large ball-bearing
Squeeze bottle (plastic) for chocolate sauce and fruit purees
Strainers: fine and coarse, metal or nylon
Tea towels
Zip-locking bags

EQUIVALENT MEASUREMENTS

1 pound flour	4 cups flour
1 pound confectioners' sugar	3½ cups
1 pound granulated sugar	2 cups
1 pound brown sugar	2¼ packed cups
12 ounces chocolate chips	2 cups chips
1 ounce chocolate	1 square chocolate
1 pound shelled walnuts	4 cups chopped walnuts
4 ounces butter	1 stick or ½ cup butter
1 tablespoon	3 teaspoons
⅛ cup	2 tablespoons
¼ cup	4 tablespoons
⅓ cup	5⅓ tablespoons
½ cup	8 tablespoons
¾ cup	12 tablespoons
1 pint	2 cups
1 quart	4 cups or 2 pints
½ gallon	2 quarts
1 gallon	4 quarts

PAN VOLUMES

PAN SIZE	VOLUME
2½ × 1¼-inch muffin cup	¼ cup
8½ × 4½ × 2½-inch loaf pan	5–6 cups
9 × 5 × 3-inch loaf pan	8 cups
8 × 8 × 1½-inch square pan	5 cups
9 × 9 × 1½-inch square pan	6 cups
9 × 1-inch pie pan	4 cups
11 × 7 × 2-inch rectangular pan	6 cups
13 × 9 × 2-inch rectangular pan	8 cups
15½ × 10½ × 1-inch jelly roll pan	8 cups
8 × 2-inch round cake pan	4½ cups
10 × 2-inch round cake pan	6½ cups
8 × 8 × 2-inch square pan	5 cups
10 × 10 × 2-inch square pan	8 cups

GLUTEN-FREE BAKING: TIPS AND TECHNIQUES

THROUGHOUT THIS COOKBOOK, a number of baking techniques are used. Rather than describe the method each time, I have collected them here for easy reference. If you are an experienced baker, most of these terms will be familiar to you, but you might want to review them quickly to note any differences in techniques used in gluten-free baking. If you are not an experienced baker, I recommend trying out the techniques; don't be intimidated. It is worth the effort to learn new techniques.

Before you begin baking, read the recipe directions thoroughly and measure all your ingredients.

Beating Egg Whites: Bring eggs to room temperature first to get greater volume when beating egg whites. The addition of an acid, such as cream of tartar, vinegar, or lemon juice, helps develop a more stable foam and will whiten somewhat yellow whites. If you are using a copper bowl, however, no acid is needed. The bowl, the whisk, and the egg whites must not contain any fat. A balloon whisk is best if you are beating by hand. Overbeating egg whites will make folding them into a batter difficult, resulting in loss of volume in gluten-free baked goods. Use beaten egg whites immediately.

Blanching: Briefly boiling in water helps to remove the skins from nuts, fruits, and tomatoes. To remove the skins from almonds, place the nuts in a pot and cover with water. Cover and bring to a boil. Drain immediately. Rub the nuts together in a towel to loosen the skins. Then, one by one, remove the skins. Blanched almonds can also be purchased. To remove the skins from tomatoes, peaches, or apricots, cut a small × in the bottom of the fruit or tomato. Plunge into boiling water. As soon as the skin around the × begins to pull away, remove. Cool until easy to handle, then peel.

Blending Dry Ingredients: Because gluten-free flours are very light, it is important to measure and whisk the flours and other dry ingredients together before mixing in the liquid ingredients. Add all liquids on *slow* speed. The moisture in the air will make a difference in how much liquid is needed.

Blind Baking: A method of prebaking a pastry shell. It is either partially baked or completely baked before filling to help prevent a soggy bottom crust.

Caramelizing: Heating sugar in a pan with some water and an acid such as lemon juice until it is syrupy and deep golden brown. This can also be done under the broiler.

Chiffonade: A julienne of leafy vegetables or herbs. To cut into chiffonade, bunch up the leaves and shred them into very thin strips with your chef's knife.

Clarified Butter: Pure butterfat with all the solids and water removed; known as *ghee* in India. To clarify butter, slowly melt butter in a pan over low heat; do not boil. Once melted, let it stand for 20 minutes. Spoon off the layer of foam on the top (known as casein), and then spoon off the butterfat and place it into a clean bowl. At the bottom will be a milky liquid, which is the whey; discard. The casein can be used to cook vegetables. Store clarified butter either at room temperature or in a very tightly sealed container in the refrigerator.

Creaming: "Creaming the butter" means that room-temperature butter is whipped until almost white. This technique introduces air into the butter; then any sugar is added and the creaming continues. The whey in the butter dissolves the sugar. Creaming is important in gluten-free cakes, cookies, and quick breads to add air and lightness to the baked goods. Be sure not to melt the butter before creaming.

Curdle: To coagulate or separate into liquids and solids. Milk and egg mixtures tend to curdle if overheated or heated too quickly. Or if fresh chives or raw onions are present in a milk or egg mixture, curdling can happen. Cook the onions or dust fresh chives with cornstarch to eliminate the problem. Tomatoes and lemon juice can also cause curdling.

Doneness: Always check baked goods for doneness before taking them out of the oven. I recommend using a cake tester, a thin metal skewer, or a small paring knife. Insert the tester into almost the center of the baked good, but not all the way to the bottom. Let it stay there for the count of 3. Pull it out and quickly touch your wrist. It should be hot to the touch and clean. Be certain to check before the allotted time, as overdone baked goods tend to be dry.

Egg Wash: Also known as a *dorure,* an egg wash gives a golden brown glaze to pastries. Mix 1 egg yolk with 2 to 3 tablespoons milk or cream and brush on pie crusts and other rich pastries. For a firm glaze, brush on an egg white.

Filling a Pastry Bag: Slip the nozzle into the bag. Twist the bag just where the nozzle is, to "lock" it. Hold the bag in the hand that you do not write with. Fold the cuff back to form a "cup." With your writing hand, take a spoon or spatula and fill the bag, but not all the way full. Close the top of the bag. Hold the top of the bag in your writing hand. You will be squeezing from the top. The fingers on your opposite hand will do the guiding, lightly holding the nozzle, guiding its movement. If you do not have a pastry bag, a heavy-duty zip-locking bag will do the trick.

Folding: A way to incorporate a foam, such as beaten egg whites or whipped cream, into a batter while losing the least amount of air. A large rubber spatula is the best tool for the job, but you might want to try a spoon/spatula combination called a "spunala" for folding. The heaviest ingredient should be on the bottom. The foam should be on top and folded into the heavy base. Cut down through the center of the foam and batter with your spatula. Come up the side of the bowl closest to you, up to the top, twisting your wrist without twirling the spatula as you bring the batter up and over the foam. Turn the bowl a quarter turn and repeat the procedure. Continue until the mixture is homogenous. As you get more practice and become more comfortable, this will go quickly, and your cakes, mousses, and souffles will have greater volume—important in gluten-free baking. Overfolding will deflate the air that has been creamed, ribboned, or whipped into the ingredients.

Freezing: Gluten-free baked goods freeze well. Since they tend to stale and spoil quickly, either eat while fresh or freeze in small amounts. Wrap in plastic wrap or zip-locking bags and then either put in a freezer bag or wrap well with freezer paper. Always label and date the item. A microwave easily thaws and refreshes frozen baked goods.

Frosting a Layer Cake: Place one of the cake layers, flat side up, on a cardboard round the same size as the cake. (You can purchase these rounds at party stores. It is also helpful to have a cake decorating stand.) Put 1 cup of the filling on this layer. Using an icing spatula, spread the filling to the edges. If the filling is chocolate or a pudding, pipe some frosting around the edge of the cake. This will keep the filling from seeping out. Now place the second cake layer, flat side up, on top of the filling. Make sure that the cake layers are aligned. It is important to take the next step, called the crumb coat. Spread a thin layer of frosting on the sides and top of the cake. Wait 5 to 10 minutes before continuing. This step will adhere the crumbs, allowing you to frost the cake more easily and neatly. If you are using French buttercream, refrigerate for the allotted time. A flexible thin spatula will make this job much easier. Hold the spatula perpendicular to the cake and frost the sides. Put frosting on the top and smooth the frosting evenly over it. Practice makes perfect. You can press lightly toasted chopped nuts on the sides to hide any flaws. Run a pastry comb over the top of the cake to add a professional look.

Greasing Baking Pans: Lightly spray with a gluten-free baking spray or butter, then either line the pans with a piece of parchment paper or dust with rice flour.

Grinding Nuts: Use a food processor with the metal S blade. Pulse until you get the desired texture. If the recipe calls for finely ground nuts, add a few tablespoons of the sugar called for in the recipe. It is very easy to end up with nut butter, but the sugar will help prevent this happening.

High-Altitude Cake Baking (higher than 3,000 feet):

For high-fat cakes, reduce the butter by 1 to 2 tablespoons.

For every 1 cup liquid, increase by 1 to 4 tablespoons.

For every 1 cup of sugar, reduce by 1 to 3 tablespoons.

For every 1 teaspoon baking powder, reduce by ⅛ to ¼ teaspoon.

Jelly Roll: Bake a sponge cake in a jelly roll pan (a rectangular cookie sheet with raised sides). Invert the cake onto a clean towel sprinkled with confectioners' sugar (or cocoa for chocolate cakes). Trim the edges of the cake. Loosely roll the cake up in the towel and cool. Once the cake is cooled, unroll very gently and fill. Reroll. Dust with confectioners' sugar or pipe or spread an icing over the cake.

Marbling: When a recipe requires the batter to be marbled, pour the main batter into the prepared dish or pan. Drizzle with the second, contrasting batter. Using a table knife, swirl the two together.

Measuring Dry Ingredients: Use dry measuring cups. Fill the cups and level off with a knife or spatula.

Measuring Liquid Ingredients: Use a glass or clear plastic liquid measuring cup.

Melting Chocolate: Because chocolate is a starch, it must be buffered with hot water to ensure that the starches do not scorch during melting. Always use a double boiler, or place the chocolate in a bowl and then put it over hot water. If you are using a microwave to melt chocolate, do it in increments of seconds. Chop the chocolate first to speed up the melting. If melted butter is called for in the recipe, melt it with the chocolate. Never let water mix with chocolate to be melted. It will seize (become hard) and cannot be rescued.

Nut Flours: Use nut flours to enhance the flavor and texture of baked goods. They can be purchased at specialty shops or by mail order, but you can make your own easily at home. A coffee grinder produces the best results, but a food processor can be used. You may need to add a little sugar to keep from making a nut butter.

Parchment Paper: A must for gluten-free baking—your new best friend. It saves cleanup time, prevents sticking, and eliminates the need to grease and flour pans. Parchment paper can be purchased at cookware shops, through mail order, and in bulk at wholesale paper suppliers.

Preheating: It takes about 15 minutes to properly preheat an oven. Baked goods need to go into a hot oven. Use an oven thermometer to check the oven temperature and then adjust accordingly if necessary. If the oven temperature is off by 50 degrees, call a service person to recalibrate.

Ribboning: When a recipe says "beat the egg yolks and sugar until lemon colored and thick," that is incorrect. It should say "beat the egg yolks and sugar until thick and pale and they form a ribbon." Ribboning is very important in baking. By whisking the egg yolks and sugar together, you are combining the capacity of the fat in the yolks to trap air with the capacity of the sugar to attract the moisture in the yolks. The moisture will make a heavy syrup with the sugar, which will help trap more air. As the beating goes on, the mixture will get heavier and stickier and increase in volume. Some recipes call for a very heavy ribbon, one that will actually fall from the whisk in a flat stream, forming ribbons that fold onto themselves. Others may call for a thin ribbon. Ribboning adds air to the batter, which acts as a leavening agent and also evenly disperses the egg yolk through the batter.

Room Temperature: Between 68° and 77°F. Many recipes call for room-temperature eggs or butter. Remove the items from the refrigerator and allow them to come to room temperature.

Scalding: Heating to just below boiling, about 185°F. Usually used when referring to cooking milk or cream.

Sifting: Use a mesh strainer to remove any lumps or undesirable particles from dry ingredients.

Skinning Hazelnuts: Preheat the oven to 350°F. Place the hazelnuts on a cookie sheet and bake in the oven for 10 minutes. The skins will crack. While the nuts are still warm, rub them with a tea towel to remove the skins.

Slicing a Cake into Layers: Place the cake on a cardboard circle. To make this easier have the cake on a cake stand or lazy Susan. Using a sharp serrated knife, make a small notch down the side of the cake. Decide how many layers you can slice. Start at the top of the cake. Hold the knife parallel to the counter. Begin slicing and turning the cake. As you turn the cake, move the knife through the cake. Make sure to keep the knife parallel. Lift the cut layer off and place it cut side down on the counter or on a piece of waxed paper or parchment paper. If you're making more than 2 slices, continue this process. When you begin filling the cake, make sure you line up the notches as you place the slices on top of the filling.

Sugar Syrups: Sugar and water cooked together. To prevent crystallization, a little acid, corn syrup, fat, or egg white is added to specific recipes. There are several stages sugar syrups go through. Use a candy thermometer or have a glass of cold water handy to drizzle the syrup into:

- Thread stage—2-inch threads; used for syrups; 230°–234°F (110°–112°C)
- Soft ball stage—ball that flattens; used for fudge, pralines, and fondant; 234°–240°F (112°–115°C)
- Firm ball stage—ball that holds its shape; used for caramels; 244°–248°F (118°–120°C)
- Hard ball stage—firm and hard ball; used for nougat or divinity; 250°–266°F (121°–130°C)
- Soft crack stage—hard and pliable threads; used for taffy; 270°–290°F (132°–143°C)
- Hard crack stage—hard and brittle threads; used for lollipops and brittles; 300°–310°F (149°–154°C)
- Caramel stage—syrups that are golden or brown; used for pots de crème, flans, caramel stages; 320°–350°F (160°–177°C)

Tempering Egg Yolks: It is unwise to use raw eggs because of the danger of salmonella, so when a recipe calls for raw eggs, they should be tempered, which is quite easy to do in a microwave oven. The following directions for tempering eggs are adapted from Jimmy Schmidt's book, *Jimmy Schmidt's Cooking Class.* Jimmy is a talented chef, restaurateur, and columnist/author who attended Madeleine Kamman's Modern Gourmet Cooking School in Boston with me.

1. Have a number of clean forks or whisks available to prevent cross-contamination. Put the egg yolks in a microwave-safe bowl. Whisk until smooth and then add 1

tablespoon lemon juice, 3 tablespoons water, and a pinch of salt. Cover with plastic wrap and microwave on full power (high) for 45 seconds or until the mixture begins to rise. Remove from the microwave.

2. Using a different clean whisk or fork, whisk the mixture again, cover with wrap, and return to the microwave. Cook 8 to 10 seconds longer and remove from the microwave.
3. Beat with another clean whisk or fork until smooth. Cover again and return to the microwave for 10 seconds or until the mixture begins to rise.
4. With yet another clean whisk or fork, whisk again, cover with wrap, and return to the microwave for 8 to 10 seconds. Remove from the microwave and beat again. The yolks are now tempered and safe to use.
5. Check the yolks with a thermometer to ensure that they have reached a temperature of 180°F. If they have not, repeat the steps above until they reach the desired temperature, making sure to use a clean whisk or fork each time. When the temperature is reached, set aside for 1 minute. The tempered eggs will be thick—the texture is that of hollandaise sauce.

Toasting Nuts: Preheat the oven to 350°F. Place the nuts on a cookie sheet. Bake for 5 to 8 minutes. Toasting enhances the flavor of the nuts. Be careful not to overtoast. To toast in a microwave oven, place the nuts in a 2-cup liquid measuring cup. Cook, uncovered, on full power (high) for about 2 minutes; stir, cook another 30 seconds, and stir again. Do this until the nuts are golden brown: 2 to 3 minutes for ½ cup pecans, 2 to 3 minutes for 1 cup almonds, 3 to 4 minutes for 1 cup pecans, 3 to 4 minutes for ½ cup raw peanuts or walnuts. Cool on paper towels.

Whipping Cream: Heavy cream will stiffen the way egg whites do. Whipping incorporates air and causes the butterfats to cling to each other around the air. Make sure that everything is cold to hasten the thickening. One cup of cream will double in volume. On a hot day, place the bowl of cream in ice.

Whisking: Beat with a whisk or fork to aerate dry ingredients or to lightly mix liquids together. Whisking is particularly important in gluten-free baking to put "lift" into baked goods.

Zest/Grated Rind: The colored outer rind, or zest, of citrus fruits is filled with flavorful oils. When grating, do not grate into the white pith, which is bitter.

SUPPLIERS

EQUIPMENT AND COOKWARE

Chef's Catalog Co.
3215 Commercial Avenue
Northbrook, IL 60062-1920
Phone: 800-338-3232
www.chefscatalog.com

New York Cake and Baking Distributors
56 West 22nd Street
New York, NY 10010
Phone: 212-675-2253
Decorating equipment, pans, chocolates

Sur la Table
Pike Place Farmers Market
84 Pine Street
Seattle, WA 98101
Phone: 800-243-0852
www.surlatable.com
Baking equipment

Von Snedaker's Magic Baking Sheets
12021 Wilshire Boulevard, Suite 231
Los Angeles, CA 90025
Phone: 310-395-6365
Reusable flexible baking sheets

Williams-Sonoma
Mail Order Department
P.O. Box 7456
San Francisco, CA 94120-7456
Phone: 800-541-2233
www.williamssonoma.com

BAKING SUPPLIES AND PRODUCTS

American Spoon Foods Inc.
P.O. Box 566
Peloskey, MI 49770
Phone: 800-222-5886
Fax: 800-647-2512 or 231-347-2512
www.spoon.com
Dried fruits, nuts, jams, dried mushrooms

Authentic Foods
1850 West 169th Street, Suite B
Gardena, CA 90247
Phone: 800-806-4737
Fax: 310-366-6938
www.authenticfoods.com
Gluten-free flours, mixes, baking supplies

Bickford Flavors
19007 St. Clair Avenue
Cleveland, OH 44117-1001
Phone: 800-283-8322
Gluten-free flavorings

Bob's Red Mill Natural Foods
5209 SE International Way
Milwaukie, OR 97222
Phone: 503-654-3215
Fax: 503-563-1339
www.bobsredmill.com
Gluten-free flours

Chukar Cherries Company
P.O. Box 510
Prosser, WA 99350-0510
Phone: 800-624-9544

Fax: 509-786-2591
www.chukar.com
Dried fruits, candies

Cybros, Inc.
P.O. Box 851
Waukesha, WI 53187-0851
Phone: 800-876-2253
www.cybrosinc.com
Gluten-free flours

Dairy Fresh Candies
57 Salem Street
Boston, MA 02113
Phone: 800-336-5536 or 617-742-2639
Nuts, chocolates, dried and candied fruits, candies

De-Ro-Ma
1118 Berlier
Laval, Quebec H7I 3R0
Canada
Phone: 514-990-5694 or 800-363-DIET
Fax: 450-629-4781
www.glutino.com
Prepared foods

Dietary Specialties, Inc.
865 Centennial Avenue
Piscataway, NJ 08854
Phone: 888-636-8123
Prepared foods

Eden Foods
701 Clinton-Tecumseh Highway
Clinton, MI 49236
Phone: 313-973-9400
www.eden-foods.com
Prepared foods

Ener-G Foods
P.O. Box 84487
Seattle, WA 98124-5787
Phone: 800-331-5222; in state, 800-325-9788
www.ener-g.com
Prepared foods, baking supplies

Gluten-Free Pantry
P.O. Box 840
Glastonbury, CT 06033
Phone: 800-291-8386 or 860-633-6853
Fax: 860-633-6853
www.glutenfree.com
Prepared foods, gluten-free flours, baking supplies

Gluten Solutions, Inc.
737 Manhattan Beach Boulevard, Suite B
Manhattan Beach, CA 90266
Phone: 888-845-8836
www.glutensolutions.com
Online grocery store and catalog

King Arthur Flour Company
The Baker's Catalogue
P.O. Box 876
Norwich, VT 05055-0876
Phone: 800-827-6836
Fax: 800-343-3002
e-mail: info@KingArthurFlour.com
www.kingarthurflour.com
Baking supplies

Miss Roben's
P.O. Box 1149
Frederick, MD 21702
Phone: 800-891-0083
Fax: 301-631-5954
www.missroben.com
Gluten-free flours, prepared foods

The Really Great Food Company
P.O. Box 3319
Malverne, NY 11565

Phone: 800-5935377
Fax: 516-593-9522
Prepared foods, supplies, and equipment

Special Foods
9207 Shotgun Court
Springfield, VA 22153
Phone: 703-644-0991
Fax: 703-644-1006
e-mail: kslimak@ix.netcom.com
www.specialfoods.com
Supplies, prepared foods, information

INFORMATION AND RESOURCES

Allergy Resources, Inc.
P.O. Box 888
Palmer Lake, CO 80133
Phone: 800-873-3529

American Academy of Allergy, Asthma & Immunology
611 E. Wells Street
Milwaukee, WI 53202
Help line: 800-822-2762
Phone: 414-272-6071
www.aaaai.org

Celiac Disease Foundation
13251 Ventura Boulevard, Suite 3
Studio City, CA 91604-1838
Phone: 818-990-2354
Fax: 818-990-2379
e-mail: cdf@celiac.org
Elaine Monarch: CDFoundtn@aol.com.
or Miles Perlmutter: thinker@earthlink.net
www.celiac.org

Celiac Sprue Association/USA
P.O. Box 31700
Omaha, NE 68131-0700
Phone: 402-558-0600 or 643-4340
Fax: 402-558-1347
e-mail: celiacs@csaceliacs.org
www.csaceliacs.org

Food Allergy Network
10400 Eaton Place, Suite 107
Fairfax, VA 22030-5647
Phone: 703-691-3179
Fax: 703-691-3179
e-mail: fan@worldwide.net
www.foodallergy.org

Gluten-Free Living (newsletter)
P.O. Box 105
Hastings-on-Hudson, NY 10706
Phone: 914-969-2018
Fax: 914-969-2018

Gluten Intolerance Group
Gluten Intolerance Group of NA-GIG
15110 10th Avenue SW, Suite A
Seattle, WA 98166-1820
Phone: 206-246-6652
Fax: 206-246-6531
e-mail: info@gluten.net or gig@accessone.com
www.gluten.net

The Natural Gourmet Cookery School
48 West 21st Street
New York, NY 10010
Phone: 212-645-5170
www.naturalgourmetschool.com

Sully's Living Without (magazine)
P.O. Box 132
Clarendon Hills, IL 60514-0132
Phone: 630-415-3378
Fax: 847-816-6045
e-mail: Pwagener@livingwithout.com
www.livingwithout.com

MUFFINS, QUICK BREADS, AND COFFEE CAKES

Basic Muffins
Apple Muffins
Cornmeal Muffins
Coconut Raspberry Muffins
Dairy-Free Banana Muffins
Cardamom Muffins
Raisin Cream Scones
Cornmeal Scones
Scone Pizzas
Sweet Potato Scones
Shortcakes
Chocolate Shortcakes
Banana Bread
Eleanor's Banana Bread
Banana Peanut Butter Bread
Pumpkin Bread
Cranberry Orange Bread
Date Nut Bread
Carrot Spice Bread
Blueberry Cake
Sour Cream Coffee Cake
Spice Coffee Cake
Cherry Kuchen
Carrot Cake
Apple Cream Cheese Coffee Cake
Cherry Streusel Coffee Cake
Lemon Poppy Seed Bread
Upside-Down Armenian Coffee Cake

Muffins, quick breads, and coffee cakes

are a good place to start fine-tuning your gluten-free baking skills. Not only are these baked goodies delicious, but they are easy to make gluten-free. While we often think of quick breads and muffins as sweet, there are a number of recipes in this chapter that are savory, such as corn bread and scones, and can be served with your main meal. In addition, I have cut back on the sugar in several recipes to bring out the natural sweetness of the ingredients.

You will note that a number of recipes in this chapter call for lining the bottom of the pan with parchment paper. This chef's secret aids easy removal of baked goods from the pan. In addition to parchment, I also give the pan a quick spritz of cooking spray to ensure quick release. When you are making muffins and not all the cups are filled, put a few tablespoons of water in the empty ones to ensure the heat disperses evenly.

Quick breads and muffins freeze quite well. Sometimes I make smaller loaves of bread or extra muffins and freeze them. When I am ready to serve them, I thaw them in the refrigerator overnight and warm slightly in the microwave before serving. Most of the items in this chapter freeze and reheat well.

Muffins are fast and easy. One celiac I know makes a quantity of her own basic muffin mixes ahead of time and has muffins "on hand" for months. The first recipe in this chapter provides a basic muffin and many variations to add variety. Mixing and making gluten-free muffins is not much different from making muffins with gluten. Be sure to mix the dry ingredients first, then add the moist ingredients. The rising agent, such as baking powder or baking soda, reacts instantly to moisture and starts to work immediately. When you add the liquid, be certain not to beat the batter too much; just mix until it is moistened and fill the muffin cups two-thirds full. The "perfect" muffin should be straight on the sides and rounded on top. After they are baked, remove the muffins to a cooling rack immediately to prevent soggy bottoms.

The good news is that quick breads and coffee cakes are lower in fat than cakes. The bad news is that they tend to be drier. Adding nuts and dried fruits, however, helps moisten breads and coffee cakes—and serving them with butter, honey, jam, or my personal favorite, a schmear of cream cheese, adds moistness and enhances the flavor. Don't be alarmed if your loaf breads develop a lengthwise crack during baking. This fissure is characteristic of tea breads.

Sometimes I think that baking is very much like high school chemistry class. Here's a case in point: You'll notice that the quick bread recipes that contain acid ingredients such as yogurt, sour cream, honey, molasses, chocolate, cocoa powder, or brown sugar also include baking soda in combination with baking powder. One-half teaspoon of baking soda will neutralize 1 cup of the acid ingredient. Remember that baking soda is four times as potent as baking powder. Use 1 teaspoon baking powder per 1 cup flour or ¼ teaspoon baking soda per cup of flour. When baking at high altitudes, reduce the baking powder or soda by one-fourth, but do not reduce the amount to less than half if there is sour cream or buttermilk in the recipe.

I would like to go on record as a strong advocate of a morning or afternoon tea break. In my opinion, this highly civilized custom offers us all a chance to catch our breath, collect our thoughts, and, well, eat more scones. These delicacies from the British Isles are richer and sweeter than biscuits and are just delicious served piping hot out of the oven with clotted cream, whipped cream, or butter and jam. I've included a number of scone recipes and variations in this chapter and invite you to join my tradition.

BASIC MUFFINS *Makes 12 muffins*

Here is a basic muffin mix chock-full of possibilities. A number of variations are listed, but since this is a good recipe to experiment with, you should try developing your own muffin specialty. Make a large quantity of the mix and put it in a Baggie to have on hand. I love to eat these as soon as they are out of the oven, even before they have had a chance to cool. Reheated in the microwave for just a few seconds is almost as good as straight from the oven.

- 1 cup brown rice flour
- ½ cup cornmeal, preferably stone-ground
- ½ cup tapioca starch or arrowroot
- 2 teaspoons gluten-free baking powder
- 1 teaspoon Egg Replacer
- ½ teaspoon xanthan gum
- ½ teaspoon baking soda
- ½ cup corn or canola oil
- ½ cup honey
- ½ cup hot milk
- 1 egg
- 1 tablespoon lemon juice

Preheat the oven to 375°F. Grease 12 muffin cups and dust with rice flour.

Mix together the brown rice flour, cornmeal, tapioca starch, baking powder, Egg Replacer, xanthan gum, and baking soda. Make a well in the dry ingredients.

Whisk together the oil, honey, hot milk, egg, and lemon juice. Pour into the well in the dry ingredients and stir until the batter is blended. Spoon into the prepared pan. Bake on the middle rack for 18 to 20 minutes or until done.

Substitutions:

To make the muffins egg-free, replace the egg with one of the following:

Flax: Bring ½ cup water to a boil. Whisk in 1½ teaspoons flax meal. Cook until slightly thick, like an egg white. Cool. Use in place of the egg.

Tofu: Mash ¼ cup soft or firm tofu with a fork until it looks like ricotta cheese. Use in place of the egg.

VARIATIONS

APPLE WALNUT MUFFINS

Replace the milk with apple juice. Add 1 teaspoon cinnamon to the dry ingredients. Gently stir ½ cup chopped toasted walnuts and 1 peeled, cored, and grated apple into the batter.

CRANBERRY APPLE MUFFINS

Add 1 teaspoon cinnamon and ⅛ teaspoon ginger to the dry ingredients. Gently stir 1 cup fresh cranberries and 1 grated small apple into the batter.

CRANBERRY PECAN MUFFINS

Add ⅛ teaspoon cloves to the dry ingredients. Replace the milk with ½ cup orange juice. Gently stir 1 cup chopped fresh cranberries and ½ cup chopped lightly toasted pecans into the batter.

DRIED FRUIT MUFFINS

Gently stir 1 cup chopped dried fruit of your choice and ½ cup chopped toasted nuts of your choice into the batter.

FRESH BLUEBERRY LEMON MUFFINS

Add 1 teaspoon grated lemon zest with the liquids. Gently fold 1 cup fresh blueberries into the batter.

RASPBERRY MUFFINS

Gently fold 1 cup fresh raspberries into the batter.

APPLE MUFFINS *Makes 12 muffins*

Soy flour makes these muffins a healthy choice for breakfast or for a snack after school. They freeze well.

- ¾ cup soy flour
- ½ cup potato starch
- ¼ cup brown rice flour
- 1 teaspoon gluten-free baking powder
- ¾ teaspoon baking soda
- ½ teaspoon cream of tartar
- ½ teaspoon xanthan gum
- 1 teaspoon cinnamon
- ¼ teaspoon nutmeg
- ¼ teaspoon allspice
- ¼ teaspoon salt
- ⅓ cup melted unsalted butter or oil
- ⅔ cup sugar
- 2 large eggs
- ½ cup grated raw apple
- Cinnamon sugar for sprinkling

Preheat the oven to 350°F. Lightly grease 12 muffin cups or a 9 × 5-inch loaf pan.

Mix together the soy flour, potato starch, brown rice flour, baking powder, baking soda, cream of tartar, xanthan gum, cinnamon, nutmeg, allspice, and salt. Make a well in the dry ingredients.

Mix the melted butter, sugar, eggs, and grated apple. Pour into the well in the dry ingredients and stir until the batter is blended. Spoon into the muffin pan or loaf pan. Sprinkle the top with cinnamon sugar and bake the muffins for 15 to 18 minutes or the loaf for 40 minutes or until done.

CORNMEAL MUFFINS *Makes 12 muffins*

These are very moist corn muffins, and unlike so many others, they don't have the aftertaste of baking powder. The second day they are as moist and yummy as the first. Simply microwave them for 20 seconds and you will think they just came out of the oven. If you like a crisper corn muffin, preheat the pan before you fill it with the batter. Try these with a bowl of chili.

- 1½ cups brown rice Basic Gluten-Free Mix (page 16)
- 1 cup cornmeal
- ½ cup almond flour
- ⅓ cup sugar
- 1 tablespoon gluten-free baking powder
- ¾ teaspoon xanthan gum
- ⅛ teaspoon salt
- 1¼ cups half-and-half
- 1 stick unsalted butter, melted
- 1 egg

Preheat the oven to 400°F. Lightly grease 12 muffin cups or line with paper liners.

Mix together the gluten-free mix, cornmeal, almond flour, sugar, baking powder, xanthan gum, and salt. Make a well in the dry ingredients.

Whisk together the half-and-half, melted butter, and egg. Pour into the well in the dry ingredients. Whisk together until well mixed. The batter will be thick. Fill the muffin cups three-quarters full. Bake on the middle rack for 15 to 18 minutes or until done. Remove the muffins from the pan and cool.

COCONUT RASPBERRY MUFFINS *Makes 12 muffins*

I love muffins with a "surprise" jam filling, and the combination of coconut and raspberry is especially nice. Experiment with your favorite jams or preserves, such as grape, orange marmalade, blueberry, or strawberry.

- 1¾ cups brown rice Basic Gluten-Free Mix (page 16)
- ¼ cup almond flour
- ½ cup sugar
- 2 teaspoons gluten-free baking powder
- ½ teaspoon xanthan gum
- ⅛ teaspoon salt
- ½ cup hot milk
- 2 eggs
- 1 stick unsalted butter, melted
- 1 cup shredded sweetened coconut
- 12 teaspoons raspberry preserves
- Confectioners' sugar for dusting

Preheat the oven to 375°F. Grease 12 muffin cups well and dust with rice flour.

Mix together the gluten-free mix, almond flour, sugar, baking powder, xanthan gum, and salt. Make a well in the dry ingredients.

Whisk the milk, eggs, and melted butter together. Pour into the well in the dry ingredients and stir until the batter is blended. Fold in the shredded coconut.

Place ¼ cup of the batter in each muffin cup. Dot with 1 teaspoon preserves. Cover with more batter. Bake on the middle rack for 15 to 20 minutes or until done. Turn the muffins out onto a rack to cool. Dust with confectioners' sugar before serving.

DAIRY-FREE BANANA MUFFINS *Makes 12 muffins*

A great muffin for anyone who is also sensitive to dairy products.

- 1½ cups Basic Gluten-Free Mix (page 16)
- ¾ cup packed brown sugar
- 1 tablespoon gluten-free baking powder
- 1 teaspoon cinnamon
- ½ teaspoon xanthan gum
- ⅛ teaspoon salt
- 2 bananas, peeled and mashed
- ½ cup gluten-free rice or soy milk
- ⅓ cup canola oil
- 2 egg whites
- 1 teaspoon lemon juice
- 1 cup chopped lightly toasted walnuts
- Cinnamon sugar for sprinkling

Preheat the oven to 350°F. Lightly grease 12 muffin cups.

Mix together the gluten-free mix, brown sugar, baking powder, cinnamon, xanthan gum, and salt. Make a well in the dry ingredients.

Whisk together the bananas, rice milk, oil, egg whites, and lemon juice. Pour into the well in the dry ingredients and stir until blended. Fold in the nuts. Spoon the batter into the muffin cups. Sprinkle with cinnamon sugar. Bake on the middle rack for 20 minutes or until done.

CARDAMOM MUFFINS *Makes 12 muffins*

Don't let the rich taste of these muffins fool you—they are low in fat. The exotic Indian spice cardamom is a nice change from cinnamon or nutmeg.

- 1½ cups Basic Gluten-Free Mix (page 16)
- ½ cup packed brown sugar
- ½ teaspoon cinnamon
- ½ teaspoon gluten-free baking powder
- Pinch of salt
- ½ stick unsalted butter, chilled and cut into pieces
- ¼ cup toasted walnuts
- 1 teaspoon cardamom
- 1 cup brown rice flour
- ½ teaspoon baking soda
- ¼ teaspoon xanthan gum
- 1¼ cups buttermilk

Preheat the oven to 375°F. Grease 12 muffin cups well.

Mix together the gluten-free mix, brown sugar, cinnamon, baking powder, and salt. Add the butter and use your fingertips to work it into the dry ingredients, forming a coarse meal. Measure out ¼ cup of the mixture and put it in a food processor. Add the nuts and cardamom and pulse together. Set aside.

Mix the brown rice flour, baking soda, and xanthan gum with the remaining flour mixture. Stir in the buttermilk. Spoon the batter into the greased muffin cups. Sprinkle with the reserved nut crumb topping. Bake on the middle rack for 20 minutes or until done.

RAISIN CREAM SCONES *Makes 6 (3-inch) scones*

After you mix the dough, you can pat it out with your hands, or roll it out and cut into round or wedge shapes.

- 1 cup brown rice flour
- ½ cup sweet rice flour or tapioca starch
- ½ cup almond flour
- ¼ cup potato starch
- 2¼ teaspoons gluten-free baking powder
- ¼ teaspoon xanthan gum
- ¼ teaspoon salt
- ½ stick unsalted butter, chilled and cut into pieces
- ½ cup golden raisins, soaked for 10 minutes in hot water and drained
- 2 eggs
- 1 tablespoon honey
- ⅓ to ½ cup heavy cream
- Cinnamon sugar for sprinkling

Preheat the oven to 400°F. Line a cookie sheet with parchment paper or lightly grease the cookie sheet and dust it with rice flour.

Mix together the brown rice flour, sweet rice flour, almond flour, potato starch, baking powder, xanthan gum, and salt. Add the butter and use your fingertips to work it into the dry ingredients, forming a coarse meal. Toss in the raisins. Make a well in the dry ingredients. Break the eggs into the well. Add the honey and some of the cream. Using a fork, begin mixing the wet ingredients together and then slowly incorporate the dry. Add more cream to form a soft but not wet dough.

Remove the dough from the bowl and place on a lightly floured counter. Press into a flat cake about ½ inch thick. Using a biscuit cutter, cut out the dough. Place the scones on the cookie sheet. Brush with some cream and sprinkle with cinnamon sugar. Bake on the middle rack for 12 to 15 minutes. Check the bottoms of the scones; they should be golden brown when done.

VARIATIONS

CHERRY ORANGE SCONES

Add 1 teaspoon grated orange zest and replace the raisins with dried cherries.

CHOCOLATE SCONES

Add ⅓ cup chopped walnuts and replace the raisins with ½ cup chocolate chips.

CRANBERRY WALNUT SCONES

Replace the raisins with ½ cup dried or chopped fresh cranberries and add ½ cup chopped walnuts.

BLUEBERRY SCONES

Replace the raisins with ¾ cup dried, frozen, or fresh blueberries

WALNUT CURRANT SCONES

Add ½ cup chopped walnuts and replace the raisins with currants plumped in 2 tablespoons warm water.

RAISIN ORANGE SCONES

Add ¼ cup chopped candied orange peel and ⅛ teaspoon ginger.

CORNMEAL SCONES *Makes 7 or 8 (3-inch) scones*

If any of these scones are left over, you can use them for a delicious savory bread pudding (pages 211–13).

1 cup brown rice flour
¾ cup cornmeal
⅓ cup potato starch
3 tablespoons tapioca starch
4 teaspoons gluten-free baking powder
½ teaspoon baking soda
⅛ teaspoon salt
1 stick unsalted butter, chilled and cut into pieces
2 tablespoons honey
1 egg, lightly beaten
½ to ⅔ cup buttermilk
Cinnamon sugar for sprinkling (optional)

Preheat the oven to 400°F. Line a cookie sheet with parchment paper.

Mix together the brown rice flour, cornmeal, potato starch, tapioca starch, baking powder, baking soda, and salt. Add the butter and use your fingertips to work it into the dry ingredients, forming a coarse meal. Make a well in the dry ingredients.

Mix together the honey, egg, and ½ cup of the buttermilk. Pour into the well in the dry ingredients. Stir with a fork. I like to use my hands at this point to gather everything up and form a soft but not sticky dough. If it is too dry, add more buttermilk. Lightly flour the counter with rice flour and pat the dough into a cake ½ inch thick. Cut out pie-shaped pieces or use a biscuit cutter and cut out rounds. Place on the cookie sheet. Sprinkle with cinnamon sugar, if you like, or leave plain. Bake on the middle rack for 12 to 15 minutes or until the bottoms are golden.

VARIATIONS

CHERRY CORN SCONES

Add 1 cup dried cherries after the butter has been incorporated into the dry ingredients.

LEMON CORN SCONES

Add 1 teaspoon grated lemon zest and ½ cup golden raisins after the butter has been incorporated into the dry ingredients.

SCONE PIZZAS

My testers Kay Lawrence and Tess Craine, a mother/daughter team, made a pizza using the Cornmeal Scones (page 45) recipe for the crust. Their toppings were tomato sauce, fresh spinach, soy pepperoni, anchovies, and soy mozzarella. The variations below are also delicious.

Tomato sauce
Fresh basil
Chopped fresh garlic
Grated mozzarella

Or:

Tomato sauce
Cooked broccoli
Sautéed sliced mushrooms
Chopped fresh garlic
Grated mozzarella and provolone

Tomato sauce
Sautéed onion
Chopped cooked bacon
Grated cheddar cheese and mozzarella

Or:

Tomato sauce
Sautéed sliced onion and colored peppers
Fresh basil
Grated mozzarella and fontinella

Pat the dough into a pizza pan lined with parchment paper. Bake it for 5 minutes at 400°F. Spread the toppings on and continue baking for another 10 minutes.

SWEET POTATO SCONES *Makes 6 (3-inch) scones*

Try this savory scone with turkey, lamb, or sausage dishes. It's a welcome addition to everyone's basket of breads and rolls, especially on the Thanksgiving table.

- 1 cup brown rice flour
- ½ cup sweet rice flour or tapioca starch
- ½ cup almond flour
- ¼ cup potato starch
- 2 tablespoons brown sugar
- 2¼ teaspoons gluten-free baking powder
- ½ teaspoon baking soda
- ½ teaspoon ginger
- ¼ teaspoon allspice
- ¼ teaspoon xanthan gum
- ¼ teaspoon salt
- ⅛ teaspoon nutmeg
- ½ stick unsalted butter, chilled and cut into pieces
- ½ cup golden raisins
- 1 egg
- 1 tablespoon honey
- 1 cup mashed cooked sweet potato
- ¼ cup buttermilk
- Cinnamon sugar for sprinkling

Preheat the oven to 400°F. Line a cookie sheet with parchment paper.

Mix together the brown rice flour, sweet rice flour, almond flour, potato starch, brown sugar, baking powder, baking soda, ginger, allspice, xanthan gum, salt, and nutmeg. Add the butter and use your fingertips to work it into the dry ingredients, forming a coarse meal. Toss in the raisins. Make a well in the dry ingredients. Break the egg into the well. Add the honey, mashed sweet potato, and some of the buttermilk. Using a fork, begin mixing the wet ingredients together and then slowly incorporate the dry. Add more buttermilk to form a soft but not wet dough.

Remove the dough from the bowl and place on a lightly floured counter. Press into a flat cake about ½ inch thick. Using a biscuit cutter, cut out the dough. Place the scones on the cookie sheet. Brush with some cream and sprinkle with cinnamon sugar. Bake on the middle rack for 12 to 15 minutes. Check the bottoms of the scones; they should be golden brown when done.

VARIATION Add ½ cup lightly toasted and chopped pecans.

SHORTCAKES *Makes 7 or 8 (3-inch) shortcakes*

What better way to celebrate strawberry season than with strawberry shortcake? These shortcakes, however, will be a hit all year. When ready to serve, split each shortcake in half. Spoon cut-up strawberries over the bottom half and dollop with a spoonful of whipped cream. Top with the top half of the shortcake and spoon on more whipped cream if you like. For a change, try mixing blueberries and sliced nectarines or peaches together to serve with the shortcakes.

- 2¾ cups Basic Gluten-Free Mix (page 16)
- ¼ cup sugar
- 4 teaspoons gluten-free baking powder
- 1 teaspoon Egg Replacer
- ¾ teaspoon xanthan gum
- ¼ teaspoon salt
- 1¼ sticks unsalted butter, chilled and cut into pieces
- ¾ to 1 cup heavy cream

Preheat the oven to 400°F. Lightly grease a cookie sheet and line it with parchment paper or dust with rice flour.

Mix together the gluten-free mix, sugar, baking powder, Egg Replacer, xanthan gum, and salt. Add the butter and use your fingertips to work it into the dry ingredients, forming a coarse meal. Slowly mix in enough cream until you have a soft but not sticky dough.

Turn the dough out onto a lightly floured surface. Gently knead a few times. Pat or roll into a flat cake about 1 inch thick. Using a 3-inch biscuit cutter, cut out the dough. Place the shortcakes on the cookie sheet. Bake for 15 to 18 minutes. Cool on a rack.

CHOCOLATE SHORTCAKES *Makes 7 or 8 (3-inch) shortcakes*

Serve these as scones or split them in half and fill with lightly sweetened whipped cream and sweet strawberries or sliced bananas.

- 2 cups Basic Gluten-Free Mix (page 16)
- ¾ cup unsweetened cocoa powder
- ¼ cup sugar
- 4 teaspoons gluten-free baking powder
- 1 teaspoon Egg Replacer
- ¾ teaspoon xanthan gum
- ¼ teaspoon salt
- 1½ sticks unsalted butter, chilled and cut into pieces
- ⅓ cup chopped semisweet chocolate
- ¾ to 1 cup heavy cream

Preheat the oven to 400°F. Lightly grease a cookie sheet and line it with parchment paper or dust with rice flour.

Mix together the gluten-free mix, cocoa powder, sugar, baking powder, Egg Replacer, xanthan gum, and salt. Add the butter and use your fingertips to work it into the dry ingredients, forming a coarse meal. Mix in the chopped chocolate. Slowly stir in enough cream until you have a soft but not sticky dough.

Turn the dough out onto a lightly floured surface. Gently knead a few times. Pat or roll into a flat cake about 1 inch thick. Using a 3-inch biscuit cutter, cut out the dough. Place the shortcakes on the cookie sheet. Bake for 15 to 18 minutes. Cool on a rack.

BANANA BREAD *Makes 1 (8½ × 4½-inch) loaf or 12 muffins*

Here's a great way to add soy to your diet—and no one will guess there is soy flour in this recipe. Remember that soy flour is perishable and needs to be stored in the refrigerator.

This cake is delicious even without icing.

¾ cup soy flour
½ cup potato starch
¼ cup rice flour
1 teaspoon cinnamon
1 teaspoon gluten-free baking powder
¾ teaspoon baking soda
½ teaspoon cream of tartar
½ teaspoon xanthan gum
¼ teaspoon nutmeg
¼ teaspoon allspice
Pinch of salt
2 eggs
⅓ cup melted unsalted butter or oil
⅔ cup sugar
½ cup mashed banana
Cinnamon sugar for sprinkling

ICING:

1 cup confectioners' sugar
2 tablespoons lemon or orange juice

Preheat the oven to 350°F. Lightly grease an 8½ × 4½-inch loaf pan or 12-cup muffin pan and dust with rice flour, or use paper liners in the muffin pan.

Mix the soy flour, potato starch, rice flour, cinnamon, baking powder, baking soda, cream of tartar, xanthan gum, nutmeg, allspice, and salt together. Make a well in the center of the dry ingredients.

Mix the eggs, butter or oil, sugar, and banana. Pour into the well in the dry ingredients and stir until blended. Spoon the batter into the loaf pan or muffin cups. Sprinkle the top with cinnamon sugar and bake until done: 40 minutes for the loaf or 15 to 18 minutes for the muffins.

To make the icing, whisk the sugar and juice together until smooth. Pour over the bread as it cools on a rack.

ELEANOR'S BANANA BREAD *Makes 1 (9 × 5-inch) loaf*

When I started the Madd Apple Café, Eleanor was one of my favorite cooks. She would use any extra bananas to make her wonderful banana bread. David Lake, a friend of my son, gave me the idea to add blueberries to this bread. It's a great combination.

2 cups Basic Gluten-Free Mix (page 16)
1 teaspoon baking soda
½ teaspoon xanthan gum
⅛ teaspoon salt
1 stick unsalted butter
1 cup sugar
2 eggs
3 ripe bananas, peeled and mashed
½ cup chopped lightly toasted walnuts

Preheat the oven to 350°F. Lightly grease a 9 × 5-inch loaf pan and dust with rice flour or line with parchment paper.

Mix together the gluten-free mix, baking soda, xanthan gum, and salt.

Cream the butter until white. Add the sugar and beat until fluffy, about 5 minutes. Add the eggs, one at a time. Stir in the mashed bananas. Add the dry ingredients and stir until blended. Fold in the nuts. Spoon the batter into the pan. Bake for 1 hour or until done.

VARIATION Fold 1 cup fresh blueberries into the batter with the walnuts.

BANANA PEANUT BUTTER BREAD *Makes 1 (9 × 5-inch) loaf*

I did a short stint as the on-line "Ask the Chef" for an Internet site. One of the first questions I received was how much peanut butter to use in banana bread. Peanut butter? In banana bread? Then I actually made it and got the answer. I e-mailed the answer to the questioner and thanked her for the idea. This bread is the result—one of my tasters ate one-third of it at one sitting!

You can also make this recipe as muffins; bake for 15 to 18 minutes in 12 paper-lined muffin cups.

- 1 cup brown rice flour
- ⅔ cup potato starch
- ⅓ cup sweet rice flour
- 1 teaspoon gluten-free baking powder
- ¾ teaspoon baking soda
- ½ teaspoon xanthan gum
- ⅛ teaspoon salt
- 1 stick unsalted butter
- 1 cup packed light brown sugar
- ½ cup chunky or creamy peanut butter
- 2 eggs
- 2 ripe bananas, peeled and mashed

Preheat the oven to 350°F. Lightly grease a 9 × 5-inch loaf pan and dust it with rice flour or line with parchment paper.

Mix together the brown rice flour, potato starch, sweet rice flour, baking powder, baking soda, xanthan gum, and salt.

Cream the butter until white. Add the sugar and beat until fluffy, about 5 minutes. Add the peanut butter and blend well. Add the eggs, one at a time. Stir in the mashed bananas. Gently stir in the dry ingredients. Spoon the batter into the pan. Bake for 40 to 45 minutes or until done.

VARIATION Omit the peanut butter and blend 2 tablespoons unsweetened cocoa powder into the dry ingredients.

PUMPKIN BREAD *Makes 1 (9 × 5-inch) loaf, 3 (5 × 3-inch) loaves, or 12 muffins*

A "must" during the holidays. This bread is moist and very flavorful. It makes a good hostess gift, and you don't even need to confess that it is gluten-free.

- 1¾ cups Basic Gluten-Free Mix (page 16)
- 1 teaspoon baking soda
- 1 teaspoon xanthan gum
- ½ teaspoon cinnamon
- ¼ teaspoon gluten-free baking powder
- ¼ teaspoon cloves
- ⅛ teaspoon nutmeg
- Pinch of ginger
- ⅓ cup unsalted butter
- 1⅓ cups packed light brown sugar
- 2 eggs
- 1 cup pumpkin puree
- ⅓ cup milk
- ½ cup chopped nuts, dried or fresh cranberries, dates, or raisins (optional)

Preheat the oven to 350°F. Lightly grease a 9 × 5-inch loaf pan and dust it with rice flour or line it with parchment paper, or line 12 muffin cups with paper liners.

Mix together the gluten-free mix, baking soda, xanthan gum, cinnamon, baking powder, cloves, nutmeg, and ginger.

Cream the butter until white. Add the sugar and beat until fluffy, about 5 minutes. Add the eggs, one at a time. If the mixture appears cracked, add 1 or 2 tablespoons of the dry ingredients until it looks smooth. Stir in the pumpkin puree. Add the dry ingredients in two parts, alternating with the milk. Add the chopped nuts or fruit, if using. Spoon the batter into the prepared loaf pan(s) or muffin cups. Bake the loaf for 1 hour; the small loaves for 25 minutes; or the muffins for 15 to 18 minutes.

CRANBERRY ORANGE BREAD *Makes 1 (8½ × 4½-inch) loaf or 12 muffins*

I love this bread because it is not too sweet. It is sweetened by the natural flavor of the orange, a tasty foil for the cranberry.

- 1 cup brown rice flour
- ⅔ cup potato starch
- ¼ cup packed brown sugar
- 3 tablespoons tapioca starch
- 2 tablespoons almond flour
- 2 teaspoons gluten-free baking powder
- 1 teaspoon Egg Replacer
- ¾ teaspoon xanthan gum
- Pinch of salt
- ¾ cup hot milk
- 4 tablespoons melted unsalted butter or oil
- 2 eggs
- Grated zest of 1 orange
- 1 cup dried or fresh cranberries, chopped
- Cinnamon sugar for sprinkling

Preheat the oven to 350°F. Lightly grease an 8½ × 4½-inch loaf pan and line it with parchment paper or sprinkle it with rice flour, or line 12 muffin cups with paper liners.

Mix together the brown rice flour, potato starch, brown sugar, tapioca starch, almond flour, baking powder, Egg Replacer, xanthan gum, and salt.

Whisk together the milk, butter, and eggs. Whisk into the dry ingredients. Fold in the orange zest and cranberries. Spoon the batter into the loaf pan or muffin cups and sprinkle the top with cinnamon sugar. Bake the loaf for 30 to 40 minutes or the muffins for 12 to 15 minutes.

VARIATIONS

Omit the cranberries and fold one of the following into the batter:

½ cup chopped walnuts
1 cup blueberries plus 2 teaspoons grated lemon zest
1 cup chopped apple plus ½ teaspoon cinnamon
1 cup dried cherries

Replace the milk with 1 cup plain or lemon gluten-free yogurt, and add ½ teaspoon baking soda to the dry ingredients.

DATE NUT BREAD *Makes 1 (8½ × 4½-inch) loaf or 12 muffins*

I grew up on cream cheese on date nut bread sandwiches, which are still a favorite at my house.

1 cup bean flour (page 17) or brown rice flour
⅔ cup potato starch
½ cup packed brown sugar
⅓ cup tapioca starch
2 teaspoons gluten-free baking powder
½ teaspoon xanthan gum
¼ teaspoon salt
1 egg, lightly beaten
1 cup milk
2 tablespoons oil
½ teaspoon gluten-free vanilla
⅓ cup chopped lightly toasted walnuts
⅓ cup chopped dates

Preheat the oven to 350°F. Lightly grease an 8½ × 4½-inch loaf pan and dust it with rice flour, or line 12 muffin cups with paper liners.

Mix together the bean flour or brown rice flour, potato starch, brown sugar, tapioca starch, baking powder, xanthan gum, and salt.

Beat the egg and milk together. Add the oil and the vanilla. Pour into the dry ingredients and mix well. Fold in the nuts and dates.

Spoon the batter into the loaf pan or muffin cups and bake the loaf for 40 minutes or the muffins for 18 to 20 minutes.

VARIATIONS

APPLE APRICOT BREAD

Replace the dates and walnuts with ⅓ cup chopped dried apricots, plumped in 2 tablespoons orange juice, and 1 peeled and diced apple.

FIG WALNUT BREAD

Replace the dates with ⅓ cup chopped mission figs.

APRICOT ALMOND BREAD

Replace the dates and walnuts with ⅓ cup chopped dried apricots and ⅓ cup chopped lightly toasted almonds.

GOLDEN RAISIN WALNUT BREAD

Replace the dates with ½ cup golden raisins, plumped in 2 tablespoons orange juice.

PEACH PECAN BREAD

Replace the dates and walnuts with ⅓ cup chopped dried peaches, plumped in 2 tablespoons orange juice, and ⅓ cup chopped lightly toasted pecans.

CARROT SPICE BREAD *Makes 1 (9 × 5-inch) loaf*

This moist recipe is also wonderful baked in a cake pan (8-inch square or 9-inch round) and covered with a cream cheese frosting. Use any type of oil you wish. Once when I had only olive oil, I used it for this bread and it was great.

1½ cups Basic Gluten-Free Mix (page 16)
1½ teaspoons baking soda
¾ teaspoon xanthan gum
½ teaspoon cinnamon
⅛ teaspoon cloves
⅛ teaspoon salt
Pinch of nutmeg
2 eggs
1 cup canola oil
¾ cup packed brown sugar
1 teaspoon gluten-free vanilla
1½ cups grated carrots
1½ cups chopped walnuts

Preheat the oven to 350°F. Lightly grease a 9 × 5-inch loaf pan and dust it with rice flour or line with parchment paper.

Mix together the gluten-free mix, baking soda, xanthan gum, cinnamon, cloves, salt, and nutmeg.

Mix the eggs, oil, brown sugar, and vanilla together. Stir the dry ingredients into the wet mixture. Fold in the carrots and nuts.

Spoon the batter into the prepared loaf pan. Bake for 1 hour or until done.

VARIATIONS Omit the carrots and walnuts and add 2 cups chopped mango, or ½ cup chopped mango and ½ cup shredded coconut.

BLUEBERRY CAKE *Makes 1 (8-inch) square cake, 1 (8½ × 4½-inch) loaf, or 12 muffins*

This recipe makes the moistest cake, bread, or muffins. The batter is very thick, so fold in the blueberries gently. If you bake it in a cake pan, pour the lemon sauce over the warm cake for fabulous results. If you want to dress up the loaf or muffins, frost with Lemon Cream Cheese Frosting (page 148). Unfrosted, this cake freezes well.

- 1¼ cups Basic Gluten-Free Mix (page 16)
- ½ cup almond flour
- 1 teaspoon gluten-free baking powder
- ½ teaspoon xanthan gum
- ⅛ teaspoon salt
- ¾ stick unsalted butter
- 1 cup sugar
- 2 eggs, at room temperature
- 1 tablespoon grated lemon zest
- ½ cup warm milk
- 1½ cups fresh or frozen blueberries
- Lemon Sauce (recipe follows)

Preheat the oven to 325°F. Lightly butter an 8-inch square baking pan or 8½ × 4½-inch loaf pan and line it with parchment paper, or line 12 muffin cups with paper liners.

Mix together the gluten-free mix, almond flour, baking powder, xanthan gum, and salt.

Cream the butter until white. Add the sugar and beat until fluffy, about 5 minutes. Add the eggs, one at a time. Stir in the lemon zest. Add the dry ingredients in 2 parts, alternating with the milk. Gently fold in the blueberries. If using frozen berries, dust with some gluten-free mix first.

Spoon the batter into the pan and bake the square cake for 40 to 45 minutes, the loaf for 1 hour, or the muffins for 18 minutes.

Pour the lemon sauce over the hot cake. Cool the cake in the pan.

LEMON SAUCE

⅓ cup sugar
3 tablespoons lemon juice

Bring to a boil in a nonaluminum pot.

SOUR CREAM COFFEE CAKE *Makes 1 (9-inch) Bundt cake*

This coffee cake reminds me very much of the Eastern European coffee cakes my dear friend Ethel Goralnick makes.

STREUSEL TOPPING:

⅔ cup Basic Gluten-Free Mix (page 16)
½ cup granulated sugar
½ stick unsalted butter
⅓ cup chopped lightly toasted walnuts
⅓ cup shredded sweetened coconut
⅓ cup mini chocolate chips

CAKE BATTER:

1½ cups Basic Gluten-Free Mix
½ cup almond flour
1 teaspoon Egg Replacer
1 teaspoon gluten-free baking powder
1 teaspoon baking soda
½ teaspoon xanthan gum
¼ teaspoon salt
1 stick unsalted butter
1 cup packed brown sugar
3 eggs
1 cup sour cream
1 teaspoon gluten-free vanilla
¼ teaspoon almond extract

Preheat the oven to 350°F. Butter well a 9-inch Bundt pan or tube pan. Dust with rice flour.

To make the streusel, mix the gluten-free mix with the granulated sugar. Using your fingertips, pinch in the butter. Mix in the nuts, coconut, and chocolate chips. Set aside.

To make the cake batter, mix together the gluten-free mix, almond flour, Egg Replacer, baking powder, baking soda, xanthan gum, and salt.

Cream the butter until white. Add the brown sugar and beat until fluffy, about 5 minutes. Beat in the eggs, one at a time. Slowly add the sour cream, vanilla, and almond extract. Fold in the dry ingredients.

Spread two-thirds of the batter in the prepared pan. Sprinkle half of the streusel topping over the batter. Carefully cover the streusel with the remaining batter. Sprinkle the remaining streusel over the top. Bake for 1 hour in the Bundt pan or 45 to 50 minutes in the tube pan. Cool in the pan for 15 minutes. Turn out onto a rack and cool completely before serving.

SPICE COFFEE CAKE *Makes 1 (8-inch) round cake or 1 (8½ × 4½-inch) loaf*

Serve this at your next brunch or coffee klatsch. Or frost with a cream cheese icing to serve at teatime or for dessert.

- 1⅓ cups Basic Gluten-Free Mix (page 16)
- ⅓ cup granulated sugar
- ⅓ cup packed light brown sugar
- 2 teaspoons gluten-free baking powder
- 1 teaspoon Egg Replacer
- 1 teaspoon cinnamon
- ½ teaspoon baking soda
- ¼ teaspoon xanthan gum
- ¼ teaspoon salt
- ⅛ teaspoon nutmeg
- ⅛ teaspoon cloves
- 1 egg
- ½ cup milk
- 2 tablespoons canola oil
- 2 tablespoons applesauce

Preheat the oven to 350°F. Butter an 8 × 2-inch round cake pan or an 8½ × 4½-inch loaf pan. Line the bottom with parchment paper.

Mix together the gluten-free mix, both sugars, baking powder, Egg Replacer, cinnamon, baking soda, xanthan gum, salt, nutmeg, and cloves. Beat together the egg, milk, oil, and applesauce, then blend into the dry ingredients.

Spoon into the prepared pan. Bake for 20 minutes in the cake pan or 40 minutes in the loaf pan. Let the cake cool in the pan for 5 minutes and then remove to a cooling rack.

VARIATIONS Omit the cinnamon, nutmeg, and cloves and add 1¼ teaspoons Chinese five-spice mix and ⅛ teaspoon ginger.

COCONUT SPICE CAKE

Stir 1 cup shredded sweetened coconut into the batter. Sprinkle chopped nuts and cinnamon sugar on top before baking.

STREUSEL SPICE COFFEE CAKE

2 tablespoons brown rice flour
4 tablespoons sugar
1 tablespoon unsalted butter
⅓ cup chopped walnuts

Mix the brown rice flour and sugar together. Using your fingertips, pinch in the butter to form a crumb texture. Stir in the walnuts. Sprinkle this over the cake batter just before baking.

CHERRY KUCHEN *Makes 1 (9-inch) round cake*

A kuchen is a coffee cake that makes a wonderful treat for breakfast or a late-morning coffee break. Try it with different fruit combinations.

1 cup Basic Gluten-Free Mix (page 16)
1 teaspoon gluten-free baking powder
1 teaspoon Egg Replacer
¼ teaspoon xanthan gum
⅛ teaspoon salt
½ stick unsalted butter
½ cup sugar
1 egg
½ teaspoon gluten-free vanilla
Grated zest of 1 lemon (optional)
⅓ cup warm milk
1 cup pitted fresh cherries or drained pitted unsweetened canned cherries
Cinnamon sugar for sprinkling

Preheat the oven to 375°F. Lightly grease a 9-inch round cake pan or springform pan and line the bottom with greased parchment paper.

Mix together the gluten-free mix, baking powder, Egg Replacer, xanthan gum, and salt.

Cream the butter until white. Add the sugar and beat until fluffy, about 5 minutes. Add the egg, vanilla, and lemon zest. Stir in the dry ingredients in 2 parts, alternating with the warm milk.

Spoon the batter into the buttered cake pan. Arrange the cherries on top. Sprinkle with the cinnamon sugar. Bake for 15 to 18 minutes.

CARROT CAKE *Makes 1 (8-inch) round cake*

This carrot cake bakes much better in a cake pan than in a loaf pan. Dense and very moist, it will not rise a lot. This is a great recipe for those who are also on dairy-free and egg-free diets.

½ cup golden raisins
⅓ cup orange juice
¾ cup brown rice flour
¼ cup sweet rice flour
1 teaspoon gluten-free baking powder
1 teaspoon baking soda
1 teaspoon cinnamon
½ teaspoon xanthan gum
¼ teaspoon salt
⅓ cup canola oil
⅔ cup maple syrup
4 ounces soft tofu, mashed
1½ cups grated carrots
⅔ cup chopped lightly toasted walnuts

Preheat the oven to 325°F. Lightly grease an 8-inch round cake pan and line it with parchment paper.

Soak the raisins in the orange juice for 10 minutes. Drain.

Mix together the brown rice flour, sweet rice flour, baking powder, baking soda, cinnamon, xanthan gum, and salt.

Whisk the oil, maple syrup, and tofu until smooth. Stir into the dry ingredients. Fold in the grated carrots, nuts, and raisins.

Spoon the batter into the prepared pan. Bake for 1 hour or until done. Let the cake cool for 5 minutes before inverting onto a cooling rack.

APPLE CREAM CHEESE COFFEE CAKE *Makes 1 (9-inch) round cake*

This is a very rich coffee cake. A little goes a long way.

1 cup rice flour or brown rice flour
⅓ cup potato starch
¼ cup almond flour
3 tablespoons tapioca starch
1 teaspoon Egg Replacer
½ teaspoon gluten-free baking powder
¼ teaspoon xanthan gum
⅛ teaspoon salt
1 stick unsalted butter
1¾ cups sugar
8 ounces cream cheese
1 teaspoon gluten-free vanilla
2 eggs
2 teaspoons cinnamon
3 cups peeled, thinly sliced Granny Smith apples

Preheat the oven to 350°F. Butter a 9-inch springform pan. Line the bottom with parchment paper.

Mix together the rice flour, potato starch, almond flour, tapioca starch, Egg Replacer, baking powder, xanthan gum, and salt.

Cream the butter until white. Add 1½ cups of the sugar and beat until fluffy, about 5 minutes. Beat in the cream cheese and vanilla. Add the eggs, one at a time. Slowly stir the dry ingredients into the creamed mixture.

Blend the remaining ¼ cup sugar and the cinnamon together. Toss the apples with 2 tablespoons of this cinnamon sugar. Fold the apples into the batter. Spoon into the prepared pan. Sprinkle the remaining cinnamon sugar over the batter. Bake for 40 to 50 minutes or until done. Cool for 10 minutes before removing the sides, then allow to cool completely.

CHERRY STREUSEL COFFEE CAKE *Makes 2 (8-inch) square or round cakes*

The Sunday paper, a cup of coffee, and a piece of Cherry Streusel Coffee Cake—a match made in heaven! Thank you, Judith Friedlaender, for suggesting I translate your favorite recipe into a gluten-free version. The cake freezes well.

- 1⅓ cups brown rice flour
- ⅓ cup potato starch
- ¼ cup tapioca starch
- 1½ tablespoons quinoa flour
- 1½ teaspoons Egg Replacer
- 1½ teaspoons gluten-free baking powder
- ½ teaspoon xanthan gum
- ⅛ teaspoon salt
- 1½ sticks unsalted butter
- 1 cup sugar
- 2 eggs
- 1 (16-ounce) can unsweetened pitted cherries, drained

STREUSEL TOPPING:

- ½ cup brown rice flour
- ¼ cup sugar
- ½ stick unsalted butter
- ½ cup slivered almonds
- ½ teaspoon cinnamon

Preheat the oven to 350°F. Lightly grease two 8-inch square or round baking pans.

Mix together the brown rice flour, potato starch, tapioca starch, quinoa flour, Egg Replacer, baking powder, xanthan gum, and salt.

Cream the butter until white. Add the sugar and beat until fluffy, about 5 minutes. Add the eggs and beat until smooth. Slowly mix in the dry ingredients. Do not overmix. Spoon the batter into the prepared pans. It is rather thick, so you will need to use a spatula or the back of a spoon to spread and smooth it evenly.

Mix all the streusel ingredients together. Sprinkle 2 tablespoons of the mixture over the batter in each pan. Arrange the cherries in concentric circles over the top. Sprinkle the remaining streusel mixture over the cherries. Bake on the middle rack for 30 minutes. Check for doneness. Continue baking 5 minutes more at a time, if needed. Remove the cakes from the oven and cool slightly before removing them from the pans.

VARIATION

PLUM COFFEE CAKE

Omit the cherries and streusel topping and arrange 12 Italian plums, pitted and quartered, over the cake batter and bake.

LEMON POPPY SEED BREAD *makes 2 (9 × 5-inch) loaves*

I adapted this recipe from *The Moosewood Cookbook.* It has taken me a while to perfect it, but it is now so good that I use it for wedding cakes. I fill the layers with Lemon Curd (page 199) and frost with a Lemon Buttercream. (page 145).

- 1 cup milk
- ¾ cup poppy seeds
- 2¾ cups Basic Gluten-Free Mix (page 16)
- ½ cup almond flour
- 1 tablespoon gluten-free baking powder
- ¾ teaspoon xanthan gum
- ⅛ teaspoon salt
- 2 sticks unsalted butter
- 1⅓ cups packed brown sugar
- 3 eggs
- ½ teaspoon gluten-free vanilla
- Grated zest of 2 lemons

Preheat the oven to 350°F. Lightly grease 2 (9 × 5-inch) loaf pans and line with parchment paper. Sometimes I have extra batter, so I make a half-dozen muffins too. Use paper liners for the muffin cups.

Heat the milk and add the poppy seeds. Let cool until just warm.

Mix together the gluten-free mix, almond flour, baking powder, xanthan gum, and salt.

Cream the butter until white. Add the brown sugar and beat until fluffy, about 5 minutes. Add the eggs, one at a time. Add the dry ingredients in 2 parts, alternating with the poppy seed and milk mixture. Stir in the vanilla and lemon zest.

Spoon the batter into the prepared loaf pans. Bake for 40 minutes or until done; the top should spring back when pressed gently. The muffins will take 15 to 18 minutes to bake.

UPSIDE-DOWN ARMENIAN COFFEE CAKE *Makes 1 (8-inch) round cake*

When I was the chef at Café l'Orange, a small restaurant in Concord, Massachusetts, Carolyne Lynch, who became my partner in my first catering business, gave me this recipe. It has been in her family for years, and now it's one of my favorites.

- 2 cups Basic Gluten-Free Mix (page 16)
- 2 cups packed dark brown sugar
- ½ teaspoon xanthan gum
- 1 stick unsalted butter
- 1 teaspoon nutmeg
- 1 teaspoon baking soda
- 1 cup sour cream
- 1 egg, lightly beaten
- 1 cup chopped walnuts
- 1 to 2 teaspoons cinnamon

Preheat the oven to 350°F. Lightly butter an 8-inch round baking pan.

Mix together the gluten-free mix, brown sugar, and xanthan gum. Using your fingertips, work in the butter until the mixture is the consistency of gravel. Sprinkle 1½ cups of the mixture over the bottom of the prepared pan. This will be the topping of your upside-down coffee cake. Add the nutmeg and baking soda to the remaining mixture. Stir in the sour cream and the egg.

Spoon the sour cream mixture over the mixture in the pan. Sprinkle the chopped walnuts and cinnamon over the top. Bake for 50 minutes. Cool for 10 minutes, then turn upside down on a serving dish without removing the pan. After 5 minutes, remove the pan and cool completely.

COOKIES AND BARS

Toll House Cookies
Toll House Pizza
Graham Crackers
Old-Fashioned Molasses Cookies
Peanut Butter Cookies
Crisp Ginger Molasses Cookies
Reilly's Chocolate Chip Cookies
Almond Butter Cookies
Scottish Shortbread Cookies
Pumpkin Spice Cookies
White Chocolate Pumpkin Cookies
Golden Carrot Macaroons
Hazelnut Cookies
Ceci Cookies
Linzer Cookies
Florentines
Walnut Orange Biscotti
Biscotti Morbida
Chocolate Biscotti Morbida
Biscotti Morbida with Fig Filling
Biscotti di Prato
Biscotti di Fruitti
Brownies
Hazelnut Brownies
Mint Bars
Cliff's Brownies
Butterscotch Bars
Lemon Squares
Coconut Lemon Squares
Almond Lemon Squares

Mmmmmm. Cookies are everyone's favorite snack and dessert. Just ask the next person you see, and I'll bet they can recall a special cookie memory—coming home from school to the smell of peanut butter cookies fresh from the oven or getting a care package when they were far away from home, full of Mom's chocolate chip cookies, or in my case, eating an entire recipe of Gran-mère's unbaked Christmas cookie dough with my sister—and the, *ahem,* deep trouble that resulted. Baking gluten-free cookies is not any more difficult than baking traditional cookies, and this chapter is chock-full of traditional favorites like chocolate chip and peanut butter—plus some out-of-the-ordinary cookies for you to try.

Let's first take a minute to review a few cookie-making "basics" as they apply to gluten-free baking. First and most important, use the best ingredients. Use fine-quality chocolate and real butter. If you use margarine instead of butter, the texture and flavor of the cookie will change—and let's all agree right now that "spreads" just don't work for baking. When a recipe calls for oil, use 60 to 80 percent vegetable oil, which makes a firmer cookie than 100 percent corn oil. And try experimenting with different types of nuts: try hazelnuts, macadamias, or almonds. To toast nuts, spread them in a single layer on a greased cookie sheet in a 350°F oven for 5 to 10 minutes.

As in any baking, measure all ingredients before you begin, and mix the dry ingredients together before adding liquid. Brown sugar, both light and dark, should be measured firmly packed. As you are mixing cookies, scrape the bowl often. I like to use those terrific new spoon spatulas for this—you can mix and scrape with one utensil. Chilling the dough before dropping the cookies stiffens the butter or shortening in the dough and makes it more manageable. The dough will also retain its shape better and not spread as much.

The choice of ingredients plays a big role in the texture of cookies, as well as in how they will bake, look, and taste. Changing the fat or flour in a recipe will alter the texture. For crisper cookies, use butter and a little corn syrup. If you increase the baking soda, the color will be better. For a cakelike cookie, use shortening and change the baking powder to baking soda. Eggs help give cookies a puff. Brown sugar ensures a more moist cookie. If you decrease the amount of sugar and fat slightly, the dough will spread less while baking.

Always double-check whether a recipe calls for a greased or ungreased cookie sheet. While we are on the topic of cookie sheets, have you ever noticed that some sheets are

shiny, while others are dull? There *is* a reason. Shiny sheets are perfect for shortbreads and butter cookies, while dull sheets are an all-round good choice for baking. Nonstick sheets don't allow cookies to spread, and insulated cookie sheets work better for baking soft-centered cookies.

Call me a perfectionist, but I always bake a test cookie first. I prefer to think that this habit stems from frugality—I hate to waste good ingredients—but it allows me to check the consistency of the dough. If it spreads too much, I can add a tablespoon or two more flour. Be certain to preheat the oven for at least 15 minutes. If you live at a high altitude, you know that the higher the altitude, the more difficult it is to get good baking results. Increase the baking temperature by 25 degrees and reduce the baking time by 1 or 2 minutes. Reduce the amount of sugar by 1 to 2 tablespoons; you may also need to reduce the baking soda or baking powder by ⅛ teaspoon.

Bar cookies are, by far, the easiest to make and serve—and they are quick as well. Let bar cookies cool in the pan, set on a rack. Cut them with a sharp knife when they are cool, and try fun shapes, such as diamonds or triangles. Bars store more easily in the pan they were baked in. If you are making bar cookies in a different size pan than the recipe calls for, check the baking time; you may need to add or subtract up to 5 minutes.

Drop cookies should be uniform in size, and they should not vary from sheet to sheet. Try using an ice cream scoop or a smaller cookie scoop, found in most kitchenware stores, to keep a consistent size. To make a crisper cookie, flatten the mounds of dough with a spatula or fork before you put the pan in the oven. Note that humidity, altitude, oven calibration, and ingredients can impact the baking times, so if a recipe gives a range of times (e.g., 8 to 10 minutes), check for doneness at the shorter time and monitor the baking closely to prevent burning. Remove drop cookies from the cookie sheet immediately with a wide spatula and cool in a single layer on a rack.

Store soft and crisp cookies separately. Soft gluten-free cookies should be kept in a tight-fitting container. Add an apple, orange, or piece of gluten-free bread to the container if they dry out. Crisp cookies should be stored in a container with a loose-fitting lid. I notice that crisp cookies tend to soften after a day, and so I just pop them into a 300°F oven for 3 to 5 minutes and they crisp right up! Gluten-free cookies freeze well. Wrap the cookies first in plastic wrap, then in an airtight container. Double-wrap the container in freezer paper or foil, and the cookies can be stored for a month. If a recipe calls for frosting, freeze the cookies without it and frost them after they thaw.

The recipes in this chapter start with some favorite cookies—from molasses to peanut butter. But do not miss making the graham cracker recipe: it's a winner!

Pour yourself a glass of milk and pop a batch in the oven today.

TOLL HOUSE COOKIES *Makes 4 dozen small cookies*

The universal favorite, reinvented gluten-free. Be certain to take the time to toast the nuts—and feel free to add more chips if you like.

- 2¼ cups Basic Gluten-Free Mix (page 16)
- 1 teaspoon baking soda
- ¼ teaspoon xanthan gum
- ⅛ teaspoon salt
- 2 sticks unsalted butter, at room temperature
- ¾ cup packed brown sugar
- ¼ cup granulated sugar
- 1 egg
- 2 teaspoons gluten-free vanilla
- 1½ cups chocolate chips
- 1 cup walnuts, lightly toasted

Mix together the gluten-free mix, baking soda, xanthan gum, and salt.

Cream the butter until white. Add both sugars and beat until fluffy, about 5 minutes. Add the egg and vanilla. Blend well. Slowly incorporate the dry ingredients. Stir in the chocolate chips and nuts. Cover and refrigerate for at least 1 hour before baking.

Preheat the oven to 350°F. Line cookie sheets with parchment paper.

Using an ice cream scoop, place mounds of the cookie dough on the cookie sheet, leaving 3 inches between the mounds. Bake for 10 to 12 minutes. The edges will be set but the centers will be soft. Transfer the cookies to a cooling rack.

VARIATIONS

DOUBLE CHOCOLATE CHIP COOKIES

Add to the Toll House recipe an additional ½ cup chocolate chips and 1 cup chopped lightly toasted walnuts.

SPICED DOUBLE CHOCOLATE CHIP COOKIES

Add to the dry ingredients for the Double Chocolate Chip Cookies 1½ teaspoons cinnamon and 1½ teaspoons ginger.

TOLL HOUSE PIZZA *Makes 1 10-inch pizza*

Let your children and their friends be creative with this. It's almost like having a "make your own pizza" party.

- 1 recipe Toll House Cookies
- White frosting of your choice
- M&M's, nuts, assorted gluten-free candies and nuts
- Marshmallow Fluff

Preheat the oven to 350°F. Line a 10-inch pizza pan with parchment paper and lightly coat it with cooking spray.

Press the chilled cookie dough onto the pizza pan to make one big cookie. Bake for 15 to 20 minutes or until the cookie is done. Cool on a rack. Frost with icing and then arrange the "toppings" as you like. Microwave the fluff for a few seconds or until it thins out enough to drizzle over the cookie.

GRAHAM CRACKERS *Makes 4 dozen crackers*

As versatile as the original, these graham crackers can be used for s'mores—the classic camp treat of graham crackers, chocolate bars, and roasted marshmallows—or to make gluten-free gingerbread houses at Christmas time. Or crumble them to make a crust for a pie or cheesecake. A must for every gluten-free household, this recipe is a winner.

- 1 cup Basic Gluten-Free Mix (page 16)
- 1 cup brown rice flour
- ¼ cup quinoa flour or soy flour
- ½ cup packed brown sugar
- 1¾ teaspoons cinnamon
- 1 teaspoon gluten-free baking powder
- ¾ teaspoon xanthan gum
- ½ teaspoon baking soda
- ½ teaspoon salt
- 7 tablespoons unsalted butter, chilled and cut into pieces
- 3 to 4 tablespoons cold water
- 3 tablespoons honey
- 1 teaspoon gluten-free vanilla

Mix together the gluten-free mix, brown rice flour, quinoa or soy flour, brown sugar, cinnamon, baking powder, xanthan gum, baking soda, and salt. Using your fingertips, work the butter into the dry ingredients. Stir in 3 tablespoons water, the honey, and vanilla.

If the dough is too dry, add a little more water, a teaspoon at a time. Gather the dough into a soft, manageable ball. Refrigerate for at least 1 hour.

Preheat the oven to 325°F. Lightly grease a cookie sheet and line it with lightly greased parchment paper.

Cut off a piece of the dough and roll it out between 2 pieces of lightly floured (with rice flour) parchment paper. Roll out to ⅛ to ¼-inch thickness. Cut into 2 × 3-inch pieces and prick all over lightly with a fork. Place on the prepared cookie sheet, leaving a little space around each piece. Bake for 12 to 15 minutes or until golden brown. Let the cookies cool slightly before transferring to a cooling rack. Repeat with the remaining dough.

VARIATIONS

CINNAMON GRAHAM CRACKERS

Sprinkle cinnamon sugar over the cookies just before baking.

CHOCOLATE GRAHAM CRACKERS

Replace the quinoa or soy flour with ⅓ cup plus 3 tablespoons unsweetened cocoa powder.

OLD-FASHIONED MOLASSES COOKIES *Makes 2 dozen cookies*

It will be difficult to stop yourself from eating these hot out of the oven with a glass of cold milk. Maybe you should make a double batch—one for you and the other for your family!

- 2½ cups Basic Gluten-Free Mix (page 16)
- 1 teaspoon baking soda
- 1 teaspoon ginger
- ½ teaspoon cinnamon
- ½ teaspoon xanthan gum
- ¼ teaspoon cloves
- ⅛ teaspoon salt
- 1 stick unsalted butter
- ½ cup packed brown sugar
- ½ cup molasses
- 1 egg
- ½ cup buttermilk

Mix together the gluten-free mix, baking soda, ginger, cinnamon, xanthan gum, cloves, and salt.

Cream the butter until white. Add the sugar and beat until fluffy, about 5 minutes. Slowly pour in the molasses. Beat until creamy. Add the egg. Alternately add the buttermilk and dry ingredients in 3 additions. Refrigerate the dough for at least 1 hour.

Preheat the oven to 350°F. Lightly grease a cookie sheet and line it with parchment paper.

Using a medium or small ice cream scoop, place mounds of dough on the cookie sheet, leaving 2 inches between the mounds. Or roll the dough into 1½-inch balls, place on the cookie sheet, and flatten slightly. Bake for 8 to 12 minutes, depending upon the size. Let the cookies sit for 5 minutes on the cookie sheet before transferring to a cooling rack.

PEANUT BUTTER COOKIES *Makes 3 dozen small or 2 dozen medium cookies*

There is nothing better than coming home to the smell of freshly baked peanut butter cookies. I usually make a double batch of the dough and freeze the extra to bake another time. I prefer an organic sugar for these cookies because I find the flavor so much better, but you can use white sugar. Be careful: overbaking will make this cookie dry.

- 1 cup bean flour
- 1 cup brown rice flour
- ¾ teaspoon xanthan gum
- ½ teaspoon baking soda
- ⅛ teaspoon salt
- 1 stick unsalted butter
- ½ cup organic or granulated sugar
- ½ cup honey
- 1 cup creamy peanut butter
- Sugar for coating

Mix together the bean flour, brown rice flour, xanthan gum, baking soda, and the salt.

Cream the butter until white. Add the ½ cup sugar and honey and beat until fluffy, about 5 minutes. Add the peanut butter and blend. Slowly incorporate the dry ingredients. Allow the dough to sit, covered, for at least 1 hour before baking.

Preheat the oven to 350°F. Lightly grease a cookie sheet and line it with parchment paper.

Using a small to medium ice cream scoop, scoop a ball of dough, roll in the sugar, then place on the prepared cookie sheet. Using the tines of a fork, press each cookie to flatten slightly. Bake for 8 to 10 minutes. The cookies will seem underbaked.

VARIATIONS

PEANUT BUTTER CHOCOLATE CHIP COOKIES

Add 1½ cups chocolate chips to the finished dough.

PEANUT BUTTER AND JELLY THUMBPRINT COOKIES

Instead of pressing the dough with a fork on the cookie sheet, press your thumb into the center. Then place a teaspoon of your favorite jam in the indentation left by your thumb.

MILLION DOLLAR COOKIES

Press an unwrapped Hershey's Kiss into the center of each hot cookie. Let the cookies sit on the cookie sheet for 5 minutes. Transfer to a cooling rack.

DOUBLE CHOCOLATE PEANUT BUTTER COOKIES

4 ounces semisweet chocolate, melted
1 cup chocolate chips
½ cup blanched peanuts

Add the melted semisweet chocolate after adding the peanut butter. Then add the chips and peanuts to the finished dough.

CRISP GINGER MOLASSES COOKIES *Makes 5 dozen small cookies*

This crisp ginger cookie was a hit with my tasters because it is both easy and full of hearty flavors. Keep a roll of this cookie dough in the freezer so that you can slice and bake a dozen or two when the urge for a crisp ginger cookie hits you. These cookies also make a great crust for a cheesecake or an icebox cake.

2⅔ cups Basic Gluten-Free Mix (see page 16)
1¼ teaspoons xanthan gum
1 teaspoon cinnamon
¾ teaspoon ginger
½ teaspoon cloves
½ teaspoon baking soda
⅛ teaspoon salt
1 stick unsalted butter, melted
1 cup sugar
¼ cup molasses
1 egg
Sugar for coating

Mix together the gluten-free mix, xanthan gum, cinnamon, ginger, cloves, baking soda, and salt.

Mix the melted butter, brown sugar, and molasses together. Beat in the egg. Slowly stir in the dry ingredients. The dough will be sticky. Refrigerate for 2 to 4 hours.

Divide the dough into 3 equal parts. Roll into logs ½ to 2 inches thick, depending upon how big you want the finished cookie to be. If the dough is too sticky to shape into a log, place each portion of dough on a piece of plastic wrap. Shape the dough roughly into a log and roll it up in the plastic wrap. Roll it on the counter to make it round. Refrigerate for at least an hour longer so that the dough stiffens enough to be sliced.

Preheat the oven to 350°F. Line a lightly greased cookie sheet with parchment paper.

Slice the logs ¼ to ⅓ inch thick. Press both sides of the slice in sugar. Place on the cookie sheet, leaving 2 inches between slices. Bake for 8 to 10 minutes. Cool completely, then transfer to an airtight container to store.

REILLY'S CHOCOLATE CHIP COOKIES *Makes 18 to 20 (2½-inch) cookies*

These cookies, named for my son, are good for those who have to eliminate not only gluten but also dairy, soy, eggs, and peanuts from their diet. In the spring, stock up on Passover chocolate chips, which have no lecithin (a soy-based product), so that you can make these special treats. The flax in this recipe serves as a binder for the cookie—and adds a healthy touch.

- 1¾ cups Basic Gluten-Free Mix (page 16)
- 1 teaspoon baking soda
- 1 teaspoon Egg Replacer
- ¼ teaspoon xanthan gum
- ⅛ teaspoon salt
- ¾ teaspoon flax meal
- ¼ cup boiling water
- ½ cup maple syrup
- ⅓ cup oil
- 1 teaspoon gluten-free vanilla
- ½ cup chocolate chips

Preheat the oven to 350°F. Line a cookie sheet with parchment paper.

Mix together the gluten-free mix, baking soda, Egg Replacer, xanthan gum, and salt.

Mix the flax meal and boiling water together until slightly thick, like an egg white. Cool slightly.

Make a well in the dry ingredients. Pour in the maple syrup, oil, vanilla, and flax mixture. Blend well. Stir in the chocolate chips.

Drop the dough by spoonfuls onto the cookie sheet. This is a thick dough, so the cookies will not spread very much. You can flatten with a fork or leave mounded. Bake for 12 minutes. The cookies will be puffy and cakelike, and the bottoms will be lightly golden. Overbaking will cause the cookies to be dry.

NOTE: You can replace the flax and boiling water with 1 egg.

ALMOND BUTTER COOKIES *Makes 3 dozen cookies*

These are buttery, melt-in-your-mouth cookies.

- 2 cups almond flour
- 1 cup rice flour
- ¾ teaspoon xanthan gum
- ½ teaspoon gluten-free baking powder
- ½ teaspoon cardamom
- ¼ teaspoon salt
- 1½ sticks unsalted butter
- 1½ cups sugar
- 1 egg yolk
- 1½ teaspoons Egg Replacer mixed with 2 tablespoons water
- Confectioners' sugar for dusting

Preheat the oven to 350°F. Lightly grease a cookie sheet and line it with parchment paper.

Mix together the almond flour, rice flour, xanthan gum, baking powder, cardamom, and salt.

Cream the butter until white. Add the sugar and beat until fluffy, about 5 minutes. Whisk the egg yolk and Egg Replacer mixture together. Beat into the creamed butter and sugar. Stir in the dry ingredients.

Shape the dough into 1¼-inch balls and place on the cookie sheet. Bake on the middle rack for 15 to 20 minutes. The cookies should be golden. While still slightly warm, dust with confectioners' sugar. Cool before storing in an airtight container.

SCOTTISH SHORTBREAD COOKIES *Makes 2 dozen cookies*

I grew up on Scottish shortbread cookies, which were our favorite Christmas cookie. Before my children and I changed our kitchen into a gluten-free kitchen, I, like my mother and my grandmother, made shortbread cookies for my children. There are some traditions worth keeping, so I worked on the family recipe until I was able to re-create the same flavor and almost the same texture that I remembered my mother's cookies had.

- 2 cups brown rice flour
- ½ cup almond flour
- ¼ cup sweet rice flour
- ½ teaspoon xanthan gum
- ⅛ teaspoon salt
- 2 sticks unsalted butter, at room temperature
- ½ cup packed brown sugar
- 1 teaspoon gluten-free vanilla
- 2 tablespoons heavy cream mixed with an egg yolk, for glazing cookies (optional)

Preheat the oven to 350°F. Lightly grease a cookie sheet and line it with parchment paper.

Mix together the brown rice flour, almond flour, sweet rice flour, xanthan gum, and salt.

Cream the butter until white. Add the sugar and continue beating until fluffy, about 5 minutes. Add the vanilla. Stir in the dry ingredients. Keep mixing until you have a soft cookie dough.

For traditional shortbread cookies, divide the dough into 3 pieces. Lightly flour the counter with white rice flour. Roll the dough out into a round ⅓ to ½ inch thick. My sister and I prefer our cookies thick and somewhat soft. Thinner cookies tend to be crisper. For a golden finish, brush the dough with the egg glaze. Using a fork, prick the surface gently. Cut into wedges. Place the pieces on the cookie sheet 1 inch apart and bake for 12 to 20 minutes, depending upon the thickness. Transfer to a cooling rack.

PUMPKIN SPICE COOKIES *Makes 3 dozen small cookies*

These are wonderful soft, cakelike cookies, perfect during the fall and winter months and a nice change from soft molasses cookies. They make great giant cookies with a cream cheese frosting. Try using dried cranberries instead of golden raisins.

1 cup plus 2 tablespoons Basic Gluten-Free Mix (page 16)
1 teaspoon Pumpkin Pie Spice Mix (recipe follows)
½ teaspoon baking soda
½ teaspoon xanthan gum
Pinch of salt
½ stick unsalted butter
⅓ cup packed light brown sugar
2½ tablespoons granulated sugar
1 egg, lightly beaten
½ cup pumpkin puree
½ cup golden raisins
½ cup pecan halves, lightly toasted
Spice Icing (recipe follows)

Mix together the gluten-free mix, pumpkin pie spice, baking soda, xanthan gum, and salt.

Cream the butter until white. Add both sugars and beat until fluffy, about 5 minutes. Add the egg and blend. Mix in the pumpkin puree. Slowly mix in the dry ingredients. Fold in the raisins and nuts. Cover and refrigerate for at least 1 hour.

Preheat the oven to 350°F. Lightly grease a cookie sheet and line it with parchment paper.

Using a medium ice cream scoop, place cookies 2 inches apart on the prepared cookie sheet. Bake for 12 to 15 minutes. Cool for 10 minutes and then pour a thin coating of the icing over each cookie.

PUMPKIN PIE SPICE MIX

1 tablespoon cinnamon
1½ teaspoons ginger
¾ teaspoon nutmeg
¾ teaspoon allspice
¼ teaspoon cloves

Mix everything together.

SPICE ICING

1 cup confectioners' sugar
Pinch of Pumpkin Pie Spice Mix
Heavy cream, enough to make a thin icing, about 2 tablespoons

Whisk the sugar and spices together. Whisk in enough cream to make the icing thin enough to glaze the cookies.

WHITE CHOCOLATE PUMPKIN COOKIES

Makes 5 to 6 dozen small cookies

I adapted this recipe from one by Ethel Goralnick, a chef and food editor of the *Lawrence Eagle Tribune* in Lawrence, Massachusetts. At first this combination of ingredients may seem unusual, but it really works. Pattee Di Pietro tested this recipe for me. She didn't have white chocolate chips, so she chopped up a bar of white chocolate. Her children ate these cookies in less time than it took her to make them!

2⅓ cups Basic Gluten-Free Mix (page 16)
1 teaspoon baking soda
¾ teaspoon xanthan gum
¼ teaspoon cinnamon
⅛ teaspoon allspice
⅛ teaspoon nutmeg
⅛ teaspoon salt
1 stick unsalted butter
1 cup sugar
2 eggs
1 cup pumpkin puree
1 tablespoon gluten-free vanilla
1 cup pecans, lightly toasted then cut in half or very coarsely chopped
2 cups white chocolate chips

Mix together the gluten-free mix, baking soda, xanthan gum, cinnamon, allspice, nutmeg, and salt.

Cream the butter until white. Add the sugar and beat until fluffy, about 5 minutes. Add the eggs, one at a time, beating well after each. Mix in the pumpkin puree and vanilla. By hand, stir in the dry ingredients. Fold in the nuts and chocolate chips. Cover and refrigerate the dough for at least 1 hour.

Preheat the oven to 350°F. Lightly grease a cookie sheet or line it with parchment paper.

Drop the dough onto the cookie sheet, using a teaspoon for small cookies or a tablespoon for larger ones. Leave an inch between cookies. Bake for 12 to 15 minutes. Let the cookies sit for 5 minutes before transferring to a cooling rack.

GOLDEN CARROT MACAROONS *Makes 2 dozen macaroons*

A macaroon lover can eat these and easily rationalize the healthful vitamins to go along with the sweetness and calories. The recipe calls for quinoa flour, which is milled from a grain that is high in protein and has a nutty flavor.

¼ cup brown rice flour
¼ cup quinoa flour
¼ teaspoon xanthan gum
Pinch of salt
2 egg whites
⅛ teaspoon lemon juice
½ cup honey
2 tablespoons vegetable oil
1 teaspoon gluten-free vanilla
1 cup tightly packed, finely grated carrot
2 cups shredded unsweetened coconut

Mix together the brown rice flour, quinoa flour, xanthan gum, and salt. Beat the egg whites with the lemon juice until foamy. Slowly pour in the honey. Blend well. Add the oil and vanilla. Stir in the dry ingredients. Fold in the carrots and coconut. Let the mixture sit for 20 minutes in the refrigerator.

Preheat the oven to 325°F. Line a cookie sheet with parchment paper. Lightly spray the paper with cooking spray.

Using a medium ice cream scoop, place scoops of the mixture 2 inches apart on the prepared cookie sheet. Bake for 25 to 30 minutes. Let the macaroons sit for 5 minutes before transferring to a cooling rack.

HAZELNUT COOKIES *Makes 16 to 18 cookies*

I developed this cookie recipe for Ruth Saltzman, who is a diabetic. I was catering her granddaughter's wedding one summer, and we were to have assorted cookies with the coffee. I wanted her to have a cookie she would be able to enjoy. I don't usually use Equal for baking, but this time I did and it worked. If sugar is not an issue for you, use an equivalent amount of sugar. Make the hazelnut flour by using a coffee grinder (see page 29), or purchase it at specialty shops or via mail orders (see pages 33–35).

1¾ cups hazelnut flour
¼ cup tapioca starch
¼ teaspoon xanthan gum
¼ teaspoon gluten-free baking powder
Pinch of salt
1 stick unsalted butter
1 cup Equal Spoonful or 1 cup sugar
¾ teaspoon gluten-free vanilla
1 egg yolk

Mix together the hazelnut flour, tapioca starch, xanthan gum, baking powder, and salt.

Cream the butter until white. Add the sweetener or sugar and beat until fluffy, about 5 minutes. Add the vanilla and egg yolk. Blend. Stir in the dry ingredients. Refrigerate for at least 1 hour.

Preheat the oven to 350°F. Line a cookie sheet with parchment paper. Lightly spray the paper with cooking spray.

Make 1½-inch balls and place them on the cookie sheet, leaving 2 inches between. Bake for 15 to 20 minutes. The bottoms will have a slight golden brown color. Cool slightly before transferring to a cooling rack.

VARIATIONS Use pecan or almond flour.

CECI COOKIES *Makes 24 cookies*

Chickpea flour is quite common in Middle Eastern cuisine. While it is definitely an acquired taste, it's worth a try. This crunchy cookie is not very sweet and has a pronounced chickpea flavor, which is nutlike and very distinctive. I love it dusted with confectioners' sugar.

2½ cups Basic Gluten-Free Mix (using 1 cup chickpea flour) (page 16)
2 teaspoons cinnamon
½ teaspoon xanthan gum
Pinch of salt
2 egg yolks
2 sticks unsalted butter, melted
1½ cups confectioners' sugar
2 tablespoons heavy cream
24 whole blanched almonds
Confectioners' sugar for dusting

Preheat the oven to 300°F. Lightly grease a cookie sheet and line it with parchment paper or dust it with rice flour.

Mix together the gluten-free mix, cinnamon, xanthan gum, and salt.

Beat together 1 egg yolk, the melted butter, and the 1½ cups confectioners' sugar until smooth. Stir in the dry ingredients. Whisk together the remaining yolk and the cream in a small bowl.

Roll the dough out to ¼ inch thick between 2 pieces of parchment paper. Cut into 2-inch triangles. Brush the triangles with the egg glaze. Place an almond on each cookie. Bake for 12 to 15 minutes. You can dust these cookies with confectioners' sugar as they cool. They will soften after a few days.

LINZER COOKIES *Makes 2 to 3 dozen cookies*

While these cookies are baking, picture yourself sitting at a cozy café in the Dolomite Mountains on the border of Austria and Italy, sipping cappuccino and enjoying the wonderful combination of raspberry and hazelnuts. The cookies are best eaten soon after making, as the jam will soften them after several days. They are delicious without the jam and just dusted with confectioners' sugar.

- 1¼ cups Basic Gluten-Free mix (page 16)
- 1 cup ground toasted hazelnuts or almonds
- 2 teaspoons cinnamon
- ½ teaspoon xanthan gum
- ¼ teaspoon nutmeg
- ¼ teaspoon cardamom
- ⅛ teaspoon salt
- 1 stick unsalted butter
- 1 cup sugar
- Seedless raspberry jam, melted

Preheat the oven to 350°F. Lightly grease a 10 × 10-inch baking pan and line it with lightly greased parchment paper.

Mix together the gluten-free mix, ground nuts, cinnamon, xanthan gum, nutmeg, cardamom, and salt.

Cream the butter until white. Add the sugar and beat until fluffy, about 5 minutes. Slowly incorporate the dry ingredients.

Press the dough into the prepared pan. Bake for 15 minutes. Spread the melted jam over the crust. Bake for another 12 minutes. Cool. Cut into 2-inch squares and remove from the pan.

FLORENTINES *Makes 12 to 16 cookies*

Florentines are flat, lacy, crispy cookies with a chocolate bottom. They are a bit time-consuming and fussy to make but well worth the effort. Once the chocolate is on the cookies, they need to be eaten within a few days; otherwise, they lose their crispness.

- ⅔ cup Basic Gluten-Free Mix (page 16)
- ⅛ teaspoon xanthan gum
- 6 tablespoons unsalted butter
- ⅔ cup sugar
- ⅓ cup heavy cream
- 3 tablespoons honey
- ⅔ cup chopped dried cherries
- ⅓ cup diced candied orange peel
- ⅓ cup Grand Marnier or other orange-flavored liqueur
- 1 cup sliced almonds (chop half of them)
- 6 ounces bittersweet chocolate, melted

Preheat the oven to 350°F. To prevent burning, use an insulated cookie sheet. Lightly grease the sheet and line it with parchment paper.

Mix together the gluten-free mix and xanthan gum.

Melt the butter in a medium saucepan. Add the sugar, cream, and honey and bring to a boil. Cook until the temperature on a candy thermometer reaches 230°F. (If you do not have a candy thermometer, dip a spoon into the boiling mixture and dribble it into a glass of ice-cold water; it should spin a thread.) This will take about 10 minutes. Stir in the cherries, orange peel, Grand Marnier, almonds, and dry ingredients.

Using a tablespoon or teaspoon, drop mounds of dough onto the cookie sheet, leaving about 3 inches between mounds. Dip your fingers in cold water and flatten the mounds a bit. Bake on the middle rack for 10 to 12 minutes, turning the pan halfway through the cooking time. Let the cookies cool on the cookie sheet, then transfer very carefully to a cooling rack.

Once the cookies have cooled, brush the melted chocolate on the bottom of each one. Turn the cookies top side down on the rack to allow the chocolate to set. As the chocolate begins to set, use a fork to make wavy lines. Store in a cool place. These cookies are fragile, so handle with care.

WALNUT ORANGE BISCOTTI *Makes 3 dozen or more cookies*

These biscotti are my all-time favorites. My friends wish that I would start a biscotti business so that they would have these all the time.

- 1½ cups Basic Gluten-Free Mix (page 16)
- ¼ cup sweet rice flour
- 1 teaspoon xanthan gum
- ½ teaspoon baking soda
- ½ teaspoon gluten-free baking powder
- ⅛ teaspoon salt
- 1 stick unsalted butter, at room temperature
- 1 cup sugar
- 2 eggs
- 2 teaspoons grated orange zest
- 1 teaspoon gluten-free vanilla
- 1½ cups chopped lightly toasted walnuts

Mix together the gluten-free mix, sweet rice flour, xanthan gum, baking soda, baking powder, and salt.

Cream the butter until white. Add the sugar and beat until fluffy, about 5 minutes. Blend in the eggs, one at a time. Add the orange zest and vanilla, then stir in the nuts. Slowly incorporate the dry ingredients to form a soft dough. Refrigerate the dough for at least 1 hour. I find the dough bakes better if refrigerated overnight.

Preheat the oven to 375°F. Lightly grease 2 cookie sheets and line with parchment paper.

Divide the dough into 3 equal pieces. Roll each piece into a log 1½ to 2 inches thick. Place 2 logs on one cookie sheet, leaving enough space between them for the dough to spread while baking. Place the third log on the other cookie sheet. Bake the logs for 20 minutes.

Remove the cookie sheet from the oven and let sit for 5 to 10 minutes. Slice the logs on a slight diagonal about ¾ inch thick. Place the slices, cut side down, on the cookie sheets. Lower the oven temperature to 350°F and bake the slices for 10 to 12 minutes. Cool on a cooling rack. Store in an airtight container.

VARIATIONS Along with the nuts, add one of the following:

- ½ to 1 teaspoon black pepper
- 1 cup dried cranberries or dried cherries
- 1 cup chocolate chips
- Any combination of the above

BISCOTTI MORBIDA *Makes 3 dozen cookies*

This is a soft biscotti. *Deliciosa!*

1 cup brown rice flour
1 cup almond flour
½ cup potato starch
¼ cup tapioca starch
¼ cup sweet rice flour
1 teaspoon xanthan gum
½ teaspoon baking soda
½ teaspoon gluten-free baking powder
1 stick unsalted butter
1 cup sugar
2 eggs
1 egg white

Mix together the brown rice flour, almond flour, potato starch, tapioca starch, sweet rice flour, xanthan gum, baking soda, and baking powder.

Cream the butter and sugar together until white and fluffy. Add the eggs, one at a time. Then slowly incorporate the dry ingredients to form a soft dough. Cover and refrigerate for 1 hour or, even better, overnight.

Preheat the oven to 375°F. Lightly grease 2 cookie sheets and line with parchment paper.

Divide the dough into 3 equal pieces. Roll each piece into a log about 1½ inches thick. Place 2 logs on one cookie sheet, leaving enough space between them for the dough to spread while baking. Place the third log on the other cookie sheet. Lightly beat the egg white, then lightly brush it on the logs. Bake on the middle rack of the oven for 20 minutes. Remove from the oven and let the logs sit for 5 minutes before slicing. Slice each log on a slight diagonal about ½ inch thick. For longer cookies, increase the diagonal. Cool before storing.

CHOCOLATE BISCOTTI MORBIDA *Makes 3 to 4 dozen cookies*

My family loves soft biscotti and were delighted when I made this chocolate version. They disappear as fast as I can make them.

- 1½ cups Basic Gluten-Free Mix (page 16)
- ½ cup almond flour
- ½ cup unsweetened cocoa powder
- ¼ cup sweet rice flour
- ½ teaspoon baking soda
- ½ teaspoon gluten-free baking powder
- ½ teaspoon xanthan gum
- ⅛ teaspoon salt
- 1 stick unsalted butter
- 1 cup sugar
- 2 eggs
- 1½ teaspoons gluten-free vanilla

Mix together the gluten-free mix, almond flour, cocoa powder, sweet rice flour, baking soda, baking powder, xanthan gum, and salt.

Cream the butter until white. Add the sugar and beat until fluffy, about 5 minutes. Add the eggs, one at a time. Mix in the vanilla. Then slowly incorporate the dry ingredients to form a soft dough. Cover and refrigerate for 1 hour or, even better, overnight.

Preheat the oven to 350°F. Lightly grease 2 cookie sheets and line with parchment paper.

Divide the dough into 3 equal pieces. Roll each piece into a log 1½ to 2 inches thick. Place 2 logs on one cookie sheet, leaving enough space between them for the dough to spread while baking. Place the third log on the other cookie sheet. Bake on the middle rack for 20 minutes. Remove from the oven and let the logs sit for 5 to 10 minutes. Slice the logs on a slight diagonal about ¾ inch thick. Cool before eating.

VARIATIONS Replace the almond flour with hazelnut or pecan flour.

BISCOTTI MORBIDA WITH FIG FILLING *Makes 3 dozen cookies*

Fig Newton lovers, this is for you.

- Dough for Biscotti Morbida (page 83)
- Fig Filling (recipe follows)
- 1 egg white

Preheat the oven to 375°F. Lightly grease 2 cookie sheets and line with parchment paper.

Divide the dough into 3 equal pieces. Roll each piece into a log about 1½ inches thick. Using your index finger, make an indentation along the length of each log. Press one-third of the fig filling into each indentation. Then pinch the dough up and together to cover the filling. Place 2 logs, seam side down, on one cookie sheet, leaving enough space between them for the dough to spread while baking. Place the third log on the other cookie sheet. Lightly beat the egg white, then lightly brush it on the logs. Bake on the middle rack of the oven for 20 minutes. Remove from the oven and let the logs sit for 5 minutes before slicing. Slice each log on a slight diagonal about ¾ inch thick. For longer cookies, increase the diagonal. Cool before storing.

FIG FILLING

- ¾ cup orange juice
- 3½ tablespoons brown sugar
- Grated zest of 1 orange
- 1 tablespoon lemon juice
- 1 tablespoon cornstarch or arrowroot
- 8 ounces dried figs, finely chopped
- 1 tablespoon finely chopped candied ginger

Mix all the ingredients together in a small nonaluminum saucepan. Cook over low heat until thick, being careful not to scorch. Cool completely before using.

BISCOTTI DI PRATO *Makes 3 to 4 dozen cookies*

From the village of Prato in the hills of Tuscany comes this dunking cookie. At the end of a meal, Italians enjoy this hard cookie with a small glass of Vino Santo, a sweet wine.

1¾ cups Basic Gluten-Free Mix (page 16)
1 cup almond flour
¼ cup sweet rice flour
¾ teaspoon xanthan gum
½ teaspoon baking soda
½ teaspoon gluten-free baking powder
⅛ teaspoon salt
1 stick unsalted butter
1 cup sugar
2 eggs
½ cup lightly toasted blanched almonds, each cut into 3 pieces
1½ teaspoons gluten-free vanilla
1 egg white, lightly beaten

Mix together the gluten-free mix, almond flour, sweet rice flour, xanthan gum, baking soda, baking powder, and salt.

Cream the butter until white. Add the sugar and beat until fluffy, about 5 minutes. Add the eggs, one at a time. Add the almonds and vanilla. Slowly incorporate the dry ingredients. Refrigerate the dough for at least 1 hour or overnight.

Preheat the oven to 350°F. Lightly grease 2 cookie sheets and line with parchment paper.

Divide the dough into 3 equal pieces. Roll each piece into a log 1½ inches thick. Place 2 logs on one cookie sheet, leaving enough space between them for the dough to spread while baking. Place the third log on the other cookie sheet. Brush the logs with the egg white. Bake for 15 to 20 minutes or until the logs are golden brown.

Remove the cookie sheet from the oven and let sit for 5 minutes. Slice the logs on a slight diagonal about ¾ inch thick. Place the slices, cut side down, on the cookie sheet. Bake the slices for 10 to 12 minutes. Cool on a cooling rack. Store in an airtight container.

VARIATION

CHRISTMAS BISCOTTI

Substitute pistachios for the blanched almonds and add 1 cup dried cranberries or cherries.

BISCOTTI DI FRUITTI *Makes 3 to 4 dozen*

An acclaimed expert on the history, culture, and food of Boston's North End Italian neighborhood, Michelle Topor made these dried fruit biscotti during a cooking class at my kitchen one summer. So I revised her recipe, making them gluten-free.

- 1½ cups Basic Gluten-Free Mix (page 16)
- ¾ cup sugar
- ¼ cup sweet rice flour
- ¼ cup almond flour
- 2 teaspoons grated lemon or orange zest
- 1 teaspoon baking soda
- 1 teaspoon gluten-free baking powder
- ¾ teaspoon nutmeg or cinnamon
- ½ teaspoon xanthan gum
- ⅛ teaspoon salt
- ½ cup dried cherries, cut in half if large
- ½ cup dried figs, stemmed and diced
- ½ cup golden raisins, chopped
- ¼ cup brandy, cognac, rum, or orange juice
- 2 egg whites, plus 1 whole egg
- 1 egg white, for glazing

Mix together the gluten-free mix, sugar, sweet rice flour, almond flour, zest, baking soda, baking powder, nutmeg or cinnamon, xanthan gum, and salt.

Place the dried cherries, figs, raisins, and brandy or juice in a bowl. Cover and macerate for 15 to 20 minutes.

Whisk 2 egg whites until frothy. Stir in the dry ingredients; the consistency will be coarse and crumbly. Add the whole egg and fruits; now the dough will be sticky. Cover and refrigerate for 1 hour or overnight.

Preheat the oven to 350°F. Lightly grease a cookie sheet and line it with parchment paper.

Flour your hands and the counter with rice flour. Divide the dough into 3 equal pieces. Shape each piece into a log about 12 inches long. Place the logs 3 inches apart on the prepared cookie sheet. Slightly flatten the logs until ½ inch thick and 2 inches wide. Lightly beat the remaining egg white, then brush it on each log. Bake the logs for 20 minutes or until golden. Let cool for 5 to 10 minutes. Lower the oven temperature to 300°F. Slice the logs on a slight diagonal about ½ inch thick. Stand the slices upright on the cookie sheet. Return to the oven to dry out for 25 minutes. Cool.

BROWNIES *Makes 12 to 16 brownies*

These brownies are easy to make. The trick is not to overbake them, as they are best a bit underdone. Substitute melted butter for the oil for even richer brownies. They freeze well.

- 1 cup Basic Gluten-Free Mix (page 16) or Bette Hagman's gluten-free mix
- 1 teaspoon xanthan gum
- 4 eggs
- 2 cups sugar
- ⅛ teaspoon salt
- 1 cup oil, such as canola, or 2 sticks melted unsalted butter
- 1 teaspoon gluten-free vanilla
- 4 ounces unsweetened chocolate, melted and slightly cooled

Preheat the oven to 350°F. Lightly grease a 9-inch square baking pan and line the bottom with parchment paper, or sprinkle with rice flour or cocoa powder.

Mix together the gluten-free mix and xanthan gum.

Beat the eggs, sugar, and salt until pale yellow and thick (see "Ribboning," page 30). Pour in the oil or butter and the vanilla. Blend. Stir in the melted chocolate. Sprinkle the dry ingredients on top and fold in.

Pour into the prepared pan. Bake on the middle rack for 20 to 25 minutes. Cool for 5 minutes before removing from the pan. Cool before cutting.

VARIATIONS After the dry ingredients are folded in, add one of the following:

- 1 cup chocolate chips (milk chocolate, white chocolate, semisweet chocolate, or a mixture)
- 1 cup chopped lightly toasted walnuts or hazelnuts
- 1 cup chocolate chips and ½ cup chopped lightly toasted walnuts or hazelnuts

You can also sprinkle ½ cup chopped nuts over the top before baking.

HAZELNUT BROWNIES *Makes 12 to 16 brownies*

I make these brownies when I want to indulge myself. They are very rich and dense, almost cakelike. In fact, you can bake the batter in a 9-inch springform pan and serve a slice of it with whipped cream or (if you *really* want to indulge) French vanilla ice cream and hot fudge sauce. The brownie will sink once it cools. Be sure to wait until it is thoroughly cool before slicing; otherwise, it will be crumbly.

- 2 cups hazelnut flour
- ¼ teaspoon xanthan gum
- 2 sticks unsalted butter, at room temperature
- ⅓ cup granulated sugar
- ⅓ cup packed light brown sugar
- Pinch of salt
- 3 eggs
- 1 teaspoon gluten-free vanilla
- 8 ounces extra bittersweet chocolate, melted and cooled
- ¾ cup chopped lightly toasted hazelnuts (optional)

Preheat the oven to 350°F. Lightly butter a 9-inch square pan and line it with parchment paper.

Mix together the hazelnut flour and xanthan gum.

Cream the butter until white. Add the sugars and beat until fluffy, about 5 minutes. Add the salt, eggs, and vanilla. Beat until well blended. Stir in the cooled and melted chocolate. Fold in the dry ingredients and add the nuts, if using.

Pour into the prepared baking pan. Spread evenly. Bake for 25 to 30 minutes or until a paring knife comes out clean and hot when inserted into the center of the brownie. Cool completely.

VARIATION Substitute almond flour and almonds for the hazelnuts.

MINT BARS *Makes 5 to 6 dozen bars*

Peggy Osher attended classes at my cooking school/catering business during the 1980s and was always very generous with her recipes. Her mint bars became a favorite of mine and a hit at my catering functions. I thought about it for two years before I attempted to adapt her recipe to gluten-free baking—and they are delicious! I keep the baked cookies frozen and eat them straight from the freezer; they thaw very quickly.

CRUST:

½ cup Basic Gluten-Free Mix (page 16)
½ cup almond flour
Pinch of salt
⅛ teaspoon xanthan gum
1 stick unsalted butter
⅔ cup sugar
2 eggs
2 ounces unsweetened chocolate, melted
½ teaspoon gluten-free vanilla

MINT ICING:

½ stick unsalted butter
2 cups sifted confectioners' sugar
3 to 6 tablespoons heavy cream
½ to 1 teaspoon mint extract

GLAZE:

2 ounces unsweetened chocolate
2 tablespoons unsalted butter

Preheat the oven to 350°F. Lightly grease a 9-inch square pan for thick cookies or a small jelly roll pan for thinner ones. Line it with parchment paper.

To make the crust, mix together the gluten-free mix, almond flour, salt, and xanthan gum.

Cream the butter until white. Add the sugar and beat until fluffy, about 5 minutes. Add the eggs and beat until well blended. Stir in the melted chocolate and vanilla. Stir the dry ingredients into the chocolate mixture.

Pour into the prepared pan and spread evenly. Bake for 15 minutes or until the tip of a sharp knife comes out hot to the touch and clean. Cool completely.

To make the icing, cream the butter and the confectioners' sugar together. Add the mint extract and enough cream to make an icing thin enough to spread. Spread over the chocolate crust.

To make the glaze, melt the chocolate and then whisk in the butter. Spread it over the mint icing.

Allow the glaze to harden before cutting the bars. Cut one way across the pan into 1-inch-wide slices, then cut on the diagonal, making diamond-shaped pieces.

CLIFF'S BROWNIES *Makes 2 to 3 dozen brownies*

I always encourage experimentation in gluten-free baking—and I practice what I preach. This recipe was created when we mixed all the dry ingredients together and added them to the eggs and the oil by mistake. There was no ribboning of sugar and egg, so there wouldn't be any leavening agent to make the brownies rise. Because I couldn't bear to throw away the mix and I wasn't willing to fiddle with the ingredients, I decided to bake the brownies and see what would happen. They came out flat and fudgy, but I layered them with mint filling and iced them with more chocolate. They were the hit of the party.

1 cup Basic Gluten-Free Mix (page 16) or Bette Hagman's gluten-free mix
2 cups sugar
1 teaspoon xanthan gum
Pinch of salt
4 eggs
1 cup canola oil
1 teaspoon gluten-free vanilla
4 ounces unsweetened chocolate, melted and slightly cooled

FILLING:

6 tablespoons unsalted butter
3 cups confectioners' sugar
4 to 6 tablespoons heavy cream
1½ teaspoons mint extract

GLAZE:

4 ounces unsweetened chocolate
½ stick unsalted butter

Preheat the oven to 350°F. Lightly grease a 13 × 9-inch baking pan and line the bottom with parchment paper.

Mix together the gluten-free mix, sugar, xanthan gum, and salt.

Lightly beat together the eggs, oil, and vanilla. Mix in the melted chocolate. Sprinkle the dry ingredients on top and fold in.

Pour the batter into the prepared pan. Bake on the middle rack for 20 to 25 minutes. Cool for 5 minutes before removing from the pan.

To make the filling, cream the butter until white and then add the confectioners' sugar. Add just enough heavy cream to make a mixture that is easy to spread. Flavor with the mint extract. Cut the brownie in half. Spread the filling over one of the halves. Place the second half on top of the filling.

To make the glaze, melt the chocolate and then whisk in the butter. Spread it over the brownie and chill until the chocolate is set before cutting. These are best served straight from the refrigerator.

BUTTERSCOTCH BARS *Makes 2 to 3 dozen bars*

Made in a smaller pan (8 to 9 inches square), these are almost a candylike bar. That was the way I first made this recipe. My daughter and her friends were delighted. If you prefer a cakelike bar, use a larger pan (13 × 9 or 10½ × 15 × 1 inch).

- 2½ cups Basic Gluten-Free Mix (page 16)
- ¾ teaspoon xanthan gum
- ½ teaspoon salt
- 1 ½ sticks unsalted butter
- ¾ cup packed light brown sugar

TOPPING:

- ⅓ cup unsalted butter
- 2 tablespoons light brown sugar
- 1 cup semisweet chocolate chips
- ⅔ cup light Karo syrup
- 1 tablespoon heavy cream
- 2½ cups chopped walnuts or pecans

Preheat the oven to 350°F. Lightly grease an 8- or 9-inch square baking pan or a 15½ × 10½ × 1-inch jelly roll pan. Line the bottom of the pan with parchment paper.

Mix together the gluten-free mix, xanthan gum, and salt.

Cream the butter until white. Add the brown sugar and beat until fluffy, about 5 minutes. Slowly incorporate the dry ingredients into the creamed butter and sugar. The mixture will be somewhat crumbly.

Press into the prepared pan. Prick the dough all over with a fork. Bake for 6 to 8 minutes or until lightly browned. Cool.

To make the topping, melt the remaining butter and brown sugar together in a small pan. Add the chocolate chips, Karo syrup, and cream. Stir over medium heat until the chips are melted and everything is well blended.

Once the crust is baked and cooled, pour the chocolate over the crust and sprinkle the nuts on top. Bake for another 10 to 12 minutes. Cool completely before cutting into 2-inch squares.

LEMON SQUARES *Makes 16 to 24 squares*

When I started working with Cynthia Murfey and Gail Hunter in their catering business, Gail was the lemon square expert. She was gracious enough to share her secret and her recipe with me. Here is the result of adapting her recipe to make a gluten-free treat for you lemon square lovers.

CRUST:

1 cup Basic Gluten-Free Mix (page 16)
½ cup almond flour or hazelnut flour
⅓ cup confectioners' sugar
¼ teaspoon xanthan gum
⅛ teaspoon salt
1 stick unsalted butter, chilled and cut into pieces

FILLING:

3 eggs
1½ cups granulated sugar
⅓ cup fresh lemon juice

Confectioners' sugar for dusting

Preheat the oven to 325°F. Lightly grease a 13 × 9-inch baking pan for thin bars or an 8-inch square pan for thicker bars. Line the pan with buttered parchment paper.

To make the crust, mix together the gluten-free mix, almond flour, confectioners' sugar, xanthan gum, and salt. Using your fingertips, work the butter into the dry ingredients. Do not overmix. You want to have a crumbly texture. Press the mixture into the prepared pan and bake for 20 minutes or until slightly golden.

To make the filling, beat the eggs and sugar together. Add the lemon juice. Whisk together.

Pour the filling over the hot crust. Return to the oven and bake for another 20 minutes. The edges will begin to brown. Cool before dusting with confectioners' sugar. Cut into about 2-inch squares.

COCONUT LEMON SQUARES *Makes 16 squares*

Who doesn't like lemon squares? Add coconut and you have a winning combination.

You can make coconut powder by grinding unsweetened shredded coconut in a coffee grinder.

CRUST:

¾ cup Basic Gluten-Free Mix (page 16)
¼ cup almond flour
¼ cup coconut powder or confectioners' sugar
¼ teaspoon xanthan gum
Pinch of salt
6 tablespoons unsalted butter, chilled

FILLING:

2 eggs
1 cup sugar
2 tablespoons fresh lemon juice
½ teaspoon gluten-free baking powder
½ cup shredded sweetened coconut

Confectioners' sugar or coconut powder for dusting

Preheat the oven to 350°F. Lightly grease an 8- or 9-inch square pan and line it with parchment paper.

To make the crust, mix together the gluten-free mix, almond flour, coconut powder, xanthan gum, and salt. Using your fingers, pinch the butter into the dry ingredients. Press the mixture into the baking pan. Bake for 15 to 20 minutes or until light golden.

To make the filling, beat the eggs, the sugar, lemon juice, and baking powder together. Stir in the coconut.

Pour the filling over the hot crust. Return to the oven and bake for another 20 to 25 minutes. The edges will begin to brown. Remove from the oven and cool. Dust with confectioners' sugar or more coconut powder. Cut into 2-inch squares.

ALMOND LEMON SQUARES *Makes 16 squares*

When it is your turn to bring dessert, try these almond lemon squares and no one will even guess that they are gluten-free.

CRUST:

¾ cup Basic Gluten-Free Mix (page 16)
¼ cup almond flour
¼ cup confectioners' sugar
¼ teaspoon xanthan gum
pinch of salt
6 tablespoons butter, chilled

FILLING:

2 tablespoons sifted confectioners' sugar
½ cup marzipan (almond paste)
3 eggs
1½ cups granulated sugar
⅓ cup fresh lemon juice

Confectioners' sugar for dusting

Preheat the oven to 350°F. Lightly grease an 8- or 9-inch square pan and line it with parchment paper.

To make the crust, mix together the gluten-free mix, almond flour, confectioners' sugar, xanthan gum, and salt. Using your fingertips, pinch the butter into the dry ingredients. Press the mixture into the baking pan. Bake for 15 to 20 minutes or until light golden. Cool slightly.

To make the filling, mix the confectioners' sugar into the marzipan. Roll out until large enough to fit on top of the crust. Place it on top of the cooled crust.

Beat together the eggs, granulated sugar, and lemon juice. Pour over the marzipan and crust. Return to the oven and bake for another 20 to 25 minutes. The edges will begin to brown. Remove from the oven and cool. Dust with confectioners' sugar. Cut into 2-inch squares.

VARIATION

RASPBERRY LEMON SQUARES

Make the crust for the lemon squares. Do not cover with marzipan. Melt 1 cup seedless raspberry jam and spread over the hot crust. Make the lemon filling and proceed with the recipe.

CAKES

Basic Cake
Butter Cake
Pound Cake
Chocolate Butter Cake
Cocoa Genoise
Carrot Almond Cake
Sponge Cake
Lemon Orange Sponge Cake
Biscuit aux Noix
Almond Biscuit
Walnut Cake
Ladyfingers
Meringue Shells
Nut Meringue Shells
Chocolate Meringue Shells
Fresh Fruit Pavlova
Lemon Pavlova
Guilt-Free Pavlova
Japonaise Base
Chocolate Torte
Chocolate Pecan Torte
Basic Yummy Cheesecake
Chocolate Cheesecake
Nondairy Chocolate Cheesecake
Savory Pesto Cheesecake
Warm Chocolate Hazelnut Cake
Chocolate Applesauce Cake
Chocolate Apricot Cake
Black Forest Cake

Boston Cream Pie
Bûche de Noël
Chocolate Praline Torte
Chocolate Raspberry Genoise
Chocolate Torte
Coconut Butter Cake
Dobos Torte
Fresh Nectarine Almond Cake
Lemon Icebox Cake
Chocolate Mousse Cake
Mocha Cream Torte
Hazelnut Pinwheel
Ravani
Sachertorte
Sicilian Cassata
Chocolate Cassata
S'more Cake
Southern Belle
Strawberry Cream Cake

As with the proverbial chicken and egg,

I am not certain which comes first: the cake or the celebration. Of this I am sure—the cakes in this chapter will make any meal, snack, or occasion a delight. One of the silver linings of gluten-free baking, from my point of view, is that it eliminates the temptation to pick up a mix amidst the dizzying options in the cake aisle at the supermarket. It gives us the chance to be creative and, best of all, to master some of the basics from classic cuisine, such as the sponge cake, biscuit, and genoise, and turn them into memorable desserts.

The key to the cakes in this chapter is understanding the technique used to make them. What makes a cake rise light and fluffy is the trapped air in beaten eggs or the gas formed by baking powder or soda. Incorporating air demands that the baker use such methods as ribboning, whipping, and folding, which are described on pages 28–32. I've also included a number of meringues in this chapter; creating perfect meringues is simplicity itself once you master the technique of beating egg whites (see page 26).

I advise bakers to use the finest ingredients for their creations—and cakes are no exception. Oil makes cakes tender and moist but cannot hold the air for leavening. Sugar, like fat, helps tenderize the cake, while honey or brown sugar helps cakes stay moist. Because the sugar is already dissolved in syrups, cakes made with syrup will brown at lower temperatures, so adjust the heat accordingly. An extra egg white will help to raise a flat cake. Careful measurement is critical to creating the delicate balance of ingredients that ensures a cake will rise. The environment for cake baking is important—your room should be 70°F or "room temperature" during baking.

Having the right equipment on hand is just as important as using the finest ingredients. But how do you choose the right pan? Standard round cake pans are 9 inches across and 1½ inches deep, but a 2-inch-deep pan is better to use and more versatile. It is best to have two or three round cake pans of the same diameter, one springform pan for cheesecake, and a ring mold. For many of the cakes in this chapter, creating a cake roll is a delightful departure from the traditional—and for that you'll need a 17 (or 18) × 13-inch jelly roll pan. I also like to use a pan with a decorated bottom so that I can invert the cake and dust it with confectioners' sugar for a simple and elegant finish. The material for baking pans depends on your preference. Aluminum heats most evenly. Nonstick pans release cakes easily. Nonstick pans of aluminum and steel combine these qualities and are a favorite among commercial bakers.

If you are not sure if your pan is the right size for your batter, fill the pan with water, measure the water, then add up the quantity of the ingredients in the recipe: 2 cups flour plus 1 cup sugar plus 1 egg (¼ cup) and so on. I use a trusty tool—my finger—to tell if there is enough batter in a pan. Up to the first knuckle of my index finger is about 1 inch deep. Fill cake pans one-half to two-thirds full. Loaf pans and tubes, however, can be filled fuller. If beaten egg whites are called for in a recipe, be certain to beat them last (unless you are beating sugar into the whites). And make sure that when you begin beating the whites, the pan is prepared and that the oven is preheated so you can put the cake directly into the oven.

Just before baking, tap the bottom of the cake pan to free air bubbles that may be trapped, then place the pan in the center of the oven. Be sure to close the oven door gently and do not, I repeat, *do not* open the door during the first 15 minutes of baking or your cake will sink in the middle.

When cooling a cake, keep in mind that the type of cake dictates the cooling method. In general, cool plain cakes in the pan for 5 minutes, then invert them onto a cooling rack. Richer cakes, like pound or other butter cakes, should sit for 10 minutes in the pan and then be unmolded onto a cooling rack and turned right side up. Genoise and sponge cakes are removed from the pan, inverted, and cooled immediately. Angel food cakes should cool upside down in the pan; if the pan does not have feet, you can set its center hole over a funnel or a bottle. To avoid imprinting cooling rack marks on the top of a cake, place a towel on the rack and invert the cake onto the towel. Then turn it onto another rack.

Not all cakes need to be frosted; a dusting of confectioners' sugar or a garnish of fruit makes a nice finish. But when the cake is for a gift or special occasion, take the opportunity to be creative. Select one of the frostings from the next chapter to complement the cake in taste, texture, and appearance. Try your hand at decorating with one of the many cake-decorating accessories on the market—and think about taking a decorating class for fun. Using a turntable or lazy Susan makes the process of icing a cake much easier; simply place the cake on a round of cardboard and then on the turntable. Apply a thin layer of frosting, the crumb coat, then frost and decorate the cake. Carefully lift it off the turntable onto a serving dish.

Baking is both a science and an art; it is more precise and scientific than any other kind of cooking. Mastering the classic techniques will give you a fabulous sense of pleasure and accomplishment. The satisfaction you will feel when your family is begging for one of your cakes will be just reward, and I hope it will encourage you to tackle even the most complex of recipes.

BASIC CAKE *Makes 1 (9-inch) round or 1 (11 × 7-inch) rectangular cake*

One sunny June Sunday, I had a craving for a white cake to go with the bowl of fresh strawberries my mother had prepared for dessert. So I created this very versatile cake, which tastes even better the next day. Dust with confectioners' sugar, serve plain, or cover with your favorite frosting.

2½ cups Basic Gluten-Free Mix (page 16)
1 cup maple sugar or brown sugar
½ cup almond flour
1½ tablespoons gluten-free baking powder
1 teaspoon Egg Replacer
¾ teaspoon xanthan gum
⅛ teaspoon salt
1½ cups hot milk
½ cup almond oil or vegetable oil
1 teaspoon gluten-free vanilla

Preheat the oven to 350°F. Lightly grease a 9-inch round cake pan or an 11 × 7-inch baking pan and line the bottom with parchment paper.

Mix together the gluten-free mix, maple sugar, almond flour, baking powder, Egg Replacer, xanthan gum, and salt.

Whisk together the hot milk, oil, and vanilla. Slowly incorporate the dry ingredients into the milk mixture. Whisk until the batter is smooth. Pour into the prepared pan and let sit for 5 minutes before placing in the oven.

Bake for 20 to 22 minutes or until done. Do not overbake or the cake will be very dry. Let the cake sit in the pan for 10 minutes, then turn it out onto a cake rack. Remove the parchment paper and turn the cake right side up. Cool completely before serving.

VARIATIONS

- Omit the maple sugar. Add ½ cup maple syrup when mixing the hot milk and oil, and add ⅛ teaspoon baking soda to the dry ingredients.
- To make a chocolate cake, omit ½ cup of the gluten-free mix; add ½ cup unsweetened cocoa powder and ⅛ teaspoon baking soda to the dry ingredients.
- To create a checkerboard cake, make one recipe of the basic cake and one of the chocolate variation. Use special pans for a checkerboard cake.

BUTTER CAKE *Makes 1 (8-inch) round cake*

This is another basic cake that is great as a birthday cake. As with all butter cakes, do not refrigerate because it will dry out in the refrigerator. Just wrap well and leave on the counter for up to two days.

- ⅔ cup brown rice flour
- ⅓ cup potato starch
- 1 tablespoon sweet rice flour or tapioca starch
- 1 teaspoon Egg Replacer
- ½ teaspoon gluten-free baking powder
- ¼ teaspoon xanthan gum
- ⅛ teaspoon salt
- 1 stick unsalted butter
- ½ cup sugar
- 2 eggs
- ½ teaspoon gluten-free vanilla
- 2 to 3 tablespoons milk

Preheat the oven to 350°F. Butter an 8-inch round cake pan and line it with buttered parchment paper.

Mix together the brown rice flour, potato starch, sweet rice flour, Egg Replacer, baking powder, xanthan gum, and salt.

Beat the butter until white. Add the sugar and beat until fluffy, about 5 minutes. Add the eggs, one at a time, and beat until smooth. Add 1 tablespoon of the dry ingredients if the mixture appears to be curdled or broken. Stir in the remaining dry ingredients and the vanilla and milk.

Spoon the batter into the prepared cake pan. Bake for 15 to 20 minutes or until done. Let sit for 10 minutes before inverting onto a cooling rack.

POUND CAKE *Makes 1 (8½ × 4½-inch) loaf*

The original recipe for this classic butter cake called for equal weights of eggs, butter, flour, and sugar, otherwise known as *quatre-quatre.* Sturdy and moist, it can support the addition of dried fruits and nuts. It is important to cream the butter and sugar very well.

- 1 cup Basic Gluten-Free Mix (page 16)
- 1½ cups almond flour
- 1 teaspoon Egg Replacer
- ½ teaspoon xanthan gum
- ½ teaspoon gluten-free baking powder
- ¼ teaspoon freshly grated nutmeg
- ⅛ teaspoon salt
- 1 stick unsalted butter
- 1 cup sugar
- 1 teaspoon gluten-free vanilla
- 5 eggs
- 4 ounces mascarpone cheese

Preheat the oven to 350°F. Butter an 8½ × 4½-inch loaf pan and line with buttered parchment paper.

Mix together the gluten-free mix, almond flour, Egg Replacer, xanthan gum, baking powder, nutmeg, and salt.

Cream the butter until white. Add the sugar and beat until fluffy, about 5 minutes. Add the vanilla and 1 egg. Beat until smooth. Blend in the mascarpone. Alternate adding the remaining eggs with the dry ingredients.

Pour the batter into the prepared pan. Bake for 45 to 50 minutes or until done. Cool the cake in the pan for 25 minutes, then invert onto a cooling rack. Remove the parchment paper and cool completely.

VARIATIONS

Omit the nutmeg and add 1 tablespoon grated fresh ginger or 2 teaspoons ground ginger.

Add ¾ cup mini chocolate chips

CHOCOLATE BUTTER CAKE *Makes 1 (8-inch) round cake*

One day while testing my basic chocolate cake and the butter cake, my cooking friend Cynthia Murfey volunteered to taste the results. Although she liked both, she wondered if it would be possible to make a chocolate cake that tasted more like the butter cake. I decided to give it a try. With much coaxing, my daughter left a piece for me to take to Cynthia, who heartily approved. Make it special with a ganache filling (page 150) and a French buttercream frosting (page 145).

¾ cup Basic Gluten-Free Mix (page 16)
¼ cup unsweetened cocoa powder
1 teaspoon Egg Replacer
½ teaspoon baking soda
¼ teaspoon xanthan gum
⅛ teaspoon salt
1 stick unsalted butter
½ cup confectioners' sugar
2 eggs, at room temperature
½ teaspoon gluten-free vanilla
2½ tablespoons milk

Preheat the oven to 350°F. Butter an 8-inch round cake pan and line it with parchment paper.

Mix together the gluten-free mix, cocoa powder, Egg Replacer, baking soda, xanthan gum, and salt.

Cream the butter until white. Add the confectioners' sugar and beat until fluffy, about 5 minutes. Add the eggs, one at a time, and beat until smooth. Add 1 tablespoon of the dry ingredients to the mixture if the batter appears to be cundled or broken. Stir in the remaining dry ingredients and the vanilla and milk.

Spoon the batter into the prepared cake pan. Bake for 15 to 20 minutes or until done. Let the cake sit for 10 minutes before inverting onto a cooling rack.

COCOA GENOISE *Makes 1 (8-inch) round cake*

The French butter sponge cake called genoise is a basic cake you will want to master. It is leavened by using a technique called ribboning. Once you have mastered the recipe and technique, try doubling it to make a layer cake or cake roll. For a layer cake, raise the oven temperature to 350°F.

- 2 tablespoons potato starch
- 6 tablespoons sifted unsweetened cocoa powder
- 1 tablespoon arrowroot or cornstarch
- 3 eggs, at room temperature
- 6 tablespoons sugar
- ⅛ teaspoon salt
- 2 teaspoons gluten-free vanilla
- ½ stick unsalted butter, melted and clarified

Preheat the oven to 325°F. Lightly butter an 8-inch round cake pan and line it with parchment paper.

Mix together the potato starch, cocoa powder, and arrowroot or cornstarch.

Ribbon the whole eggs, sugar, and salt (see technique, page 30). Add the vanilla and reribbon. Place the dry ingredients in a sifter. Sift one-third of the dry ingredients over the batter and fold in. Repeat with the remaining dry ingredients, one-third at a time. Fold in the clarified butter.

Spoon the batter into the prepared cake pan and bake for 15 to 20 minutes or until done. Invert immediately onto a cooling rack.

CARROT ALMOND CAKE *Makes 1 (8-inch) round cake*

This cake is good enough to stand alone without icing, with just a dusting of confectioners' sugar (although a dollop of sweetened vanilla whipped cream is also a nice touch). To dress it up, try a white chocolate or vanilla buttercream icing. The baking technique for this cake is that of a genoise. It is important to have warm eggs and to ribbon the eggs and sugar heavily in order to incorporate air into the cake.

1½ cups almond flour
¼ cup potato starch
1½ tablespoons sweet rice flour
Pinch of salt
3 eggs
¾ cup packed light brown sugar
½ tablespoon gluten-free vanilla
1 cup finely grated carrots
½ stick unsalted butter, melted

Preheat the oven to 350°F. Lightly butter an 8-inch round cake pan. Line the bottom with parchment paper.

Mix together the almond flour, potato starch, sweet rice flour, and salt.

Heat a saucepan with an inch of water over low heat. Do not let the water boil. Break the eggs into a heatproof mixing bowl. Place the bowl over the hot water. Begin beating the eggs with an electric beater or by hand with a whisk. Slowly incorporate the brown sugar. Continue beating until the mixture feels warm when you stick your finger in it. Remove the bowl from the hot water and continue beating until the mixture forms a heavy ribbon (see page 30) and the tracks of the beater do not disappear right away. Add the vanilla. Fold in the carrots. Sprinkle the dry ingredients over the mixture and fold in. Fold in the melted butter.

Gently pour the batter into the prepared pan. Smooth the top. Tap the bottom of the cake pan once. Bake on the middle rack for 25 to 30 minutes or until the cake is done; it will pull away from the sides of the pan. Invert the cake onto a cooling rack. Remove the parchment paper. Cool completely before serving.

VARIATION Substitute an equal amount of hazelnut flour for the almond flour.

SPONGE CAKE *Makes 2 (8-inch) cake layers or 1 cake roll*

Aaaah, the indispensable sponge layer cake. This classic can also be baked in a jelly roll pan, filled with any preserves or jam you like, rolled up, and served with whipped cream piped on top. Or you can be more adventurous with the filling and make a mousse or buttercream or any variation that you can imagine. During the observance of Passover, make this cake with the potato starch.

4 eggs, separated
1 cup sugar
1½ teaspoons gluten-free vanilla
2 tablespoons plus ¼ teaspoon lemon juice
Pinch of salt
1 cup potato starch or rice flour

Preheat the oven to 325°F. Lightly grease two 8-inch round cake pans or a 17 × 13-inch jelly roll pan and line with parchment paper.

Ribbon the egg yolks and the sugar together until pale yellow (see technique, page 30). Add the vanilla and 2 tablespoons of the lemon juice.

Whip the egg whites with the salt and ¼ teaspoon lemon juice until soft peaks are formed. Gently fold one-fourth of the whites into the ribboned base. Slide the remaining egg whites on top. Sift the potato starch or rice flour on top of the egg whites. Fold into the base until homogenous.

Gently spoon the batter into the prepared cake pans or jelly roll pan. Tap the bottom of the pans once on the counter to remove any air pockets. Bake the cake layers on the middle rack for 20 to 25 minutes, the cake roll for 12 to 15 minutes, or until done. If making cake layers, invert onto a cooling rack; if making a cake roll, invert onto a tea towel dusted with confectioners' sugar, trim the edges, and loosely roll up lengthwise. Unroll, fill, and decorate when totally cooled.

LEMON ORANGE SPONGE CAKE

Makes 1 (10-inch) Bundt cake or 1 cake roll

This recipe was adapted from a Passover cake recipe given to me by my friend Lonnie Harris, whose father was a celiac. It is delicious served with fresh sliced strawberries and whipped cream.

1 cup finely ground toasted gluten-free bread crumbs
¼ cup potato starch
12 eggs, separated
1½ cups sugar
½ cup orange juice
Grated zest of 1 lemon and 1 orange
Pinch of salt
1 teaspoon lemon juice

Preheat the oven to 325°F. Use a nonstick 10-inch Bundt pan or line a 17 × 13-inch jelly roll pan with parchment paper.

Mix together the bread crumbs and potato starch. Ribbon the egg yolks and sugar heavily (see technique, page 30). Beat in the orange juice and the lemon and orange zest.

Whip the egg whites with the salt and lemon juice until soft peaks are formed. Gently stir one fourth of the whites into the ribboned base. Slide the remaining egg whites on top. Sprinkle the dry ingredients on top and fold into the base until homogenous.

Gently spoon the batter into the Bundt pan. Bake for 30 minutes or until done. Cool and then unmold. If making a cake roll, bake for 12 to 15 minutes. Invert onto a tea towel dusted with confectioners' sugar, trim the edges, and loosely roll up lengthwise. Cool.

VARIATIONS

Fill the cake roll with 1 cup whipped cream and 1 cup sliced strawberries. Roll up like a jelly roll. Using a pastry bag fitted with a fluted nozzle, pipe 1 cup whipped cream on top and decorate with whole berries and fresh mint leaves.

Flavor the whipped cream with 1 tablespoon Grand Marnier and garnish the roll with orange slices instead of strawberries.

Instead of whipped cream, spread the cake roll with 1½ to 2 cups Lemon Curd (page 199).

BISCUIT AUX NOIX *Makes 1 cake roll or 2 (8-inch) cake layers*

In winter, make this cake with half walnuts and half almonds, then fill it with coffee-flavored whipped cream. In summer, use almonds and fill with sweetened whipped cream and strawberries.

- 2 cups finely chopped nuts of your choice
- ¼ cup sifted cornstarch
- 4 eggs, separated
- ½ cup sugar
- 1 teaspoon gluten-free vanilla
- Pinch of salt
- ¼ teaspoon lemon juice

Preheat the oven to 325°F. Lightly grease a 15½ × 10½ × 1-inch jelly roll pan or two 8-inch round cake pans and line with parchment paper.

Mix together the nuts and cornstarch and set aside.

Ribbon the egg yolks and sugar until pale yellow (see technique, page 30). Add the vanilla.

Whip the egg whites with the salt and lemon juice until soft peaks are formed. Gently stir one fourth of the whites into the ribboned base. Slide the remaining whites on top. Sprinkle the nuts over the egg whites and fold into the base until homogenous.

Gently pour the batter into the prepared pan. Tap the bottom once on the counter to remove any air pockets. Bake the cake roll on the middle rack for 12 to 15 minutes or until done. If making a cake roll, invert it onto a tea towel sprinkled with confectioners' sugar. Trim the edges, loosely roll up lengthwise and cool. If making cake layers, bake for 15 to 20 minutes and turn them out onto a cooling rack.

ALMOND BISCUIT *Makes 1 (11 × 7-inch) cake*

A *biscuit* (pronounced "biss-KWEE") is a sponge cake made with separated eggs. The egg yolks are ribboned with sugar, and the whites are beaten and folded in, oh so very gently, to create a light cake.

- ¼ cup potato starch
- ¾ cup almond flour
- 1 teaspoon Egg Replacer
- 3 eggs, separated
- ½ cup confectioners' sugar
- 1 teaspoon gluten-free vanilla
- ¼ teaspoon lemon juice
- ⅛ teaspoon salt
- 1 tablespoon granulated sugar
- ⅓ cup butter, melted

Preheat the oven to 375°F. Lightly grease an 11 × 7 × 1½-inch jelly roll pan or a 15½ × 10½ × 1-inch jelly roll pan. Line with parchment paper.

Mix the potato starch, almond flour, and Egg Replacer together.

Ribbon the egg yolks with the confectioners' sugar (see technique, page 30). Add the vanilla and ribbon again. In a clean bowl with a whisk begin beating the egg whites with the lemon juice and salt. As soon as the whites are a thick foam, add the granulated sugar. Beat until stiff peaks are formed. Gently stir one-fourth of the whites into the ribboned base. Slide the remaining whites on top. Sprinkle the dry ingredients over and fold into the base until homogeneous. Quickly but gently fold in the melted butter.

Pour the batter onto the prepared pan. Spread the batter evenly over the pan. Tap the bottom of the pan once on the counter to remove any air pockets. Bake on the middle rack for 12 to 14 minutes or until done. Invert the cake onto a tea towel dusted with confectioner's sugar. Remove the parchment and let cool.

WALNUT CAKE *Makes 2 (9-inch) cake layers or 1 cake roll*

During training, professional chefs are taught not to waste anything in cooking—and to use everything. I collect leftover bread crumbs, cake crumbs, and cookie crumbs in my freezer, waiting for just the right recipe to come along. I use leftover gluten-free cookie crumbs to make this cake. I fill and ice it with either a coffee-flavored whipped cream or French buttercream (page 145).

- 2 cups finely ground lightly toasted walnuts
- ¾ cup gluten-free cookie crumbs
- 6 eggs, separated
- ¾ cup sugar
- 1 tablespoon rum
- ¼ teaspoon lemon juice

Preheat the oven to 325°F. Lightly grease two 9-inch round cake pans or a 17 × 13-inch jelly roll pan and line with parchment paper.

Mix the nuts and the cookie crumbs together.

Ribbon the egg yolks and sugar until thick and pale yellow (see technique, page 30). Add the rum and ribbon again.

Whip the egg whites and lemon juice until soft peaks are formed. Gently stir one-fourth of the whites into the ribboned base. Slide the remaining whites on top. Sprinkle the nuts and cookie crumbs on top and fold into the base until homogenous.

Gently spoon the batter into the prepared pans. Tap the bottom of the pans once on the counter to remove any air pockets. Bake on the bottom rack for 20 minutes or until done. Cool on a rack. If making a cake roll, invert the cake onto a clean tea towel sprinkled with confectioners' sugar. Trim the edges and loosely roll up lengthwise. Cool, unroll, and fill.

LADYFINGERS *Makes 48 to 50 ladyfingers*

I have always enjoyed making desserts featuring ladyfingers, the oblong-shaped sponge cakes, so I set my mind to perfecting a gluten-free recipe. These are not as puffy as the store-bought ones you may be familiar with, but the flavor is right, and they are perfect for icebox cakes, mousse cakes, tiramisu, or trifle.

⅔ cup potato starch
⅓ cup almond flour
1 teaspoon gluten-free baking powder
4 eggs, separated
½ cup sugar
⅛ teaspoon salt
1 teaspoon gluten-free vanilla
⅛ teaspoon lemon juice
Confectioners' sugar for dusting

Preheat the oven to 350°F. Line 2 or 3 cookie sheets with parchment paper.

Mix together the potato starch, almond flour, and baking powder.

Ribbon the egg yolks with the sugar, salt, and vanilla heavily (see technique, page 30).

Whip the egg whites with the lemon juice until soft peaks are formed. Gently stir one-fourth of the whites into the ribboned base. Slide the remaining whites on top. Sprinkle dry ingredients over the whites and fold into the base until homogenous.

Fit a pastry bag with a plain ½-inch nozzle. Stuff the pastry bag with the batter and pipe 3-inch-long ladyfingers onto the parchment paper, leaving a few inches between them. Dust the ladyfingers with the confectioners' sugar. Bake one cookie sheet at a time, refrigerating the second (and third) one while the first batch bakes. This will slow down the deflation of the whites. Bake for 7 to 8 minutes or until the ladyfingers are golden. Transfer to a cooling rack.

VARIATIONS

Spoon the batter into a pastry bag fitted with a ½-inch plain nozzle. Pipe 1½-inch rounds onto parchment-lined cookie sheets. Bake for 12 minutes. Cool. Sandwich 2 cakes together with a filling of sweetened and flavored whipped cream, Ganache, Cream Cheese Frosting (page 148), or Buttercream (page 146).

MERINGUE SHELLS *Makes 2 (8- or 10-inch) shells*

Meringue shells are a versatile, low-fat base for desserts; you can dress them up with fruit, fruit sauces, or a rich chocolate sauce. If you are adept with a pastry bag, you can make meringues into baskets, swans, hearts, or a design of your own. Once made, if stored properly, they last for a long time. If you make a recipe calling for egg yolks only, freeze the whites for later use in meringues.

4 egg whites, at room temperature
Pinch of salt
⅛ teaspoon lemon juice
Scant 1 cup sugar
1 teaspoon gluten-free vanilla

Preheat the oven to 225°F. Lightly butter 2 cookie sheets and dust with rice flour or line them with parchment paper. Trace two 8- or 10-inch circles (or more smaller ones) on the prepared cookie sheets.

Using an electric mixer, beat the egg whites, salt, and lemon juice on low speed until soft mounds form. Add the sugar. Increase the speed to medium-high, add the vanilla, and beat until the meringue is glossy and forms stiff peaks. Divide the meringue in half and spread within the circles you have drawn on the cookie sheets, going over the lines just a little. Bake for 2 to 3 hours or until the meringues are dry. Cool on a rack.

NUT MERINGUE SHELLS *Makes 2 or 3 (8-inch) shells*

When I bake meringues with nuts, I always use a higher temperature than for other meringues. Because I am usually using nut meringues in a cake recipe with a filling, I want the meringues to be crisp because the filling will soften them. At a higher temperature, the meringue will brown up, which is okay.

6 egg whites
Pinch of salt
Drop of lemon juice
1¼ cups superfine granulated sugar
2 cups nuts of your choice, ground finely with 9 tablespoons sugar
1 tablespoon gluten-free vanilla

Preheat the oven to 325°F. Lightly butter 2 cookie sheets and dust with rice flour, or line them with parchment paper. Trace two or three 8-inch rounds on the prepared cookie sheets.

Using an electric mixer, beat the egg whites, salt, and lemon juice until soft mounds form. Add the sugar. Increase the speed to medium-high and beat until the meringue is glossy and forms stiff peaks. Fold in the nuts and vanilla.

Fit a pastry bag with a plain nozzle and fill it with the meringue. Pipe a ring around the shapes traced on the cookie sheets. Fill in with the meringue. Smooth out with a spatula. Bake for 20 to 25 minutes. Cool, then remove to a rack.

CHOCOLATE MERINGUE SHELLS *Makes 2 (8- to 10-inch) shells*

6 egg whites
Pinch of salt
¼ teaspoon lemon juice
⅔ cup superfine granulated sugar
⅔ cup sifted confectioners' sugar
½ cup sifted unsweetened cocoa powder

Preheat the oven to 225°F. Lightly butter 2 cookie sheets and dust with rice flour, or line them with parchment paper. Trace two 8- or 10-inch circles (or more smaller shapes) on the prepared cookie sheets.

Using an electric mixer, beat the egg whites, salt, and lemon juice on low speed until soft mounds form. Gradually add the superfine sugar. Increase the speed to medium-high and beat until the meringue is glossy and forms stiff peaks. Fold in the confectioners' sugar. Sift the cocoa powder over the whites and fold in. Spread the meringue within the circles you have drawn on the cookie sheets, going over the lines just a little. Bake for 2 to 3 hours or until the meringues are dry. Cool on a rack.

FRESH FRUIT PAVLOVA *Makes 6 to 8 servings*

A Pavlova is a meringue shell filled with whipped cream and fresh fruit. Legend has it that a chef in Adelaide (located in south Australia) created the Pavlova after he saw famed ballerina Anna Pavlova perform, saying that he wanted to create a dessert that was as light and airy as her dancing. Here are three Pavlova recipes using meringue shells.

1 cup heavy cream
1 to 2 tablespoons confectioners' sugar
½ teaspoon gluten-free vanilla
1 cup blueberries
2 cups hulled and quartered strawberries
1 cup raspberries
1 (8- or 9-inch) meringue shell or 8 to 9 (3-inch) shells (page 111)

Whip the cream with the confectioners' sugar and vanilla. Mix all the berries together in a bowl. Refrigerate the cream and berries until you are ready to assemble the dessert.

Spoon the whipped cream over the meringue shell(s) or fit a pastry bag with a large fluted nozzle, fill with the whipped cream, and pipe over the meringue shell. Spoon the fruit on top or pass the bowl of fruit separately.

VARIATION Instead of the berries, use 4 cups of any prepared fresh seasonal fruit.

LEMON PAVLOVA *Makes 6 to 8 servings*

1 recipe Lemon Curd (page 199)
1 (8- or 9-inch) meringue shell (page 111)
1 cup heavy cream
1 to 2 tablespoons confectioners' sugar
½ teaspoon gluten-free vanilla
1 recipe Raspberry Sauce (page 152)

Spread the lemon curd over the meringue shell. Whip the cream with the confectioners' sugar and vanilla. Spoon the whipped cream over the lemon curd or fit a pastry bag with a large fluted nozzle, fill with the whipped cream, and pipe over the lemon curd.

With a serrated or very sharp knife, cut the filled meringue shell into individual slices. Place on dessert plates and serve. Pass a pitcher of the raspberry sauce, or pool the sauce in the middle of each dessert plate before placing the slice of Pavlova on it.

GUILT-FREE PAVLOVA *Makes 8 servings*

1 to 2 tablespoons honey
½ teaspoon gluten-free vanilla
1 recipe Yogurt Cheese (recipe follows)
1 (8- or 9-inch) meringue shell (page 111)
4 cups fresh seasonal fruits of your choice
⅓ cup apricot preserves, melted and strained

Whisk the honey and the vanilla into the yogurt cheese. Spread this over the meringue shell. Cut the fruit into slices and arrange it in concentric rings on top of the cheese. Brush with the apricot preserves.

YOGURT CHEESE *Makes 1 cup*

1 quart plain low-fat yogurt

Double a length of cheesecloth, moisten, and line a strainer with it. Place the strainer over a bowl. Spoon the yogurt into the lined strainer. Refrigerate overnight.

In the morning, the yogurt will have released most of the whey and will be thick, almost like cream cheese. You can use this "cream cheese" for dips or sweeten it with honey for a treat on your bagel for breakfast.

JAPONAISE BASE *Makes 3 (8-inch) bases*

These nut meringue bases are so versatile, creating a new dessert is as easy as varying the fillings and icings.

2 cups almonds, lightly toasted
1½ cups sugar
½ cup cornstarch
9 egg whites
Pinch of salt
⅛ teaspoon lemon juice
1 teaspoon gluten-free vanilla

Preheat the oven to 325°F. Lightly butter 2 cookie sheets and dust with rice flour, or line them with parchment paper. Trace the outline of three 8-inch cake pans on the cookie sheets.

Put the almonds in a food processor and chop. Add 1 cup of the sugar and grind finely. Mix in the cornstarch. Set aside.

Using an electric mixer, beat the egg whites on low speed until soft mounds form. Add the remaining ½ cup sugar, the salt, and lemon juice. Add the vanilla, increase the speed to medium high, and beat until the meringue is glossy and forms stiff peaks. Sprinkle the nut mixture over the whites and fold in. Spoon the meringue onto the prepared cookie sheets and spread to fill in the traced circles. Bake for 30 to 35 minutes or until the meringues are firm to the touch. Cool on the pan before removing. Store in a cool, dry place. Do not refrigerate.

VARIATIONS

An equal amount of other toasted nuts, such as pecans, pistachios, walnuts, hazelnuts, or peanuts, can be used instead of the almonds.

CHOCOLATE JAPONAISE BASE

Mix in ¼ cup grated bittersweet chocolate with the nut mixture.

CHOCOLATE TORTE *Makes 12 to 15 servings*

3 cups heavy cream
1 recipe Chocolate Japonaise Base (above)
¼ cup confectioners' sugar
¼ cup sifted unsweetened cocoa powder
1 tablespoon rum
Semisweet chocolate shavings for garnish

Whip the cream until soft mounds form. Add the confectioners' sugar and cocoa powder and mix until they are completely combined. Stir in the rum. Place 1 Japonaise base on a serving plate. Spread with one-fourth of the whipped cream. Repeat with the second base. Top with the third base. Cover the sides of the torte with whipped cream. Cover the top of the torte or fit a pastry bag with a fluted nozzle, fill with the remaining whipped cream, and pipe rosettes over the top. Sprinkle the shaved chocolate over the top. Refrigerate until ready to serve.

NOTE: Remember that cocoa powder stiffens the cream, so do not overbeat the cream before adding the cocoa powder.

CHOCOLATE PECAN TORTE *Makes 12 to 16 servings*

This torte combines two of my favorite flavors: chocolate and pecans. Pecan meringues, though rich in flavor, are a light way to end a heavy meal.

1 recipe Chocolate Japonaise Base (page 115), with lightly toasted pecans used in place of the almonds
1 recipe French Buttercream (page 145)
1 recipe Ganache (page 150)
Whole toasted pecans

With a sharp paring knife, trim the baked Japonaise bases to make 8-inch rounds. Put some of the buttercream in a pastry bag fitted with a plain nozzle. Pipe buttercream around the edge of 2 rounds. Set the other round aside. When the ganache begins to thicken and set, spread it inside the piped buttercream on the two rounds. Save a little for decoration.

Place one of the rounds on top of the other. Place the reserved plain round, flat side up, on top as the top layer. Spread a thin coating of buttercream over the top and sides of the torte. Refrigerate for 5 minutes. Spread another layer of buttercream, making it as smooth as possible. Refrigerate for another 5 minutes. Spread a final coat of buttercream over the torte. Place whole pecans around the base of the cake. Melt the ganache just enough so that you can drizzle it over the top of the torte. Refrigerate. Remove from the refrigerator at least 20 minutes before serving.

BASIC YUMMY CHEESECAKE *Makes 1 (10-inch) cheesecake*

Cheesecake was a perennial favorite on the dessert menu at my restaurant, Madd Apple Cafe. It was great fun creating different flavors for our guests, and my cooks came up with a long list of winning combinations.

To make your own gluten-free graham crackers, see the recipe on page 69.

CRUST:

1½ cups gluten-free graham cracker or cookie crumbs
¼ teaspoon cinnamon
1 stick unsalted butter, melted

FILLING:

2 pounds cream cheese, at room temperature
1½ cups sugar
1 tablespoon grated orange zest
5 eggs, lightly beaten
2 cups sour cream
2 tablespoons cornstarch
1 teaspoon gluten-free vanilla

Preheat the oven to 350°F.

To make the crust, mix the graham cracker crumbs, cinnamon, and melted butter together. Press onto the bottom and halfway up the sides of a 10-inch springform pan. Bake for 10 minutes and set aside to cool while making the filling. Lower the oven temperature to 250°F.

To make the filling, cream together the cream cheese and sugar until very fluffy. Stir in the orange zest. Add the eggs and beat well. Beat in the remaining ingredients.

Pour the filling into the springform pan and bake for 2 to 3 hours or until the top is golden and set like a custard. Turn the oven off, open the door ajar, and leave the cheesecake in the oven for an hour before removing. Cool and then refrigerate.

VARIATIONS

APRICOT CHEESECAKE

Crumble Scottish Shortbread Cookies (page 75) or Crisp Ginger Molasses Cookies (page 72) to use in place of the graham cracker crumbs in the crust. Omit the orange zest from the filling. Add 1 pound apricot puree and 1 tablespoon lemon juice. To make the apricot puree, cover 1 pound of pitted dried apricots with boiling water. Let sit at least 1 hour. Drain and puree in a food processor.

PUMPKIN CHEESECAKE

Crush Crisp Ginger Molasses Cookies (page 72) to make crumbs for the crust. Add to the filling 1 pound pumpkin puree, 2 tablespoons finely chopped candied ginger, and 1½ teaspoons Pumpkin Pie Spice (page 76).

Serve with a fresh cranberry sauce on the side.

CRANBERRY CHEESECAKE

Use ginger snap crumbs for one crust. Add 12 ounces pureed cranberry chutney or homemade cranberry-orange relish to the filling.

MARGARITA CHEESECAKE

Increase the orange zest to 2 tablespoons. Add 6 tablespoons lime juice, 2½ tablespoons grated lime zest, 1 tablespoon Triple Sec, and a few drops of green food color.

MOCHA CHEESECAKE

- 2 tablespoons unsweetened cocoa powder
- 12 ounces semisweet chocolate
- 3 ounces unsweetened chocolate
- 2 tablespoons gluten-free instant espresso
- 2 tablespoons hot water

Add the cocoa powder to the crust.

Melt the semisweet and unsweetened chocolate together over low heat. Dissolve the instant espresso in the hot water. Stir the melted chocolate and the dissolved espresso into the cheesecake batter.

MANDARIN CHOCOLATE CHEESECAKE

2 tablespoons unsweetened cocoa powder
12 ounces semisweet chocolate
3 ounces unsweetened chocolate
1 tablespoon grated orange zest (for a total of 2 tablespoons in recipe)

Add the cocoa powder to the crust.

Melt the semisweet and unsweetened chocolate together over low heat. Stir the orange zest and melted chocolate into the cheesecake batter.

MOCHACCINO CHEESECAKE

1 tablespoon unsweetened cocoa powder
12 ounces semisweet chocolate
2 tablespoons gluten-free instant espresso
½ cup brewed coffee

Add the cocoa powder to the crust.

Melt the semisweet chocolate and espresso in the coffee. Stir enough of the chocolate mixture into the cream cheese mixture to make the batter look like café au lait. Pour this batter over the prebaked crust. Marble the rest of the chocolate mixture into the batter.

CHOCOLATE CHEESECAKE *Makes 1 (10-inch) cheesecake*

Mmmmm. Rich and delicious for dessert—or just about any time.

CHOCOLATE GRAHAM CRACKER CRUST:

1½ cups gluten-free Graham Cracker crumbs (page 69)
½ stick butter, melted
2 tablespoons sugar
2 tablespoons grated semisweet chocolate
¼ teaspoon cinnamon

FILLING:

3 eggs
1 cup sugar
1 teaspoon gluten-free vanilla
1½ pounds cream cheese, at room temperature
1 cup sour cream
12 ounces bittersweet chocolate, melted and cooled

Preheat the oven to 350°F.

Combine all the crust ingredients in a food processor and pulse until blended. Press into a 10-inch springform pan. Bake for 10 minutes and set aside to cool while making the filling. Lower the oven temperature to 325°F.

To make the filling, ribbon the eggs with the sugar and vanilla (see technique, page 30). Whip the cream cheese until fluffy. Mix the ribboned egg mixture into the cream cheese. Stir in the sour cream and melted chocolate.

Pour the filling into the springform pan and bake for 1 hour or until the sides feel firm and the center is set like a custard. Turn the oven off, open the door ajar, and leave the cheesecake in the oven for another hour. Refrigerate for at least 12 hours before removing the sides of the springform pan.

NONDAIRY CHOCOLATE CHEESECAKE *Makes 1 (9-inch) cheese cake*

This dairy-free version of the chocolate cheesecake has the added benefit of tofu.

- 1 recipe Graham Cracker Crust (page 185), made with ½ cup almonds, or Pecan Butter Crust (page 188)
- 16 ounces silken tofu
- 1 cup sugar
- ½ cup unsweetened cocoa powder
- 16 ounces soy cream cheese
- 1 egg
- 2 teaspoons gluten-free vanilla

Preheat the oven to 325°F. Lightly grease a 9-inch quiche pan.

Put the crumbs in the pan and gently tilt it to coat with the crumbs. Press the crumbs to ensure that they adhere. Bake for 10 minutes. Set aside to cool.

Put the tofu in a food processor and blend until smooth. Add the sugar, cocoa powder, and soy cream cheese and blend until smooth. Add the egg and vanilla and blend until incorporated. Pour the batter into the prepared pan. Bake for 45 minutes. Check for doneness. The edges need to be firm, the center soft. Turn the oven off and let the cheesecake cool in the oven with the door slightly open. Refrigerate for at least 3 hours before serving.

SAVORY PESTO CHEESECAKE *Makes 1 (8-inch) cheesecake*

This savory twist on the classic cheesecake makes a very nice entree for lunch or a light supper. Serve with a salad of fresh tomatoes and arugula dressed with extra virgin olive oil and balsamic vinegar. Cut into thin slices for hors d'oeuvres at a cocktail party.

1 double-crust recipe Flaky Pastry (page 183)
1 pound cream cheese
1 pound gluten-free ricotta cheese
3 eggs
⅔ cup grated Asiago or Parmesan cheese
1 cup packed basil leaves
3 tablespoons white rice flour
1 teaspoon salt
Freshly ground black pepper
3 tablespoons pine nuts

Preheat the oven to 350°F. Butter the bottom and sides of an 8-inch springform pan.

Roll out the crust to fit the bottom of the pan and lay it in the pan. Roll out more crust into a strip long enough to line the sides of the pan, leaving 1 inch at the top clean. Fit the strip of pastry around the inside and press the ends together. If the pastry is difficult to handle, just press it into the pan and up the sides. Refrigerate until ready to fill.

Put the cream cheese and ricotta in a food processor and blend until smooth. Add the eggs and blend again. Add the remaining ingredients except the pine nuts and continue blending until smooth. Pour the filling into the prepared pan. Sprinkle the pine nuts on top. Bake for about 50 minutes. The cheesecake will jiggle in the center but be firm around the edges. Turn the oven off, open the door ajar, and let the cheesecake sit in the oven for an hour. Cool on a rack and then remove the sides of the pan. Serve at room temperature.

VARIATION

NONDAIRY PESTO CHEESECAKE

In the crust, replace the butter with soy margarine. In the filling, replace the cream cheese with soy cream cheese, the ricotta with silken tofu, and the Parmesan with nondairy soy Parmesan.

WARM CHOCOLATE HAZELNUT CAKE *Makes 6 individual cakes*

These warm cakes are simple to make and literally melt in your mouth. To experience the warm, soft center characteristic of these cakes, serve them as soon as they come out of the oven. I like using individual brioche tins to bake the cakes because they are pretty and easy to unmold, but custard cups and muffin pans work too.

4 ounces bittersweet chocolate
1 ounce unsweetened chocolate
1 stick unsalted butter
2 eggs
2 egg yolks
¼ cup sugar
1 tablespoon hazelnut flour
Fruit puree sauce, soft whipped cream, or crème anglaise for serving (optional)

Preheat the oven to 450°F. Lightly coat individual brioche tins with cooking spray.

Melt the bittersweet chocolate, unsweetened chocolate, and butter together. Ribbon the eggs, egg yolks, and sugar until thick and pale yellow (see technique, page 30). Beat in the warm melted chocolate and butter. Quickly fold in the hazelnut flour. Spoon the batter into the prepared molds. (At this point, the batter can be refrigerated for several hours. Bring to room temperature and then bake.) Place the molds on a cookie sheet and bake for 6 to 7 minutes. The centers will be quite soft, but the sides will be firm.

Invert onto dessert dishes. Let the cakes sit for about 10 seconds before unmolding. Serve immediately with a fruit puree sauce, lightly whipped cream, or crème anglaise, if using.

CHOCOLATE APPLESAUCE CAKE *Makes 1 (11 × 7-inch) cake*

This recipe is so moist and dense, it reminds me of a brownie. It can easily be doubled. A very easy cake to make, and—shhh—it is low in fat too.

- ¾ cup Basic Gluten-Free Mix (page 16)
- ⅓ cup cornstarch
- 1 teaspoon gluten-free baking powder
- 1 teaspoon baking soda
- ¼ teaspoon xanthan gum
- ⅓ cup unsweetened cocoa powder
- 2 egg whites
- ⅔ cup sugar
- ½ cup warm milk
- ½ cup light corn syrup
- ¼ cup unsweetened applesauce
- 1 teaspoon gluten-free vanilla

ICING:

- 2 cups confectioners' sugar
- 2 tablespoons unsweetened cocoa powder
- 2 to 3 tablespoons milk

Preheat the oven to 350°F. Lightly grease an 11 × 7 × 1½-inch baking pan and line it with parchment paper. Lightly grease the paper.

Mix together the gluten-free mix, cornstarch, baking powder, baking soda, and xanthan gum. Sift the cocoa powder into the bowl. Whisk until the dry ingredients are well blended.

Using an electric mixer, beat the egg whites until they are foamy. Add the sugar slowly. Pour in the milk, corn syrup, applesauce, and vanilla. Whisk the dry ingredients into the wet ingredients.

Pour the batter into the prepared pan. Bake for 25 minutes or until done. Invert onto a cooling rack.

To make the icing, whisk together the confectioners' sugar and cocoa, adding just enough milk to make an icing thin enough to spread over the cake. Once the cake is cool, spread the icing over it.

CHOCOLATE APRICOT CAKE *Makes 1 (10-inch) cake*

What a sweet way to use up any leftover meringue you may have from making tortes!

- 3 tablespoons fine, soft gluten-free bread crumbs
- ⅔ cup Basic Gluten-Free Mix (page 16)
- ½ cup almond flour or meringue praline (see Note, below)
- ¼ teaspoon xanthan gum
- ⅛ teaspoon salt
- 6 ounces semisweet chocolate, chopped
- 1½ sticks unsalted butter
- ⅔ cup sugar
- 3 eggs
- 1 teaspoon gluten-free vanilla

CHOCOLATE GLAZE:

- ½ cup heavy cream
- 8 ounces bittersweet or semisweet chocolate, chopped
- 2 tablespoons unsalted butter
- ½ (12-ounce) jar apricot preserves, melted and strained
- Lightly sweetened whipped cream for serving (optional)

Preheat the oven to 350°F. Butter a 10-inch springform pan and sprinkle with the gluten-free bread crumbs.

Mix together the gluten-free mix, almond flour or meringue praline, xanthan gum, and salt and set aside. Melt the chocolate over hot water and set aside.

Beat the butter until white. Add the sugar and beat until fluffy, about 5 minutes. Add 2 of the eggs, one at a time, and beat until well blended. Stir in the melted chocolate and then beat in the last egg and the vanilla. Fold in the dry ingredients.

Gently pour the batter into the prepared pan. Bake on the middle rack for 50 minutes or until done. Let the cake cool in the pan for 15 minutes. Remove the sides and bottom of the pan.

To make the chocolate glaze, bring the cream to a boil. Remove from the heat and whisk in the chopped chocolate. Add the butter and whisk until the chocolate and butter are melted. Let the glaze cool slightly.

Cool the cake completely. Cut the cake in half and fill it with about one-third of the apricot preserves. Spread more of the preserves over the top and sides of the cake. Pour the chocolate glaze over the cake. Use a spatula to smooth and even out the glaze. Chill. Serve with whipped cream, if using.

Note: Make meringue praline by putting leftover meringues, preferably nut meringues, in the food processor and making a fine crumb. Store in an airtight container.

BLACK FOREST CAKE *Makes 1 (8- or 9-inch) layer cake*

A European classic. During my days at Le Nôtre Pâtissier in Paris, I remember having to pit fresh cherries; now I use canned ones. (Some shortcuts are acceptable.) Use a few cherries with the stems on to finish this cake. When we did the photograph for this recipe, we got carried away and put cherries between all the layers. It looked and tasted spectacular, but was a little difficult to cut!

½ cup almond flour
½ cup cornstarch
2 tablespoons unsweetened cocoa powder
1 teaspoon cinnamon
6 ounces bittersweet chocolate
6 tablespoons unsalted butter
1 cup confectioners' sugar
1 teaspoon grated orange zest
¼ teaspoon plus a pinch of salt
7 egg yolks
8 egg whites
¼ teaspoon lemon juice
¼ cup granulated sugar

KIRSCH SYRUP:
⅓ cup water
⅓ cup sugar
Drop of lemon juice
1 cinnamon stick
¼ cup kirsch

3 cups heavy cream
3 tablespoons confectioners' sugar
2 pounds fresh cherries, washed and pitted, or 1 pound 2 ounces canned pitted cherries, drained
⅓ cup grated bittersweet chocolate
Chocolate curls for decoration
Cocoa powder for dusting

Preheat the oven to 325°F. Butter two 8-inch round cake pans or two 9 × 2-inch pans. Fit the bottom of the pan(s) with parchment paper and grease lightly.

Mix together the almond flour, cornstarch, cocoa powder, and cinnamon and set aside. Melt the chocolate over hot water and set aside.

Beat the butter until white. Add the confectioners' sugar, orange zest, and ¼ teaspoon salt and beat until fluffy, 5 minutes. Add the egg yolks, one at a time, and beat until blended. Mix the melted chocolate into the creamed butter.

Using clean beaters, beat the egg whites with the pinch of salt and the lemon juice. When they are almost stiff, start adding the granulated sugar. Beat until stiff and glossy. Gently stir one-fourth of the egg whites into the chocolate batter. Slide the remaining egg whites on top. Sprinkle the dry ingredients over the egg whites and fold into the batter.

Gently pour the batter into the prepared pan(s). Bake for 25 to 30 minutes. Invert onto a cooling rack and cool completely.

To make the syrup, put the water, sugar, lemon juice, and cinnamon stick in a saucepan. Bring to a boil and simmer for 15 minutes. Cool slightly, then add the kirsch. Set aside to cool. Whip the cream, sweetening it with the confectioners' sugar.

Cut each cake in half horizontally. Place one of the layers on an 8- or 9-inch cardboard round. Sprinkle or brush some of the kirsch syrup over the cake. Set aside 1 cup of the whipped cream for decoration. Smooth one-fourth of the remaining whipped cream over this layer. Press half of the cherries into the cream. Place a second layer on top and brush it with kirsch syrup. Smooth a third of the remaining whipped cream over this layer. Place a third layer of cake on top. Brush with the kirsch syrup and smooth half of the remaining whipped cream over this cake. Press the remaining cherries into the cream. Lay the last layer on top, making sure it is the smooth bottom of one of the cakes; set it bottom side up. Brush with the kirsch syrup. Put the reserved whipped cream into a pastry bag fitted with a fluted nozzle. Pipe the whipped cream on top of the cake. Decorate with the grated chocolate and chocolate curls. Dust the cake with cocoa powder. Refrigerate for several hours before serving.

BOSTON CREAM PIE *Makes 1 (8-inch) cake*

No, this recipe is not in the wrong chapter. A Boston cream "pie" is actually a cake—a rich, gooey cake that will delight your entire family. Traditionally, this cake is made with one 8-inch round cake. However, it can be made higher by using two 8-inch cake layers. Increase the amount of pudding you use as the filling.

1 (8-inch) Butter Cake (page 102)
1 recipe Vanilla Pudding (page 196)
½ recipe Ganache Icing (page 150)

To assemble, split the cooled cake in half horizontally. Spread the pudding over one of the cut halves. Put the other half on top the pudding, cut side down. Place the cake on a cake rack set over a piece of parchment paper or a cookie sheet. Pour the ganache over the top of the cake. Let the ganache drip down the sides. Refrigerate after the icing has set.

VARIATION

CHOCOLATE BOSTON CREAM PIE

Use an 8-inch Chocolate Butter Cake (page 102), 1 recipe Chocolate Pudding (page 196), and ½ recipe Ganache Icing (page 150)

BÛCHE DE NOËL *Makes 1 cake roll*

Serving this exquisite cake is a holiday tradition in France, where Bûche de Noël takes center stage at Christmas. There are many steps to making this cake, but they can be done over several days. I would suggest you master making a cake roll first, then a buttercream, and finally meringue. Once you have done this, the cake will no longer seem like such a big project. This cake freezes well.

CAKE ROLL:

2/3 cup Basic Gluten-Free Mix (page 16)
1 teaspoon gluten-free baking powder
1/8 teaspoon xanthan gum
Pinch of salt
4 eggs, separated
3/4 cup granulated sugar
1 teaspoon gluten-free vanilla
1/4 teaspoon lemon juice
3 ounces unsweetened chocolate, melted

CHESTNUT FILLING:

1 stick unsalted butter, softened
1/2 cup confectioners' sugar
1 (1-pound) can chestnut puree
2 tablespoons kirsch (optional)

BUTTERCREAM:

3/4 cup sugar
1/4 cup water
Lemon juice
6 egg whites
1 1/2 to 2 pounds unsalted butter, softened
4 ounces unsweetened chocolate, melted and cooled

MERINGUE MUSHROOMS:

3 egg whites
Few drops of lemon juice
3/4 cup superfine granulated sugar

MARZIPAN HOLLY:

1 (7- to 8-ounce) package marzipan (almond paste)
Red food coloring
Green food coloring

To make the cake roll, preheat the oven to 350°F. Lightly grease a 10 × 15 × 1 1/2-inch jelly roll pan and either dust with cocoa powder or line with parchment paper.

Mix together the gluten-free mix, baking powder, xanthan gum, and salt. Ribbon the egg yolks and sugar until pale yellow and thick (see technique, page 30). Add the vanilla and melted chocolate. Beat the egg whites with the lemon juice just until stiff. Stir one-fourth of the whites into the egg yolk mixture. Slide the remaining whites on top. Sift the dry ingredients over the whites and fold everything together until homogenous.

Gently pour the batter into the prepared pan and spread evenly. Tap the bottom of the pan once on the counter. Bake on the middle rack for 10 minutes or until done.

While the cake is baking, sprinkle a clean tea towel with cocoa powder. When the cake is done, remove it from the oven and invert it onto the towel. Trim off the edges. Loosely roll up lengthwise (with the towel) into a long log. Let the cake cool in the towel.

To make the chestnut filling, beat the butter until white. Add the confectioners' sugar and beat until fluffy, about 5 minutes. With the mixer on slow speed, add the chestnut puree, tablespoon by tablespoon. Then add the kirsch, if using.

To make the buttercream, mix the sugar, water, and a few drops of lemon juice in a small saucepan. Bring to a boil and cook to the soft ball stage (see sugar syrups technique, page 31).

Begin beating the whites. Add ¼ teaspoon lemon juice. As soon as the whites form soft mounds, begin pouring in the hot sugar syrup in a steady stream. Beat until cold. Add the soft butter, tablespoon by tablespoon. At first the mixture will thin out—do not be alarmed—just continue adding the butter. After adding 1 pound of the butter, pour in the cooled melted chocolate. Continue adding the butter until the buttercream is almost white and the texture is silky and light. The buttercream should be refrigerated if you are not using it right away. Bring it to room temperature and rewhip when ready to use.

To make the meringue mushrooms, preheat the oven to 225°F. Grease a cookie sheet and sprinkle with rice flour or line with parchment paper. Using a mixer on high speed, whip the whites and lemon juice until the whites form soft mounds. Gradually add ½ cup of the sugar. Beat until the whites are stiff and shiny. Fold in the remaining ¼ cup of sugar. Fit a pastry bag with a no. 4 or 5 plain nozzle, fill with the beaten whites, and make small rounded meringues for the mushroom tops. For the stems, hold the bag upright, and as you squeeze, lift the bag to form strips ½ to 1 inch high with points. Bake for 1½ hours or until the meringues are firm and lift off the cookie sheet easily. Cool 15 minutes. To assemble, use a little buttercream to stick stems to the tops. You will have lots of meringue mushrooms. Store in an airtight container, not in the refrigerator.

To make the marzipan holly, color a small piece of marzipan with red food coloring, and color a larger piece green. Roll red balls for the berries, 3 per cluster. Roll out the green marzipan and cut out holly leaves, 2 per cluster. Keep the berries and leaves covered with plastic wrap until ready to use. I use a gluten-free baking spray when rolling out the marzipan to it keep from sticking to the counter.

To assemble the Bûche de Noël, gently unroll the chocolate cake. Do not panic if the cake cracks. The buttercream will hide any cracks, and no one will be the wiser. Spread the chestnut filling over the cake. Roll up. Place on a cardboard rectangle. Ice the cake with the buttercream. Do not make the icing look smooth. You can use the back of a fork to give it texture. Slice off both the cake ends at a slight angle. Place these cut ends on the cake to make it look like a log with the stumps of branches. You can ice over the ends or leave plain.

Arrange the marzipan holly and the meringue mushrooms on and around the cake. Just before serving, dust the cake lightly with confectioners' sugar. Keep refrigerated until ready to serve. Remove from the refrigerator 30 minutes before serving to allow the buttercream to soften.

CHOCOLATE PRALINE TORTE *Makes 1 (8-inch) layer cake*

A lovely cake for a birthday or other special occasion.

- 2 baked layers (8-inch) Sponge Cake (page 106)
- Gluten-free brandy
- ½ recipe Praline Buttercream (page 146)
- ½ recipe Chocolate Buttercream (page 146)

Cut each cake in half horizontally to make 2 layers. Sprinkle the layers with some brandy.

Divide the praline buttercream into thirds. Spread one-third over the top of one cake layer. Place the second layer on top. Spread another third of the buttercream over this layer. Place the third layer on top. Spread the remaining buttercream over the layer. Place the fourth layer on top, making sure the flat side, which is the bottom, faces up. Place the cake on an 8-inch cardboard cake round. Cover all the sides and the top of the cake with the chocolate buttercream.

If there is any leftover buttercream, place it in a pastry bag fitted with a fluted nozzle and pipe decorations around the edge of the top and around the bottom. Refrigerate until ready to serve. Remove the cake from the refrigerator at least 20 minutes before serving to allow the buttercream to soften a bit.

Boston Cream Pie (page 125)

Raisin Cream Scones (page 44) and Coconut Raspberry Muffins (page 42)

Plum Coffee Cake (page 62)

From left to right: S'mores (pages 139–40), Mint Bars (page 90), and Double Chocolate Chip Cookies (page 68)

Spinach and Colored Pepper Quiche (page 175)

Chocolate Pecan Torte (page 116)

Chocolate Fettuccine (page 227)

Tartlets made with Pecan Butter Crust (page 188) and assorted fillings

Black Forest Cake (pages 124–25)

CHOCOLATE RASPBERRY GENOISE *1 (8-inch) layer cake*

This is a winner for those who have a sweet tooth and a love of chocolate but have to adhere to wheat-free and dairy-free dietary restrictions. If you are not on a nondairy diet, then by all means use heavy cream and butter. I dedicate this cake to Beth Sherman, for whom I created it as her birthday cake.

GANACHE:

- 1 cup nondairy creamer, such as Farm Rich
- 8 ounces dairy-free semisweet chocolate, chopped
- 2 baked Cocoa Genoise cakes (page 104), made with soy margarine or unsalted margarine
- 2 cups seedless raspberry jam, melted

To make the ganache, bring the nondairy creamer to a boil. Pour the hot creamer over the chopped chocolate. Whisk together until the chocolate is melted and smooth. Cool the ganache until it is thick enough to spread.

Slice the baked cakes in half horizontally. Fill each cake with some of the melted jam. Spread the ganache or jam over the top of one of the cakes, then set the other cake on top of it. Brush some of the melted jam over the sides and top. As soon as the ganache is thick enough to pour, pour it over the top of the cake and let it drip down the sides. If you work quickly, you can spread the ganache over the sides or just let it fall free-form. You can also whip the ganache before it cools until it is thick, like a frosting.

CHOCOLATE TORTE *Makes 1 (8-inch) torte*

A light and elegant chocolate dessert.

FILLING:

- 3 cups heavy cream
- ¼ cup sifted unsweetened cocoa powder
- ¼ cup confectioners' sugar
- 1 tablespoon rum
- 3 baked Chocolate Japonaise Bases (page 115)
- Shaved semisweet chocolate (optional)
- 1 recipe Chocolate Sauce (page 152)

To make the filling, whip the cream until it forms soft mounds. Sift the cocoa powder and confectioners' sugar over the soft whipped cream, add the rum, and stir them in.

To assemble the cake, trim the three bases to make each 8 inches across. Stack the bases, spreading the whipped cream filling between them. Cover the sides of the cake with the whipped cream. Spoon any remaining whipped cream over the top, or fit a pastry bag with a medium fluted nozzle, fill it with the whipped cream, and pipe rosettes. Sprinkle shaved chocolate over the top, if using. Serve with Chocolate Sauce.

COCONUT BUTTER CAKE *Makes 1 (8-inch) layer cake*

Lovely any time of the year, this cake is even better served with a bowl of fresh berries or slices of kiwi or pineapple.

- 1½ cups shredded sweetened coconut
- 2 cups heavy cream
- 2 tablespoons confectioners' sugar
- 1 teaspoon gluten-free vanilla
- 2 baked 8-inch Butter Cakes (page 102) or Sponge Cakes (page 106)

Preheat the oven to 350°F. Spread the coconut on a cookie sheet. Bake for 5 to 10 minutes or until the coconut begins to brown. Cool.

Whip the cream until it forms soft mounds. Whisk in the confectioners' sugar and vanilla. Whip the cream until stiff peaks form.

Spread some of the cream over the top of one of the cakes. Place the other cake on top. Cover the sides and top of the cake with the remaining whipped cream. Press the cooled toasted coconut all over the cake. Refrigerate until ready to serve.

DOBOS TORTE *Makes 1 (9-inch) torte*

Dobos Torte is a Hungarian specialty made from many layers of sponge cake filled with buttercream. This gluten-free version is adapted from a recipe by Madeleine Kamman. It is a labor-intensive cake, but take your time and it will delight you, your family, and your friends.

You need to make each pan of cake separately instead of doubling the ingredients, because the technique is a bit tricky with 6 eggs. Make the cakes and the top layer crust the day before.

CAKE (REPEAT TO MAKE 2 CAKES):

3 eggs
½ cup sugar
1 teaspoon gluten-free vanilla
Pinch of salt
½ cup plus 1 tablespoon Basic Gluten-Free Mix (page 16)
3 tablespoons unsalted butter, melted

TOP LAYER CRUST:

6 tablespoons Basic Gluten-Free Mix
⅛ teaspoon xanthan gum
½ stick unsalted butter
¼ cup sugar
1 egg
1 teaspoon gluten-free vanilla

GLAZE:

⅔ cup sugar
¼ cup water
Few drops of lemon juice

Double recipe Chocolate French Buttercream (page 145)

To make the cake, preheat the oven to 350°F. Butter two 9-inch round cake pans and line with parchment paper.

Put the eggs in a large mixing bowl. Place the bowl over hot water. Begin beating the eggs, adding the sugar gradually. Beat until the mixture is extremely foamy and white. It will almost form a ribbon. When you touch it with a finger, it will feel warm. Remove from the heat and beat until completely cool. Mix in the vanilla and salt. Sift the gluten-free mix over the batter in 3 parts, folding each part as quickly as possible. Fold in the melted butter.

Pour the batter into one of the prepared pans. Bake on the middle rack for about 25 to 30 minutes. Invert and cool. Repeat the recipe so you have 2 cake layers.

To make the top layer crust, preheat the oven to 350°F. Invert a 9-inch round cake pan and butter the outside bottom, then dust with rice flour.

Mix the gluten-free mix and xanthan gum together.

Beat the butter until white. Add the sugar and beat until fluffy, about 5 minutes. Add the egg and vanilla. Stir in the dry ingredients. Spread the mixture over the prepared bottom of the cake pan until ⅛ inch thick. Bake on the middle rack for 8 to 10 minutes. Do not overbake. There is enough batter to make a second crust in case the first gives you trouble. Loosen the layer and cool on a rack.

To make the glaze, mix together the sugar, water, and lemon juice in a saucepan. Without stirring, cook until the sugar begins to turn golden brown. Swirl the pan to ensure even cooking. Remove the pan before the sugar burns. Pour the sugar syrup evenly over the cooled top layer crust. Using a spatula, make 12 wedges. Before the caramelized sugar hardens, cut through.

To assemble, slice each of the two cooled cakes horizontally into 3 layers. Place one of the 6 layers on a cardboard round. Spread some of the buttercream over it about ⅛ inch thick. Repeat with the other layers. Make sure that the top layer is the bottom side of a cake; place it on top, flat side up, and spread some buttercream over it. Cover the entire cake with a crumb coat (see frosting technique, page 28). Refrigerate for 10 minutes.

Set aside 1 cup of the buttercream. Smooth the remaining buttercream over the sides and top of the cake. If you like, run a cake comb along the sides. Fit a pastry bag with a fluted nozzle and fill with the reserved buttercream. Mark the top of the cake with 12 wedges. Pipe buttercream along the marks. This will support the glazed top layer wedges. Place each wedge so that it is resting on the piped buttercream, point toward the center. It will form a pinwheel. Present your creation on a cake pedestal or a beautiful cake plate worthy of this masterpiece.

FRESH NECTARINE ALMOND CAKE *Makes 1 (8-inch) cake*

When I serve this refreshing dessert cake, I dollop it with some lightly sweetened whipped cream.

- 1½ cups sugar
- 1 cup water
- 3 tablespoons amaretto liqueur
- ⅓ cup cream of rice
- ⅓ cup almond flour
- ¼ cup Basic Gluten-Free Mix (page 16)
- ¼ teaspoon xanthan gum
- ⅛ teaspoon salt
- 3 eggs, separated
- Juice and grated zest of 1 lemon
- ¼ teaspoon lemon juice
- 2 ripe nectarines, peeled and sliced
- ½ cup apricot preserves
- 1 teaspoon unsalted butter
- Lightly sweetened whipped cream (optional)

Preheat the oven to 350°F. Butter an 8-inch springform pan.

Heat 1 cup of the sugar and the water in a saucepan until the sugar is dissolved. Boil without stirring for 5 minutes. Add the amaretto. Cool.

Mix together the cream of rice, almond flour, gluten-free mix, xanthan gum, and salt.

Ribbon the egg yolks and remaining ½ cup sugar (see technique, page 30). Add the juice and zest of 1 lemon. Ribbon again.

Beat the egg whites with the ¼ teaspoon lemon juice until stiff peaks form. Gently stir one-fourth of the whites into the yolk mixture. Slide the remaining whites on top and sprinkle the dry ingredients over the whites. Fold everything together. Spoon into the prepared pan. Bake for 30 to 35 minutes.

Pour the amaretto syrup over the warm cake. Cool the cake in the pan for 20 minutes. Remove the sides. Arrange the nectarine slices over the top. Melt the apricot preserves in a saucepan over low heat. Strain the preserves and whisk in the butter. Brush over the nectarine slices. Serve with whipped cream, if desired.

LEMON ICEBOX CAKE *Makes 1 (9 × 5-inch) loaf*

When I grew up in the fifties, icebox cakes were all the rage. They are simple, quite yummy, and best of all for our busy lives today, very easy to make. Revisit this retro favorite from the rock 'n' roll era—now gluten-free.

- ⅔ cup cookie crumbs, made from Scottish Shortbread (page 75), Almond Butter Cookies (page 74), Graham Crackers (page 69), Linzer Cookies without the jam (page 80), or baked Pecan Butter Crust (page 188)
- 3 egg yolks
- ½ cup sugar
- 1 tablespoon gelatin
- ¼ cup water
- ⅓ cup fresh lemon juice
- Rind of 1 lemon
- Pinch of salt
- Powdered egg whites equivalent to 3 whites
- 1 cup heavy cream
- Whipped cream, Raspberry Sauce (page 152), or sliced fresh fruit (optional)

Line a 9 × 5-inch loaf pan with parchment or wax paper. Sprinkle half of the cookie crumbs over the bottom of the pan. Press firmly. Set aside the rest of the cookie crumbs.

Temper the egg yolks (see technique, page 31). Then ribbon the yolks with the sugar (see technique, page 30). Soften the gelatin in the water in a saucepan, then simmer until the gelatin melts. Mix the dissolved gelatin into the egg mixture. Mix in the lemon zest and all but ¼ teaspoon of the lemon juice.

Prepare the powdered egg whites according to package directions. Beat the whites with the remaining ¼ teaspoon lemon juice and the salt until soft peaks form. Gently fold one-fourth of the whites into the yolk mixture. Slide the remaining whites on top and fold in.

Whip the cream until soft mounds form. Fold the cream into the egg mixture. Gently pour the mixture into the prepared pan. Sprinkle the remaining cookie crumbs on top. Cover with plastic wrap and refrigerate overnight.

To serve, unmold onto a serving dish and slice. Top each slice with a dollop of sweetened whipped cream, raspberry sauce, or fresh fruit, if using.

CHOCOLATE MOUSSE CAKE *Makes 1 (8-inch) layer cake*

This recipe requires time because tempering the eggs is time-consuming. Usually I use powdered egg whites and freeze the egg whites from the eggs for later use in a meringue, Japonaise base, or other recipe.

- 2 baked 8-inch chocolate cakes, such as Cocoa Genoise (page 104), Chocolate Butter Cake (page 103), or Basic Chocolate Cake (page 101)
- 1 recipe Chocolate Mousse (recipe follows below)
- 1 cup heavy cream

Line the bottom of an 8-inch springform pan with an 8-inch cardboard round. Place one of the cakes in the bottom of the springform pan. Cover with half of the chocolate mousse. Place the other cake on top of the chocolate mousse. Spoon the remaining chocolate mousse over the cake. Cover with plastic wrap and refrigerate overnight.

When ready to serve, remove the plastic wrap and the sides of the springform. Whip the cream and sweeten if you like with confectioners' sugar. Fit a pastry bag with a fluted nozzle, fill with the whipped cream, and decorate the top of the cake; no frosting on the sides.

CHOCOLATE MOUSSE

- ½ cup sugar
- 5 egg yolks, tempered (see technique, page 31)
- 6 ounces bittersweet chocolate, melted
- 1 tablespoon gluten-free instant coffee powder, dissolved in 1 tablespoon hot water, rum, or coffee
- 1 teaspoon gelatin, dissolved in 2 tablespoons water
- Powdered egg whites equivalent to 5 whites
- ½ cup heavy cream

Add the sugar to the tempered egg yolks and beat until thick and a heavy ribbon forms (see technique, page 30). Stir in the warm melted chocolate, dissolved coffee, and melted gelatin.

Prepare the powdered egg whites according to package directions. Beat the whites until stiff peaks form. Gently stir one-fourth of the whites into the chocolate base. Fold in the remaining egg whites.

Whip the cream until soft mounds form. Fold the cream into the chocolate base. Refrigerate until ready to use.

MOCHA CREAM TORTE *Makes 1 (8-inch) torte*

Coffee and chocolate are the unbeatable taste sensation in this torte.

FILLING:

1 tablespoon gluten-free instant espresso powder
1½ tablespoons hot water
2 cups heavy cream
2 tablespoons confectioners' sugar
3 baked Japonaise Bases (page 114), made with finely chopped lightly toasted walnuts in place of almonds
½ recipe Ganache Icing (page 150)

Dissolve the instant espresso in the hot water. Whip the cream until it starts to form soft mounds. Add the cooled espresso and the confectioners' sugar. Whip until stiff.

To assemble the cake, trim each baked Japonaise base to an 8-inch diameter. Turn each base so that the flat side is up. Spread one-third of the whipped cream filling over 2 of the trimmed bases. Stack the bases one on top of the other and then place the third base on top, making sure that the flat side is up.

Place the torte on a rack. Put a piece of parchment paper or a cookie sheet under the rack. Pour the ganache icing over the cake and let it drip down the sides of the cake. Or let the ganache set until almost too thick to pour and spread on the top only. Refrigerate the torte until ready to serve.

HAZELNUT PINWHEEL *Makes 1 (8-inch) pinwheel cake*

Ethel Goralnick and I both trained with Madeleine Kamman. Ethel shared this recipe with me, and it became a favorite of mine for serving at small dinner parties. My clients are always delighted when I make individual pinwheel cakes.

CAKE:

½ cup hazelnuts, walnuts, or almonds
1 teaspoon gluten-free baking powder
5 eggs, separated
½ cup plus 2 tablespoons granulated sugar
⅛ teaspoon salt
¼ teaspoon lemon juice

FILLING:

2 cups heavy cream
4 tablespoons confectioners' sugar
2 tablespoons Cointreau

TOPPING:

4 mangoes, peeled, pitted, and sliced; or seasonal fruit of your choice

Preheat the oven to 350°F. Butter a 17 × 13-inch jelly roll pan and line it with parchment paper.

To make the cake, mix the nuts and baking powder in a food processor and process until finely ground.

Heavily ribbon the egg yolks, ½ cup of the granulated sugar, and the salt (see technique, page 30). Set aside.

Whip the egg whites with the lemon juice and remaining 2 tablespoons sugar until stiff peaks form. Fold one-fourth of the beaten whites into the egg yolk mixture. Slide the remaining egg whites on top. Sprinkle the nut mixture over the whites. Fold everything together.

Spread the batter over the prepared pan. Bake for 20 minutes, but check after 15 minutes to make certain that it does not overbake. Slide the cake with the paper onto a rack. Peel off the paper and let the cake cool on the rack.

To make the filling, whip the cream with the confectioners' sugar and add the Cointreau. Spread the filling over the cake. Cut the cake crosswise into 1-inch strips and then roll the strips in a spiral, joining them end to end, to make an 8-inch-wide pinwheel. Place the mango slices around the top of the cake for a garnish. Slice and serve. To make individual cakes, just roll each strip separately and garnish with the mango slices.

RAVANI *Makes 1 (8-inch) square cake*

Rhea Williams, a wonderful Greek cook, lent me her copy of a Greek cookbook published in 1955, which included a recipe for a Middle Eastern semolina sponge cake called ravani. I made it gluten-free, substituting cream of rice for the semolina and brown rice flour mix for the flour.

- ½ cup Basic Gluten-Free Mix (page 16)
- 1 tablespoon cream of rice
- 1 teaspoon gluten-free baking powder
- ⅛ teaspoon xanthan gum
- ⅛ teaspoon salt
- 4 eggs, separated
- ½ cup sugar
- ¼ teaspoon lemon juice

SYRUP:

- 1½ cups sugar
- 2 cups water
- 1 tablespoon lemon juice

Preheat the oven to 350°F. Lightly grease an 8-inch square baking pan.

Mix together the gluten-free mix, cream of rice, baking powder, xanthan gum, and salt.

Heavily ribbon the egg yolks and the sugar (see technique, page 30).

Beat the egg whites with the lemon juice until stiff peaks form. Gently stir one-fourth of the whites into the egg yolk mixture. Slide the remaining whites on top. Sprinkle the dry ingredients over the whites. Fold everything together.

Carefully pour the batter into the prepared pan. Tap the bottom of the pan on the counter. Bake on the middle rack for 20 minutes or until done.

To make the syrup, heat the sugar, water, and lemon juice in a saucepan until the sugar is dissolved. Boil without stirring for 5 minutes.

Pour the syrup over the hot cake. Cool before serving.

SACHERTORTE *Makes 1 (8- or 9-inch) torte*

In 1832 Prince von Metternich, Austria's leading statesman, ordered his pastry chef to prepare a special dessert for a gala dinner. The chief pastry chef was ill, so the task fell to his 16-year-old apprentice, Franz Sacher . . . and the rest is culinary history.

CAKE:

- ½ cup almond flour
- ½ cup cornstarch
- 2 tablespoons unsweetened cocoa powder
- 6 ounces bittersweet chocolate
- 1 stick unsalted butter
- 1 cup confectioners' sugar
- ¼ teaspoon salt
- 6 egg yolks
- 8 egg whites
- ¼ teaspoon lemon juice
- ¼ cup granulated sugar

ICING:

- 7 ounces bittersweet chocolate
- 1 cup sugar
- ⅓ cup water
- 4 drops of lemon juice

FILLING:

- ½ cup apricot or raspberry jam, strained and melted

Whipped cream for garnish

To make the cake, preheat the oven to 325°F. Butter a 9-inch springform pan or two 8-inch round cake pans. Fit the bottom of the pan(s) with lightly buttered parchment paper.

Mix together the almond flour, cornstarch, and cocoa powder.

Melt the chocolate over hot water. Cool.

Beat the butter until white. Add the confectioners' sugar and salt and beat until fluffy, about 5 minutes. Add the egg yolks, one at a time.

Using clean beaters, beat the egg whites, adding ¼ teaspoon lemon juice. When the whites are almost stiff, start adding the granulated sugar. Beat until stiff and glossy.

Mix the melted chocolate into the butter mixture. Gently stir in one-fourth of the beaten whites. Slide the remaining egg whites on top. Sprinkle the dry ingredients over the whites and fold everything together.

Gently pour the batter into the prepared pan. Bake for about 1 hour or until done. Invert onto a cooling rack and cool completely.

To make the icing, melt the chocolate over hot water. Leave the chocolate over the hot water and set aside. Heat the sugar, water, and lemon juice in a small saucepan. Cook to the thread stage (see technique, page 31). Drizzle the syrup into the melted chocolate. Let the icing cool just until it can coat the back of a spoon.

To assemble the cake, either brush the cake with the melted jam or split the cake in half and fill it with the jam. Then lightly brush the top of the cake with more jam. Place the cake on a rack over waxed paper. Pour the icing onto the very center of the cake. Using a long spatula, spread the icing over the cake. Let the icing set before serving. Serve with a generous dollop of unsweetened whipped cream.

SICILIAN CASSATA *Makes 8 to 12 servings*

A cassata is a fabulous southern Italian cake molded around sweetened ricotta and chopped fruits, nuts, and chocolate. Once you have mastered making a sponge cake, this will be a snap to make. When I first began making this cake, I made it with pound cake and a rich chocolate frosting. This recipe makes a lighter dessert.

RICOTTA FILLING:

¾ cup sugar
1½ tablespoons water
Few drops of lemon juice
1½ pounds gluten-free ricotta cheese
8 ounces semisweet chocolate, chopped
8 ounces mixed candied fruit, chopped
4 tablespoons pistachios

1 recipe Sponge Cake (page 106), flavored with 1 tablespoon orange blossom water and baked in a lightly greased 17 × 11-inch jelly roll pan lined with lightly buttered parchment paper
Maraschino liqueur
Confectioners' sugar for garnish

To make the filling, heat the sugar, water, and lemon juice in a small saucepan. Bring to a boil and boil until the sugar is thoroughly dissolved. Let cool.

Press the ricotta through a sieve (do not use a food processor). Stir in the cooled syrup. Fold in the chocolate, candied fruit, and nuts.

You will need a bowl that can hold 6 cups. Cut the cake lengthwise into 2-inch-wide strips. Sprinkle them with some maraschino. Line the bowl with the strips. Spoon in the ricotta filling. Cover the filling with more cake. Place a piece of plastic wrap over the cake. Put a plate on top of the cake and weight it down with a can of tomatoes or something similar. Set the cake in the refrigerator overnight or for several hours before unmolding. Dust the top with confectioners' sugar and serve.

CHOCOLATE CASSATA *Makes 8 servings*

This was an all-time favorite dessert at my restaurant. We nicknamed one of our regulars the "cassata lady" because she came in every single day for a slice of this delicious cake. I dedicate this recipe to her.

- 1 recipe Basic Chocolate Cake (page 101), Cocoa Genoise (page 104) or Chocolate Butter Cake (page 103), baked in a 13 × 9-inch jelly roll pan
- 1 recipe Ricotta Filling (page 138)
- 1 recipe Chocolate Sour Cream Frosting (page 148)
- 1 cup lightly toasted almond slivers or chopped walnuts

Cut the cake crosswise into thirds. Spread half of the ricotta filling over one piece. Place another piece of cake on top. Spread the remaining filling over this piece of cake. Lay the last piece of cake on top. Spread the icing over the top and sides. Press the nuts along the sides. If there is any icing left over, pipe a border along the edges of the top. Refrigerate until ready to serve.

S'MORE CAKE *Makes 1 (13 × 9-inch) cake*

Who hasn't enjoyed a s'more made around a campfire? This cake is sure to bring back some fond childhood memories of campfires and fireflies on a summer evening.

- 1½ cups crumbs made from Graham Crackers recipe (page 185)
- 1 cup Basic Gluten-Free Mix (page 16)
- 1 teaspoon gluten-free baking powder
- ½ teaspoon baking soda
- ½ teaspoon xanthan gum
- Pinch of salt
- 1 stick unsalted butter
- 1 cup packed brown sugar
- 3 eggs
- ½ cup milk
- 1 cup milk chocolate chips
- 1½ cups Marshmallow Fluff

Preheat the oven to 350°F. Lightly grease a 13 × 9-inch baking pan. Line the bottom with parchment paper.

Mix together the graham cracker crumbs, gluten-free mix, baking powder, baking soda, xanthan gum, and salt.

Beat the butter until white. Add the brown sugar and beat until fluffy, about 5 minutes. Add the eggs, one at a time. Beat until smooth. Add the dry ingredients in 2 parts, alternating with the milk. Fold in ⅔ cup of the chocolate chips. Spread the batter in the greased pan. Bake 12 to 15 minutes or until done.

While the cake bakes, melt the remaining chips in a bowl over hot water. As soon as the cake is out of the oven and hot, spread the fluff over the cake. Drizzle the melted chocolate in a pattern on top. Cool before serving.

SOUTHERN BELLE *Makes 1 (10-inch) torte*

Crunchy peanut meringue filled with dark chocolate ganache and glazed with chocolate is the ultimate in sheer decadence for lovers of chocolate and peanut butter. Try making small rounds of this meringue and filling them with chocolate ice cream topped with a hot fudge sauce.

- ⅔ cup ground lightly toasted peanuts
- 1 tablespoon potato starch
- 1½ cups sugar
- 8 egg whites
- ¼ teaspoon salt
- ¼ teaspoon lemon juice
- ½ recipe Ganache Frosting (page 149)
- 1 recipe Quick Chocolate Icing (page 150)

Preheat the oven to 325°F. Butter 2 cookie sheets and dust with rice flour. Using a 10-inch cake pan as a template, trace a circle onto each cookie sheet.

Mix the ground peanuts, potato starch, and ¾ cup of the sugar together.

Beat the egg whites, salt, and lemon juice together until foamy. Slowly add the remaining ¾ cup sugar. Beat on high speed until glossy and stiff. Sprinkle the nut mixture over the whites. Fold everything together until homogenous.

Spread the meringue evenly within the traced circles on the prepared cookie sheets. Smooth the tops and bake for 45 to 50 minutes. Cool on the pans for 5 minutes, then slide onto a cooling rack.

After the cakes are cooled, place one on a cardboard round on a rack over a tray. Cover with the ganache. Place the second cake on top. Pour the glaze over the top and let it drip over the sides. Let the glaze set before serving.

VARIATIONS

- Replace the peanuts with pecans.
- Omit the Quick Chocolate Icing. Use 1 recipe Rum Buttercream (page 146) to cover and decorate the cake.

STRAWBERRY CREAM CAKE *Makes 1 (9-inch) layer cake*

Sponge cakes make great bases for easy cream cakes. Fill the cake with strawberry jam and decorate with fresh berries. You can use any fruit jam and garnish of your choice.

1½ cups strawberry jam
½ recipe Lemon Orange Sponge Cake (page 106), baked in a 9-inch cake pan
3 cups heavy cream
3 tablespoons confectioners' sugar
1 teaspoon gluten-free vanilla
Fresh strawberries for garnish

Melt the jam in a saucepan over low heat. Strain the jam. Slice the cooled cake horizontally into 3 even layers. Spread each layer with the strained jam. Stack the layers.

Whip the cream until stiff. Sweeten with the confectioners' sugar and flavor with the vanilla. Cover the sides and top of the cake with the whipped cream. Fit a pastry bag with a fluted nozzle, fill with any leftover whipped cream, and pipe rosettes on top of the cake. Decorate with fresh strawberries.

This cake can also be made as a cake roll. Bake the ½ recipe of Lemon Orange Sponge Cake in a 13 × 9-inch jelly roll pan.

ICINGS, FROSTINGS, AND SAUCES

7-Minute Frosting
French Buttercream
Buttercream Frosting
Quick Chocolate Buttercream
Caramel Buttercream
Chocolate Sour Cream Frosting
Rich Cream Cheese Frosting
Easy Fudge Frosting
Ganache Frosting
Ganache Icing
Quick Chocolate Icing
Quick White Chocolate Buttercream
Elegant Hot Fudge Sauce
Fudge Sauce
Chocolate Sauce
Raspberry Sauce
Caramel Sauce

7-MINUTE FROSTING *Makes 2 cups*

The classic cooked frosting. Master the technique and then try the myriad variations on the theme.

- 2 egg whites, ¼ cup egg whites, or the equivalent in powdered egg whites
- 5 tablespoons water
- 1 tablespoon corn syrup
- ⅛ teaspoon lemon juice
- Pinch of salt
- 1½ cups sugar
- 1½ teaspoons gluten-free vanilla

Put everything except the vanilla in the top of a double boiler. Make sure that the water in the lower portion is rapidly boiling. Beat constantly with a wire whisk for 7 minutes. Remove from the heat, add the vanilla, and continue beating until the mixture is fluffy and of a spreadable consistency. This frosting is best used immediately. Otherwise, refrigerate and use the same day.

VARIATIONS

MINT FROSTING

Omit the vanilla and add 1 teaspoon mint extract.

ORANGE FROSTING

Omit the vanilla. Replace the water with 5 tablespoons orange juice. Add 1 teaspoon grated orange zest.

LEMON FROSTING

Omit the vanilla. Replace the water with 3 tablespoons water and ¼ cup of lemon juice. Add 1 teaspoon finely grated lemon zest.

COFFEE FROSTING

Dissolve 1 to 2 tablespoons gluten-free instant espresso powder in 1 tablespoon hot water and add with the vanilla.

NUT FROSTING

Stir in 1 cup chopped lightly toasted nuts of your choice with the vanilla.

FRENCH BUTTERCREAM *Makes 3½ cups*

¾ cup sugar
¼ cup water
Few drops of lemon juice
6 egg whites
1½ to 2 pounds unsalted butter, softened
1½ teaspoons gluten-free vanilla or other extract (optional); for other flavorings, see Variations below and on page 146

Heat the sugar, water, and lemon juice in a small saucepan. Bring to a boil and cook until the syrup reaches the soft ball stage (see technique, page 31). Remove from the heat.

Before the syrup reaches the soft ball stage, begin beating the egg whites with an electric mixer. As soon as they are foaming and the syrup is ready, slowly begin pouring the hot syrup into the egg whites. Beat until stiff and cool to the touch, about 15 minutes. Tablespoon by tablespoon, add the soft butter until the texture is satiny and the color is pale yellow to yellow-white. If the butter appears to curdle, increase the speed and add more butter. When the butter is smooth, add the vanilla or other flavoring, if desired.

VARIATIONS

CHOCOLATE BUTTERCREAM

Add 4 ounces bittersweet chocolate, melted and cooled, to the finished buttercream

WHITE CHOCOLATE BUTTERCREAM

Add 6 ounces melted and cooled white chocolate to the finished buttercream.

LEMON BUTTERCREAM

Add 2 to 4 tablespoons Lemon Curd (page 199)to the finished buttercream.

COFFEE BUTTERCREAM

Dissolve 1 to 2 tablespoons gluten-free instant coffee powder in 1 tablespoon hot water or rum. Add to the finished buttercream.

AMARETTO BUTTERCREAM

Add ⅓ cup amaretto liqueur or ½ teaspoon almond extract to the finished buttercream.

ORANGE BUTTERCREAM

Add 1 tablespoon grated orange zest to the finished buttercream.

BUTTERCREAM FROSTING *Makes 2½ cups*

1 stick unsalted butter, at room temperature
2 cups sifted confectioners' sugar
½ teaspoon gluten-free vanilla
½ to ⅔ cup heavy cream

Beat the butter until white. Add the confectioners' sugar and beat until fluffy. Add the vanilla and cream. Beat until the frosting is fluffy.

VARIATIONS

COFFEE BUTTERCREAM

Dissolve 1 to 2 tablespoons gluten-free instant espresso powder in 1 to 2 tablespoons hot water. Cool and add to the finished frosting.

CHOCOLATE BUTTERCREAM

Add 2 ounces unsweetened chocolate, melted and cooled, or 2 tablespoons unsweetened cocoa powder to the finished frosting.

MOCHA BUTTERCREAM

Dissolve 1 to 2 tablespoons gluten-free instant espresso powder in 1 to 2 tablespoons hot water and cool. Add the espresso and 2 tablespoons unsweetened cocoa powder to the finished frosting.

LIQUEUR BUTTERCREAM

Add 2 tablespoons rum, brandy, or fruit liqueur to the finished frosting.

PRALINE BUTTERCREAM

Stir ⅓ to ½ cup Praline Powder (recipe follows) into the finished buttercream.

PRALINE POWDER:

1¼ cups sugar
¼ cup water
Few drops of lemon juice
1 cup unblanched almonds or hazelnuts

Lightly grease a cookie sheet.

Put the sugar, water, and lemon juice in a heavy skillet over medium heat. Heat, without stirring, until the sugar is dissolved and the mixture is boiling. Toss in the almonds. Cover and boil until the sugar turns a caramel color.

Pour the mixture onto the greased cookie sheet. Let it cool and harden. Break the praline into coarse pieces. Pulverize in the food processor.

QUICK CHOCOLATE BUTTERCREAM *Makes 2½ cups*

An all-purpose chocolate frosting.

- 5 ounces bittersweet chocolate
- 2 ounces unsweetened chocolate
- 1½ sticks unsalted butter
- 2 cups sifted confectioners' sugar
- 1 teaspoon gluten-free vanilla

Chop both chocolates and melt over hot water. Remove the bowl from the hot water and cool. Beat the butter until white. Add the confectioners' sugar and vanilla and beat until smooth. Stir in the cooled melted chocolate. Beat on high speed for 1 minute.

CARAMEL BUTTERCREAM *Makes 3 cups*

I especially like this frosting on the chocolate Basic Cake (page 101) or the Butter Cake (page 102).

- 1½ sticks unsalted butter
- ¾ cup packed light brown sugar
- ⅓ cup heavy cream
- 2 teaspoons gluten-free vanilla
- 4 to 5 cups sifted confectioners' sugar

Melt the butter and brown sugar together in a small saucepan. Whisk in the heavy cream. Bring to a rolling boil. Boil for 1 minute. Pour the mixture into a mixing bowl. Cool slightly, then whisk in the vanilla and 1 cup of the confectioners' sugar. Continue beating in the rest of the sugar until the frosting is smooth and spreadable. This frosting is best used soon after making.

CHOCOLATE SOUR CREAM FROSTING *Makes 4 cups*

The slightly sour aftertaste of the sour cream is a good foil for sweet, dense cakes line the Butter Cake (page 102). Resist stirring this silky, shiny chocolate frosting while it is setting or it will lose its sheen.

- 16 ounces milk chocolate
- 12 ounces semisweet chocolate
- 1 teaspoon gluten-free vanilla
- 2 cups sour cream

Chop both chocolates and melt over hot water. Remove the bowl from the hot water and whisk in the vanilla and sour cream. Cool the frosting until it is thick enough to spread. Use immediately.

RICH CREAM CHEESE FROSTING *Makes 2½ cups*

A very rich frosting, perfect for carrot or any spice cake, such as pumpkin or applesauce.

- 6 tablespoons unsalted butter, at room temperature
- 8 ounces cream cheese, at room temperature
- 2 to 2½ cups sifted confectioners' sugar
- 1 teaspoon gluten-free vanilla

Beat the butter until white. Add the cream cheese and beat in. Slowly add the sugar and beat until fluffy and smooth. Flavor with the vanilla.

VARIATIONS

CHOCOLATE CREAM CHEESE FROSTING

Add 3 to 4 ounces cooled melted unsweetened chocolate.

LEMON CREAM CHEESE FROSTING

Omit the vanilla. Add 2 teaspoons grated lemon zest and 2 teaspoons lemon juice.

EASY FUDGE FROSTING *Makes 2 cups*

- 8 ounces semisweet chocolate, chopped
- 1 cup evaporated milk
- ¾ cup sugar

Melt the chocolate over hot water. Heat the milk in a small saucepan. Whisk the sugar into the heated milk and whisk until it is dissolved. Whisk the melted chocolate into the hot milk. Using an electric mixer, beat until cool.

GANACHE FROSTING *Makes 5½ cups*

Ganache looks complex, but it is very simple to create. A sophisticated frosting for any cake.

- 3 cups heavy cream
- 12 ounces bittersweet chocolate, chopped
- 12 ounces semisweet chocolate, chopped
- 2 tablespoons butter
- 2 teaspoons gluten-free vanilla

Heat the cream to the boiling point. Pour it over the chopped chocolates. Add the butter and vanilla. Whisk until smooth. Chill until the frosting is of a spreading consistency.

GANACHE ICING *Makes 1½ cups*

A very simple yet elegant frosting or filling for cakes.

8 ounces bittersweet chocolate, chopped
1 cup heavy cream

Bring the cream to a boil in a small saucepan. Pour it over the chopped chocolate. Whisk until the chocolate is melted and the mixture is smooth. Set aside until the mixture is thick yet fluid enough to pour over a cake.

To make ganache into a filling or a spreadable icing, whip it using an electric mixer before it cools. It will thicken, get light in color, and become fluffy.

QUICK CHOCOLATE ICING *Makes ½ cup*

I love to use this to dress up brownies or to put a thin chocolate glaze on a pound cake or a butter cake.

6 ounces semisweet chocolate
½ stick unsalted butter

Melt the chocolate and butter together in a saucepan over low heat or in a bowl in the microwave. Stir until smooth. Cool slightly before using.

QUICK WHITE CHOCOLATE BUTTERCREAM *Makes about 2 cups*

There is something magical about white chocolate, with its subtle but distinctive flavor. It is trickier to melt than regular chocolate; make sure that the water under the white chocolate is just hot, not boiling.

7 ounces excellent-quality white chocolate, such as Lindt
2 sticks unsalted butter
2 cups sifted confectioners' sugar
3 to 4 tablespoons heavy cream

Chop the white chocolate, put it in a bowl, and melt over hot water. Remove from the hot water and cool. Beat the butter until white. Add the confectioners' sugar. Beat until well blended. Add the cooled white chocolate and 3 tablespoons of the heavy cream. Add more cream if needed. Beat on high speed for 1 minute.

ELEGANT HOT FUDGE SAUCE *Makes 2 cups*

This sauce is thick and rich—try it on ice cream, as well as cakes and meringues.

- ⅔ cup heavy cream
- ½ stick unsalted butter
- 1 cup firmly packed light brown sugar
- Pinch of salt
- ¼ cup Droste cocoa powder
- 1 ounce unsweetened chocolate, chopped

Heat the cream, butter, sugar, and salt in a small heavy saucepan. Bring to a low boil. Remove the pan from the heat and whisk in the cocoa powder and chocolate. Serve immediately or cool and reheat. If the sauce is too thick upon reheating, whisk in more cream.

FUDGE SAUCE *Makes 1½ cups*

- 1 cup heavy cream
- ⅔ cup sugar
- Pinch of salt
- 4 ounces unsweetened chocolate, chopped
- 2 tablespoons light corn syrup
- 1 teaspoon gluten-free vanilla
- 2 tablespoons unsalted butter

In a small saucepan, whisk together the cream, sugar, and salt. Stir in the chocolate and corn syrup. Bring to a boil and, stirring constantly, boil for 5 minutes. Whisk in the vanilla and the butter. Cool, cover, and refrigerate. Reheat over low heat.

CHOCOLATE SAUCE *Makes about 2½ cups*

1⅓ cups water
Drop of lemon juice
1⅓ cups sugar
¾ cup light corn syrup
2⅔ cups unsweetened cocoa powder
1½ teaspoons gluten-free vanilla

Heat the water, lemon juice, sugar, and corn syrup in a saucepan. Bring to a boil and boil for 1 minute. Sift the cocoa powder into the sugar syrup. Whisk until smooth. Add the vanilla. Cool. Keep refrigerated.

RASPBERRY SAUCE *Makes 1½ cups*

This is an all-purpose sauce for a number of desserts. Imagine a meringue swan swimming on a gossamer pool of raspberry sauce at your next dinner party.

2 boxes frozen raspberries in syrup

Thaw the berries. Drain and reserve the juices. Puree the berries in a blender or food processor. Strain the puree through a fine sieve. Whisk in enough juice to make a sauce. Refrigerate until ready to use. Save any leftover juices in case the sauce thickens up while refrigerated. I like to use some of the juices to add to seltzer or ginger ale.

CARAMEL SAUCE *Makes 2 cups*

Serve this sauce warm with apple or pear dumplings or with cream puffs filled with ice cream.

- 1 cup sugar
- 2 tablespoons water
- Drop of lemon juice
- 1 cup heavy cream
- ½ teaspoon gluten-free vanilla

Heat the sugar, water, and lemon juice in a saucepan. Bring to a boil and boil until the sugar begins to turn a golden brown. Resist stirring while cooking; instead, swirl the pan. As soon as the sugar has turned golden brown, carefully and slowly pour in the heavy cream in a steady thin stream. Cook until the sauce has a uniform color. Stir in the vanilla. Remove from the heat and chill over ice.

PIES, TARTS, AND QUICHES

SWEET

Banana Cream Pie
Peach Pie
Pumpkin Custard Pie
French Apple Tart
Fresh Fig Tart
Italian Plum Tart
Fresh Strawberry Tart
Pear Upside-Down Tart
Plum Galette
Fresh Apricot Lattice Tartlets
Bailey's Irish Cream Pie
Chocolate Ganache Tart
Chocolate Pecan Pie
Crostata di Marmelatta
Custard Pie
Lemon Curd Tart
Lemon Mousse Tart
Nondairy Chocolate Silk Pie
Tart Tatin
Italian Cheese Pie
Crostata di Riso

SAVORY

Quiche Lorraine
Spinach and Ricotta Pie
Spinach and Colored Pepper Quiche
Fresh Spinach and Tomato Pie
Broccoli, Mushroom, and Cheddar Quiche
Carrot Quiche
Tuscan Tomato Tart
Wild Mushroom Tart
Ginger Brie Quiche
Maine Crabmeat Quiche
New England Salmon Pie

CRUSTS

Flaky Pastry
Cornmeal Crust
Pasta Frolla
Graham Cracker Crust
Meringue Crust
Oil Crust
Rich Pastry
Pecan Butter Crust
Cereal Crust

My very first memory of a homemade pie

is that of a lemon meringue pie my mother made. I misjudged the placement of her pie as I sat down on the kitchen counter where it had been set to cool. Needless to say, there was no meringue on our pie that evening.

I have always found it quite easy to create flaky pie crust. Even to this day, my mother and sister will barter with me for one of my flaky pie crusts that they can then roll out and fill. I think that with a bit of practice you will find it easy too.

The best news for reluctant pie bakers is that making gluten-free pie pastry is much easier than creating traditional pastry—there is no gluten to overwork and toughen your crust. But be certain not to work the dough too much or the warmth from your hands will melt the butter, and it's little bits of butter that make the crust flaky. You can also skip the step of allowing the crust to rest before you roll it out; without gluten, it doesn't need to rest.

There are a few tricks to working with gluten-free pastry. The pastry is fragile and won't hold its shape very well on the edges—but once you get used to it, it is very easy to mix, roll, and place in a pan. Try to pinch the edges with your fingers or the back of a fork, and butter the bottom of the pan to help the crust stay in place. Many pie makers have a "signature" for their crust. Mine is a ropelike edge—I twist and turn the edge under and then mark it with a knife to look like a rope. Experiment and try signing your gluten-free pies with your own distinctive edge.

Gluten-free pastry does not shrink as much as traditional pastry. This is important to note when blind-baking a crust. Blind baking is the technique used to prebake a crust before filling it with the ingredients. You usually do not have to line it and fill it with pie weights, as you do for conventional blind baking. Just bake the crust for 12 to 15 minutes at 400°F, let cool, then fill.

Turn a prebaked crust into a special dessert treat by filling it with cooked fruit, sweetened whipped cream topped with fresh fruit, pudding topped with whipped cream or fresh fruit, zabaglione mousse, lemon curd, lemon mousse, nondairy chocolate pudding, ganache topped with whipped cream and strawberries, or ice cream topped with syrup and kept frozen.

Fruit pies require 4 cups of fresh or 3 cups of cooked fruit filling. Try adding a squeeze of lemon to your fruit pies to enhance the flavor and add a lemony "zing." Each fruit you choose will require a different amount of sugar or sweetener, so experiment to find the level of sweetness you prefer. Because fruit pies cook down and often become too juicy, it is important to add a starch, such as cornstarch, arrowroot, or instant tapioca, to act as a thickener. When using tapioca, add 2⅔ tablespoons and ⅔ to 1 cup of sugar per 4 cups of fruit. If you prefer using cornstarch, use 2 to 4 tablespoons. When using an acidic fruit, I recommend thickening with tapioca, arrowroot, or cornstarch. Fill the pies immediately before baking; don't let fruit filling sit for more than 15 minutes.

Top crusts need a way to allow steam to escape from the pie, so cut a small "vent" hole in the top just before baking. To add a golden glazed-finish look to your pies, brush the crust with an egg glaze of egg yolk whipped with 2 tablespoons of cream or milk. Or try sprinkling cinnamon sugar on top for a sweet, crisp finish.

As a rule of thumb, begin baking pies at 425°F on the lowest rack. After 12 minutes, raise the pie to the middle rack and lower the temperature to 375°F to prevent soggy bottom crusts. Check each recipe for the specific temperature and baking time—meringues bake for 5 to 10 minutes, and custard pies bake at a lower temperature than fruit pies.

For easy cleanup, line the bottom of the oven with foil. This is a handy tip for fruit pies in particular. If you have some leftover crust, try making delicious fruit turnovers using any extra filling on hand or your favorite jam. Make mini appetizers by cutting out the dough with a 3-inch biscuit cutter and stuffing with a savory filling; bake for 15 to 20 minutes at 400°F.

One of my favorite mottoes is "Life is short—eat dessert first." As a result, this chapter is organized with sweet pies and tarts first, followed by savory quiches and tarts.

SWEET

BANANA CREAM PIE *Makes 1 (8- to 9-inch) pie*

Everyone's favorite pie and easy to make! You can mound the whipped cream over the filling if you don't have a pastry bag.

1 single-crust recipe of your choice, prebaked (pages 183–89)
1 recipe Vanilla Pudding (page 196)
3 ripe bananas
1 cup whipping cream
1 tablespoon confectioners' sugar, to taste (optional)
½ to 1 teaspoon gluten-free vanilla extract, to taste (optional)

Pour half of the pudding into the prebaked crust. Slice 2 of the bananas. Arrange the slices over the pudding. Pour the remaining pudding on top of the bananas. Cover with plastic wrap and refrigerate until thoroughly cooled.

Just before serving, slice the remaining banana and arrange the slices over the pudding. Whip the cream until stiff. If you like, sweeten with confectioners' sugar and flavor with vanilla. Fit a pastry bag with a ½-inch fluted nozzle and fill with the whipped cream. Pipe the whipped cream over the bananas.

PEACH PIE *Makes 1 (8-inch) pie*

The first time I ever made this was for Leon Berkowitz, the gentleman who first introduced me to gluten-free baking. It smelled wonderful, and Leon was thrilled when I arrived at his home with the pie still warm.

1¼ cups apricot nectar
½ cup apricot or peach preserves or jam
⅔ cup packed brown sugar
3 tablespoons cornstarch
¼ teaspoon cinnamon
⅛ teaspoon ginger
8 ripe peaches, peeled, pitted, and sliced
2 tablespoons orange juice
1 double-crust recipe Flaky Pastry (page 183), made with 2 teaspoons grated lemon zest
Egg glaze (1 egg yolk mixed with 2 tablespoons cream)

Preheat the oven to 400°F. Butter an 8-inch pie plate.

Heat the nectar in a small nonaluminum saucepan. Bring to a boil and simmer for 30 minutes or until reduced to ¾ cup. Add the preserves and whisk to combine. Strain and cool.

Mix together the brown sugar, cornstarch, cinnamon, and ginger. Place the sliced peaches in a bowl. Toss with the orange juice and the sugar mixture. Set aside.

Roll out a top and bottom crust, using 2 pieces of lightly floured (with rice flour) parchment paper. Fit one crust into the buttered pie plate. Brush the crust with the cooled preserves glaze. Carefully spoon in the peaches and any juices. Cover with the other crust, or cut pastry into ½-inch-thick strips and weave a lattice cover. Crimp the edges to form a decorative border. Brush with the egg glaze.

Bake on the bottom rack for 15 minutes. Transfer the pie to the middle rack and lower the oven temperature to 350°F. Bake for another 25 minutes. Serve warm.

PUMPKIN CUSTARD PIE *Makes 2 (9-inch) pies*

I have always loved warm pumpkin pie with whipped cream. Then I tried this recipe and discovered it was so rich and light that there is no need to garnish with whipped cream.

1 double-crust recipe Flaky Pastry (page 183)
1 cup sugar
2 tablespoons cornstarch
½ teaspoon each cinnamon, nutmeg, and ginger
4 eggs, lightly beaten
1 (29-ounce) can pumpkin puree
3¾ cups heavy cream

Preheat the oven to 425°F. Lightly butter two 9-inch pie plates.

Cut the pastry in half and roll out each piece between 2 sheets of floured (with rice flour) parchment paper. Fit the crusts into the buttered pie plates. Flute the edges.

Mix together the sugar, cornstarch, and spices. Whisk in the eggs and pumpkin puree. Pour in the cream and whisk everything until well blended. Strain the filling into the pastry.

Bake on the bottom rack for 12 minutes. Transfer the pies to the middle rack and lower the oven temperature to 375°F. Bake for another 30 minutes or until the filling is set. Cool.

FRENCH APPLE TART *Makes 1 (8-inch) tart*

This is my all-time favorite tart. It is such a simple dessert, yet the flavors are so elegant.

- 1 single-crust recipe Flaky Pastry (page 183)
- 4 to 6 Granny Smith apples, peeled, cored, and cut into ¼-inch-thick slices
- 1 tablespoon lemon juice
- 2 tablespoons cognac or brandy (optional)
- 1 tablespoon unsalted butter, melted
- 1 cup apricot preserves, melted and strained
- Unsweetened whipped cream (optional)

Preheat the oven to 375°F. Butter an 8-inch tart pan.

Roll out the pastry between 2 sheets of floured (with rice flour) parchment paper. Fit the pastry into the pan. Trim or flute the edges.

Put the apple slices in a bowl. Toss them with the lemon juice and the cognac or brandy. Arrange the apple slices in concentric circles on the pastry, overlapping slightly. Whisk the melted butter and any juices from the apples left in the bowl into the warm strained apricot preserves. At the start and every 10 minutes during the baking, brush the apples with the apricot preserves

Bake on the middle rack for 45 minutes or until the apples are brown and soft when pierced with the tip of a sharp paring knife. Be careful not to brown the apples too much. Serve with a dollop of unsweetened whipped cream, if using.

FRESH FIG TART *Makes 1 (9-inch) tart*

I wait all year for summer, when fresh figs are in season. Then I make this tart and eat figs until my craving is satisfied.

- 1 single-crust recipe Pasta Frolla (page 185) or Flaky Pastry (page 183)
- ½ cup almond or hazelnut flour (page 30)
- 1½ tablespoons brown rice flour
- Pinch of cinnamon
- ½ stick butter
- ¼ cup sugar
- 1 egg, separated
- Drop of lemon juice
- 8 fresh figs, stems removed, cut in half lengthwise
- Whipped cream sweetened with honey and flavored with mint or thyme (optional)

Preheat the oven to 375°F. Lightly grease a 9-inch porcelain quiche dish.

Roll out the pastry between 2 sheets of floured (with rice flour) parchment paper. Fit into the dish. Trim or flute the edges. Bake for 15 to 20 minutes or until slightly golden.

Mix together the almond flour, brown rice flour, and cinnamon.

Beat the butter until white. Add the sugar and beat until fluffy, about 5 minutes. Beat the egg yolk into the creamed butter and sugar. Stir the flour mixture into the creamed butter mixture.

Beat the egg white with a drop of lemon juice until it forms soft peaks. Fold into the butter-nut mixture. Spread over the pastry. Arrange the figs on top of the filling, cut side up.

Bake for 25 to 30 minutes, or until filling is firm. Serve with a dollop of whipped cream sweetened with honey and flavored with mint or thyme, if using.

ITALIAN PLUM TART *Makes 1 (8-inch) tart*

Italian plums are prune plums, smaller than our red and purple ones. I have made this pie with regular plums; they are good, but the Italian plums are superior. I like this tart best warm or at room temperature.

1 single-crust recipe Flaky Pastry (page 183)
36 Italian plums (not too ripe)
¾ cup sugar
½ teaspoon cinnamon

Preheat the oven to 400°F. Butter an 8-inch tart pan.

Cut the plums in half lengthwise without cutting all the way through and remove the pits. Arrange the opened plums side by side in concentric circles in the tart pan, standing up with their cut sides facing in toward the center.

Mix the sugar and cinnamon together. Sprinkle over the plums.

Bake for 15 minutes, then lower the oven temperature to 350°F. Continue baking for about another 25 minutes or until the plums are tender and giving up their juices.

FRESH STRAWBERRY TART *Makes 1 (8-inch) tart*

A must when strawberries are in season!

1 quart strawberries, cleaned, hulled, and left whole
¾ cup sugar
2½ tablespoons cornstarch
½ cup water
½ cup orange juice
1 single-crust recipe of your choice, prebaked in 8-inch tart pan (pages 183–89)
Unsweetened whipped cream and fresh mint (optional)

Quarter or slice 1 cup of the berries, and puree in a blender or food processor. Set aside the whole berries.

Mix together the sugar, cornstarch, water, and orange juice in a medium non-aluminum saucepan. Cook over low heat for 10 minutes. Whisk in the puree. Arrange the whole berries in the baked pastry shell. Pour the sauce over, making sure to coat the all the berries. Chill. Serve with unsweetened whipped cream and a sprig of fresh mint, if using.

PEAR UPSIDE-DOWN TART *Makes 1 (8- to 9-inch) tart*

A great way to use pears in the fall. When turning the tart onto the plate, do not hesitate or you will have tart on the floor. Make sure that the serving plate has a lip to catch any juices the pears may give off.

4 ripe yet firm pears
½ cup sugar
2½ cups dry red wine
1 cinnamon stick
1 small piece orange zest
1 single-crust recipe Flaky Pastry (page 183)
Unsweetened whipped cream (optional)

Preheat the oven to 375°F.

Peel the pears, cut in half, and core. Place the pears, cored surface up, in an 8- or 9-inch pan that can go on top of the stove as well as into the oven and that has a lid. Make sure that the pointed ends of the pears face toward the center. Remember that, when served, the bottom of the tart will be the top.

Sprinkle the sugar over the pears. Pour the wine over. Add the cinnamon stick and orange zest. Bring to a boil on the stove. Simmer, covered, until the pears are tender, about 15 minutes (less if the pears are ripe). Pour off the syrup into a saucepan and reduce until thick. Drizzle over the pears, still in the original pan.

Roll out the pastry and fit it over the pears. Tuck in the overlapping edge. Bake for 40 minutes or until the crust is brown and the juices bubble and are syrupy.

Place a large plate with a lip over the tart. Carefully invert plate and pan together. Remove the pan. Serve the tart warm with a dollop of unsweetened whipped cream, if using.

PLUM GALETTE *Makes 1 (8-inch) galette*

A galette is a free-form pie with the edges of the crust folded up over the fruit. I love the rustic way this bakes up.

2½ pounds plums, pitted and sliced
½ cup sugar
1 tablespoon cornstarch
½ teaspoon cinnamon
Pinch of cloves
1 tablespoon orange juice
1 teaspoon grated orange zest
1 double-crust recipe Flaky Pastry (page 183)
Cinnamon sugar for sprinkling

Preheat the oven to 400°F. Line a jelly roll pan with parchment paper.

Toss together the sliced plums, sugar, cornstarch, cinnamon, cloves, orange juice, and orange zest. Roll out the pastry between 2 sheets of floured (with rice flour) parchment paper into a 10 to 12-inch round and lay it on the jelly roll pan. Place the plums in the center of the pastry, leaving about 3 inches uncovered all around. Fold the uncovered pastry over the fruit, leaving the very center open. Sprinkle with some cinnamon sugar. Bake on the middle rack for 30 to 45 minutes.

FRESH APRICOT LATTICE TARTLETS *Makes 4 individual tarts*

If you are a frugal gluten-free gourmet, you will have a stash of pastry scraps in your freezer, as I do. These tartlets are a beautiful way to use up scraps of pastry. Try peaches or nectarines instead of the apricots.

4 ripe apricots
¼ cup finely ground almonds
3 tablespoons mascarpone cheese
Finely grated zest of 1 lemon
½ recipe Pasta Frolla (page 185)
2 to 3 tablespoons milk or cream

Preheat the oven to 400°F. Line a jelly roll pan with parchment paper.

Bring a pot of water to a boil. Make a small × in the bottom of each apricot. Place the apricots in the boiling water just until the skin begins to pull away from the ×. Remove from the water and cool. Peel, halve, and pit the apricots.

Blend the ground almonds, mascarpone, and lemon zest together. Spoon into each of the apricot hollows.

Roll out the pasta frolla between 2 sheets of floured (with rice flour) parchment paper. Using a pastry cutter, cut out 4 rounds slightly larger than an apricot (about 3 inches across). Place the apricots, cut side down, on the pastry rounds. Reroll the pastry and cut into thin strips. Brush the edges of the rounds with some milk or cream. Arrange the strips of pastry over the apricots to form a lattice and gently press the edges to seal. Brush the lattice with more milk or cream. Bake for 18 minutes or until the pastry turns golden brown.

BAILEY'S IRISH CREAM PIE *Makes 1 (8- or 9-inch) pie*

This is a dessert my pastry chef, Annie Woodruff, used to make at my restaurant—it was a customer favorite! Make sure you use gluten-free Heath candy bars. The Bailey's Cream is an essential part of this recipe. Distilled alcohol and caramel coloring are considered okay by many in the celiac community, but if you are among those who prefer to avoid these, then this recipe not for you.

⅔ cup sugar
¼ cup cornstarch
Pinch of salt
1 cup half-and-half or light cream
1 cup Bailey's Irish Cream
3 egg yolks
2 teaspoons gluten-free vanilla
2 tablespoons butter
1 recipe Chocolate Graham Cracker Crust, prebaked and cooled (page 186)
Unsweetened whipped cream
1 gluten-free Heath Bar, crushed

Whisk together the sugar, cornstarch, and salt in a small saucepan. Whisk in the half-and-half and Bailey's Irish Cream. Over medium heat, whisk constantly until the mixture is thickened.

In a bowl, lightly beat the egg yolks. Warm the yolks with some of the hot mixture. Whisk the warmed yolks into the remaining hot mixture. Whisking constantly, bring to a boil over medium heat. Remove from the heat and add the vanilla and butter. Strain the mixture into the cooled baked crust. Cool and chill before serving. Serve with whipped cream and crushed Heath Bar sprinkled on top.

CHOCOLATE GANACHE TART *Makes 1 (8-inch) tart*

Sometimes simple is best. Once you have mastered gluten-free pie crust, this recipe will be easy. During strawberry season, I arrange whole strawberries on top of the whipped cream.

16 ounces extra-bitter chocolate, chopped
3 cups heavy cream
1 single-crust recipe Flaky Pastry (page 183), prebaked (technique, page 157) in 8-inch tart pan
Fresh strawberries or raspberries for garnish

Place the chocolate in a heatproof bowl. Heat 2 cups of the cream to the boiling point. Pour the hot cream over the chopped chocolate. Let stand for 1 minute, then whisk together. Place over a bowl of ice water. Stir until the ganache begins to thicken. Pour into the cooled prebaked tart shell. Let set until firm, at least 1 hour. Refrigerate until ready to serve.

Whip the remaining 1 cup of cream and sweeten, if you choose. Decorate the pie with the cream or serve each slice with a dollop of the cream and fresh berries.

CHOCOLATE PECAN PIE *Makes 1 (9-inch) pie*

This winning combination was a big hit with my tester—and her entire family.

- 1 single-crust recipe Flaky Pastry (page 183)
- 2 ounces bittersweet chocolate
- ¼ cup strong brewed coffee
- 2 tablespoons butter
- 4 eggs
- ½ cup packed light brown sugar
- 1 cup light corn syrup
- 1 cup coarsely chopped pecans
- 1 cup pecan halves

Butter a 9-inch pie plate.

Roll out the pastry between 2 sheets of lightly floured (with rice flour) parchment paper. Line the pie plate with the pastry. Trim off the excess pastry and flute the edge as you like. Refrigerate until ready to fill.

Preheat the oven to 425°F.

Melt the chocolate in the coffee in a small saucepan over low heat or in a bowl in the microwave. Remove from the heat and whisk in the butter. Cool.

Beat the eggs, brown sugar, and corn syrup until fluffy. Stir in the melted chocolate. Fold in the chopped nuts. Pour the mixture into the pastry shell. Arrange the pecan halves on top.

Bake for 15 minutes. Lower the oven temperature to 375°F and bake for another 20 to 25 minutes.

CROSTATA DI MARMELATTA *Makes 1 (9-inch) tart*

When I lived in Florence, Italy, I bought a piece of this pastry almost every day to munch on while I watched my daughter play in the park. When I returned to Maine, I missed it so much that I began making it.

1 recipe Pasta Frolla (page 185)
2 cups fruit jam

Preheat the oven to 400°F. Butter a 9-inch removable-bottom tart pan.

Roll out two-thirds of the dough between 2 sheets of lightly floured (with rice flour) parchment paper until 10 to 12 inches in diameter. Fit the rolled pastry into the buttered pan to cover the bottom and sides. Trim off the excess around the edges. Bake for 15 minutes.

Spread the jam over the baked crust. Roll out the remaining dough and cut into strips. Create a lattice over the jam. Brush the lattice with some jam. Bake for 15 to 20 minutes or until the pastry is golden brown. Cool slightly, then remove the tart from the pan.

CUSTARD PIE *Makes 1 (8- or 9-inch) pie*

A New England classic. If you use 6 egg yolks, the custard will be very rich and tender. Treat yourself to the taste of nutmeg freshly grated on the top and serve a dollop of whipped cream on the side.

6 egg yolks or 3 whole eggs
½ cup sugar
Pinch of salt
2 cups light cream
1 teaspoon gluten-free vanilla
1 single-crust recipe of your choice, prebaked in 8- or 9-inch pie pan (pages 183–89)
Freshly grated nutmeg
Whipped cream and/or fresh berries (optional)

Preheat the oven to 325°F.

Beat the yolks or eggs, adding the sugar and salt. Stir in the cream and vanilla. Strain into the prebaked pie shell. Grate the nutmeg on top. Bake on the middle rack for 30 minutes or until the custard sets. Cool and serve with whipped cream, plain or with some fresh berries too, if using.

LEMON CURD TART *Makes 1 (8- or 9-inch) tart*

If you are a lemon lover, this will become your favorite dessert recipe. You can use the whites from the curd to make a meringue for the top if you like. I prefer lightly sweetened whipped cream piped on top.

- 1 single-crust recipe Flaky Pastry, prebaked in 8- or 9-inch tart pan (page 183)
- 1 recipe Lemon Curd (page 199)
- Lightly sweetened whipped cream
- Mint leaves and candied violets (optional)

Fill the prebaked shell with the lemon curd. Using a pastry bag fitted with a fluted nozzle, pipe the whipped cream on top. If you prefer, you can mound the whipped cream with a spoon. Decorate with fresh mint leaves and candied violets, if desired. Keep refrigerated until ready to serve.

LEMON MOUSSE TART *Makes 1 (8- or 9-inch) tart*

This is a very lovely, light dessert. The raspberry sauce adds color and complements the lemon.

- 1 recipe Graham Cracker Crust (page 185)
- 1 teaspoon gelatin
- 3 tablespoons water
- 1 cup Lemon Curd (page 199)
- 2 cups heavy cream
- 1 tablespoon confectioners' sugar
- 1 recipe Raspberry Sauce (page 152)

Preheat the oven to 350°F. Press the graham cracker crust mixture into an 8- or 9-inch tart pan. Bake for 10 to 12 minutes. Cool completely.

Mix the gelatin and water together in a small heatproof bowl. Place the bowl in a skillet filled with boiling water. As soon as the gelatin is melted, remove it from the boiling water. You will know when the gelatin is melted because it will appear syrupy and clear and no longer cloudy with tiny beads of the gelatin. Whisk the melted gelatin into the lemon curd.

Whip the heavy cream to the soft mound stage. Fold half of the cream into the lemon curd. Fill the cooled crust with the mousse. Refrigerate for at least 1 hour. Just before serving, sweeten the remaining whipped cream with the confectioners' sugar. Pipe or spoon the whipped cream on top of the lemon mousse. Serve the dessert with a pitcher of raspberry sauce.

NONDAIRY CHOCOLATE SILK PIE *Makes 1 (8-inch) pie*

I love to make the filling and put it in wineglasses and eat it as pudding for dessert or a snack. It is so good you will find it difficult not to feel guilty.

1 (12-ounce) package silken tofu, drained
½ cup unsweetened cocoa powder
3 tablespoons honey or maple syrup
4 tablespoons granulated Fruitsource (see Note, below)
1 recipe Graham Cracker Crust, prebaked (page 185)
Hip Whip (see Note, below)

Puree the tofu in a food processor. Add the cocoa powder, honey or maple syrup, and Fruitsource. Blend until smooth. Pour into the prebaked crust. Refrigerate for at least 2 hours. Serve with a dollop of Hip Whip.

VARIATION Use 12 ounces melted and cooled bittersweet chocolate in place of the cocoa, honey or maple syrup, and Fruitsource.

NOTE: Fruitsource is a natural sugar substitute, and Hip Whip is a soy whipped topping. Both can be found in most natural food stores.

TART TATIN *Makes 1 (9-inch) tart*

When I first apprenticed at Madeleine Kamman's Modern Gourmet in Newton Center, Massachusetts, in 1972, I assisted her with this dessert for her Classic French cooking classes. When I had my own cooking school in Portland, Maine, I taught this dessert to my students. The flavor of the apples mixed with the caramelized sugar and the butter is exquisite.

1 single-crust recipe Flaky Pastry (page 183)
¾ cup sugar
1 tablespoon water
⅛ teaspoon lemon juice
8 large Granny Smith apples, peeled, cored, and cut into ¼-inch-thick slices
1½ sticks unsalted butter, diced
Unsweetened whipped cream (optional)

Preheat the oven to 375°F.

Use a 9-inch pan, such as a skillet or sauté pan, that can go from the stove to the oven. In the pan, combine ¼ cup of the sugar, the water, and the lemon juice. Cook over medium-high heat until the mixture turns golden brown. Remove the pan from the heat and arrange a layer of the sliced apples on top of the caramelized sugar, then layer the sugar and butter and remaining apples.

Roll out the pastry between 2 sheets of floured (with rice flour) parchment paper. Lay it over the apples. Make steam holes in the pastry. Bake for 50 minutes. Cool for 5 minutes before inverting onto a serving plate. Make sure the serving plate has a lip to catch the juices from the apples.

Serve hot, at room temperature, or chilled. A dollop of unsweetened whipped cream goes very nicely with the tart.

ITALIAN CHEESE PIE *Makes 1 (9-inch) pie*

This pie is not too sweet and not as rich or filling as a slice of traditional cheesecake because it uses ricotta instead of cream cheese. I love to serve it with a small bunch of green or champagne grapes next to each slice. Be sure to look at the label to ensure that the ricotta is gluten-free.

FILLING:

5 cups (2½ pounds) gluten-free ricotta cheese
⅓ cup sugar
1 tablespoon cornstarch
⅛ teaspoon salt
1 teaspoon gluten-free vanilla
4 egg yolks
1 tablespoon golden raisins, soaked in 1 tablespoon orange juice
1 teaspoon grated orange zest
1 tablespoon each diced candied orange peel and citron

1 recipe Pasta Frolla (page 185)
2 tablespoons pine nuts
1 egg white
1 tablespoon water

Preheat the oven to 350°F. Butter a 9-inch springform pan.

Combine all the filling ingredients and mix well. Refrigerate until ready to use.

Cut off one-fourth of the pastry and put it back in the refrigerator. Roll out the remaining pastry between 2 sheets of lightly floured (with rice flour) parchment paper into a 12-inch round large enough to fit the pan, including sides. Press the pastry into the pan.

Trim off any excess pastry. Remove the reserved pastry from the refrigerator and add the trimmings to it. Roll out into a rectangle ¼-inch thick. Cut lengthwise strips about ½ inch wide.

Spoon the filling into the lined pan. Sprinkle the pine nuts over the filling. Weave the strips of pastry on top to form a lattice. Whisk the egg white and water together. Brush over the lattice.

Bake on the middle rack for 1 hour or until the pastry is golden and the filling is firm. Carefully remove the sides of the springform and cool the pie on a rack.

CROSTATA DI RISO *Makes 1 (9-inch) tart*

When I lived in Florence, I used to love to walk with my daughter on Sunday mornings to our neighborhood trattoria and order an individual crostata di riso. It's a wonderful marriage of flavors.

- ½ recipe Pasta Frolla (page 185) or 1 recipe Cornmeal Crust (page 184)
- ½ cup short-grain rice, such as Arborio
- 2 cups milk
- Small piece of lemon zest the size of a quarter
- 1 cup heavy cream
- ⅛ teaspoon salt
- ¼ cup honey
- 1 tablespoon unsalted butter
- 2 eggs, lightly beaten
- Sweetened whipped cream (optional)

Preheat the oven to 350°F. Lightly butter a 9-inch tart pan or springform pan.

Roll out the dough between 2 sheets of lightly floured (with rice flour) parchment paper into a 12-inch round large enough to fit the pan, including the sides. Fit the pastry into the buttered pan. Trim off the excess around the edges. Bake for 10 minutes. Cool while you make the filling. About 10 minutes before the filling is done, return the oven to 350°F.

Cook the rice in the milk with the lemon zest until the rice is tender, about 20 to 30 minutes, stirring occasionally. Remove the lemon zest. Blend the cooked rice with the cream, salt, honey, butter, and eggs. Pour the mixture into the prebaked shell.

Bake the tart for 10 to 12 minutes or until the filling feels firm to the touch. Cool slightly before serving. I think the tart is best served warm with a dollop of sweetened whipped cream.

SAVORY

QUICHE LORRAINE *Makes 1 (9-inch) quiche*

An all-time classic that is well worth reviving. There is no other cheese that can take the place of the Gruyère. Quiche is not a heart-healthy dish, but once or twice a year give yourself permission to enjoy the flavors of French Gruyère and bacon cooked in an egg and cream custard with just a touch of fresh nutmeg.

This recipe makes a lot of filling; you'll need a deep crust to contain it all.

- 1 single-crust recipe Flaky Pastry (page 183)
- 3 cups heavy or light cream
- 4 eggs, lightly beaten
- ¼ teaspoon salt
- Scant ⅛ teaspoon freshly grated nutmeg
- Pinch of freshly ground black pepper
- ¼ pound sliced bacon, cooked but not crisp
- ½ cup grated Gruyère cheese
- 1½ teaspoons chopped fresh parsley

Preheat the oven to 400°F. Lightly grease a 9-inch porcelain quiche dish or deep-dish pie plate.

Roll out the crust between 2 sheets of lightly floured (with rice flour) parchment paper into a 14-inch round. Fit the pastry into the greased dish. Flute the edge.

Whisk together the cream, eggs, salt, pepper, and nutmeg.

Chop the bacon and scatter it over the bottom of the pie shell. Sprinkle the cheese on top. Strain the custard over the bacon and sprinkle the top with the parsley.

Bake on the bottom rack for 15 minutes. Transfer the dish to the middle rack and lower the oven temperature to 375°F. Bake for another 30 minutes or until the custard is set. Let it cool slightly before serving.

SPINACH AND RICOTTA PIE *Makes 1 (9-inch) quiche or deep-dish pie*

I adapted this scrumptious recipe from Molly Katzen's wonderful vegetarian tome *The Moosewood Cookbook.* During the holidays I use only red peppers to give it a festive look. For hors d'oeuvres, line mini muffin tins with pastry, fill them with the filling, and bake for only 15 to 20 minutes.

2 tablespoons extra virgin olive oil plus some to drizzle on top before baking
1 cup diced colored bell peppers
1 small onion, finely chopped
1 clove garlic, chopped
1 cup gluten-free ricotta cheese
1 cup sour cream
½ cup grated Parmesan cheese
10 ounces frozen chopped spinach, thawed and squeezed dry
1 teaspoon oregano or basil
⅛ teaspoon freshly grated nutmeg
Salt and black pepper to taste
2 tablespoons potato starch or cornstarch
3 eggs, lightly beaten
1 single-crust recipe Flaky Pastry (page 183) or crust of your choice

Preheat the oven to 400°F. Lightly butter a 9-inch porcelain quiche dish or deep-dish pie plate.

Heat the oil in a medium skillet. Add the peppers, onion, and garlic and sauté until tender. Set aside.

Mix together the ricotta, sour cream, Parmesan, pepper mixture, spinach, oregano or basil, nutmeg, salt, pepper, and potato starch or cornstarch. Taste. Add more seasonings if needed, then add the eggs. Refrigerate until you are ready to fill the crust.

Roll out the pastry between 2 sheets of floured (with rice flour) parchment paper into a 14-inch round. Fit the pastry into the buttered dish. Flute the edge. Spoon the filling into the pie shell. Drizzle a little olive oil over the filling.

Bake on the bottom rack for 15 minutes. Transfer the pie dish to the middle rack and lower the oven temperature to 350°F. Bake for another 20 minutes or until the filling is firm and golden.

SPINACH AND COLORED PEPPER QUICHE

Makes 1 (9-inch) quiche or deep-dish pie

This is not only delicious but also very colorful. Great to serve around the winter holidays.

Use a deep quiche dish or pie plate—there's a lot of filling.

- 1 single-crust recipe Flaky Pastry (page 183)
- 3 cups heavy or light cream
- 1 teaspoon basil or oregano
- 1 tablespoon extra virgin olive oil
- 1 red bell pepper, thinly julienned or diced
- 10 ounces fresh spinach, washed, stemmed, and shredded
- 4 eggs, lightly beaten
- ¼ teaspoon salt
- Few grinds of black pepper
- ⅓ cup grated Parmesan or Asiago cheese

Preheat the oven to 400°F. Lightly grease 9-inch deep-dish pie plate.

Roll out the pastry between 2 sheets of floured (with rice flour) parchment paper into a 14-inch round. Fit the pastry into the greased dish. Flute the edge.

Warm the cream and basil or oregano in a small saucepan over low heat for about 10 minutes. Set aside.

Heat the oil in a medium skillet. Add the bell pepper and sauté until tender. Remove and set aside. In the same skillet, cook the spinach until it begins to stick to the pan. Stir often. Remove from the heat and cool slightly.

Whisk together the cream, eggs, spinach, salt, and pepper. Arrange the bell pepper on the bottom of the pie shell. Sprinkle the cheese on top. Pour the custard over the cheese.

Bake on the bottom rack for 15 minutes. Transfer the dish to the middle rack and lower the oven temperature to 375°F. Bake for another 30 minutes or until the filling feels firm.

FRESH SPINACH AND TOMATO PIE *Makes 1 (9-inch) pie or quiche*

When tomatoes are farm fresh, this is the pie to make.

1 single-crust recipe Flaky Pastry (page 183)
2 tablespoons olive oil
1 large onion, chopped
1 clove garlic, chopped
10 ounces fresh spinach, washed, stemmed, and chopped
¾ teaspoon salt
Freshly ground black pepper
3 eggs
1½ cups heavy cream
Pinch of nutmeg
1 cup grated Gruyère cheese
2 ripe tomatoes, thinly sliced
1 teaspoon oregano

Preheat the oven to 400°F. Lightly grease a 9-inch pie plate or quiche dish.

Roll out the pastry between 2 sheets of floured (with rice flour) parchment paper into a 14-inch round. Fit the pastry into the greased dish. Flute the edge. Refrigerate while making the filling.

Heat the oil in a medium skillet. Add the onion and garlic and sauté until the onion is translucent. Toss in the spinach and cook until it begins to stick to the pan. Season with half of the salt and some pepper.

Whisk the eggs and cream together. Add the nutmeg, remaining salt, and more pepper. Sprinkle half of the cheese over the bottom of the pie shell. Spread the spinach mixture on top. Sprinkle the remaining cheese on top. Arrange the tomato slices in concentric circles over the cheese. Strain the egg mixture over the tomatoes and cheese. Sprinkle the oregano over the top.

Bake on the bottom rack for 15 minutes. Transfer the dish to the middle rack and lower the oven temperature to 375°F. Bake for another 30 to 35 minutes or until the custard is set. Cool for 10 minutes before serving.

BROCCOLI, MUSHROOM, AND CHEDDAR QUICHE

Makes 1 (9-inch) quiche

A great vegetarian quiche for brunch, lunch, or supper.

1 single-crust recipe Flaky Pastry (page 183)
2 tablespoons vegetable oil
2 cups sliced mushrooms
1 clove garlic, chopped
¼ to ½ teaspoon salt
4 eggs
3 cups heavy cream
⅛ teaspoon nutmeg
Pinch of freshly ground black pepper
1½ cups grated sharp cheddar cheese
2 cups broccoli florets, blanched
2 tablespoons chopped fresh parsley

Preheat the oven to 400°F. Lightly grease a 9-inch deep quiche dish.

Roll out the pastry between 2 sheets of floured (with rice flour) parchment paper into a 14-inch round. Fit the pastry into the greased dish. Flute the edge and refrigerate while preparing the filling.

Heat the oil in a medium skillet. Toss in the mushrooms and garlic. Raise the heat to high. Sprinkle the mushrooms with half of the salt. Cook until the juices are released from the mushrooms and have evaporated. Remove from the heat.

Whisk the eggs and cream together. Whisk in the remaining salt and the nutmeg and pepper. Cover the bottom of the pie shell with half of the cheese. Arrange the broccoli and mushrooms over the cheese. Sprinkle the remaining cheese over the vegetables. Strain the egg mixture over the vegetables and cheese. Sprinkle the parsley on top.

Bake on the bottom rack for 15 minutes. Transfer the dish to the middle rack and lower the oven temperature to 375°F. Bake for another 30 minutes or until the custard is set. Cool for 10 minutes before serving.

CARROT QUICHE *Makes 1 (9-inch) quiche*

People are always amazed at how delicious this quiche is. Serve it with a fresh spinach salad for a lovely lunch.

- 1 single-crust recipe Flaky Pastry (page 183)
- 2 tablespoons oil of your choice
- 1 small onion, finely chopped
- 1 pound carrots, grated
- 1 tablespoon chopped fresh parsley
- 1 teaspoon fresh lemon juice
- ¼ teaspoon salt
- Pinch of freshly ground black pepper
- Large pinch of freshly grated nutmeg
- ½ cup grated Parmesan or cheddar cheese
- 3 cups heavy cream
- 4 eggs

Preheat the oven to 400°F. Lightly grease a 9-inch deep quiche pan.

Roll out the pastry between 2 sheets of floured (with rice flour) parchment paper into a 14-inch round. Fit the pastry into the quiche pan. Flute the edge and refrigerate while preparing the filling.

Heat the oil in a medium skillet with a lid. Add the onion and sauté until translucent. Add the carrots, parsley, lemon juice, salt, pepper, and nutmeg. Stir. Lower the heat and cover the pan. Cook for 12 minutes or until the carrots are soft, stirring occasionally to make sure the carrots do not stick or scorch. Taste and adjust the seasoning, if necessary.

Take the quiche pan out of the refrigerator. Spread the cooked carrots over the pastry. Sprinkle the cheese on top. Season the cream with salt and pepper. Lightly beat the eggs and whisk them into the cream. Strain the egg mixture over the carrots.

Bake on the bottom rack for 15 minutes. Transfer the quiche to the middle rack and lower the oven temperature to 375°F. Bake for another 30 minutes or until the custard is set. Cool for 10 minutes before serving.

TUSCAN TOMATO TART *Makes 1 (9-inch) tart*

During a master class with Italian chef Giuliano Bugialli, I was inspired by his tomato tart recipe. This is a wonderful dish, especially during the summer when I can get tomatoes and basil fresh at the local farmers' market.

1 single-crust recipe Flaky Pastry (page 183), flavored with ⅛ teaspoon nutmeg
2 tablespoons extra virgin olive oil
1 medium red onion, finely chopped
1 carrot, finely chopped
1 small stalk celery, finely chopped
4 cloves garlic, finely chopped
2 (28-ounce) cans imported plum tomatoes, drained and chopped
¼ cup thinly sliced fresh basil
3 tablespoons chopped fresh parsley
¾ cup grated Parmesan cheese
¼ to ½ teaspoon salt
Freshly ground black pepper to taste
4 eggs

Preheat the oven to 375°F. Lightly grease a 9 × 2-inch deep tart pan, preferably with a removable bottom.

Roll out the pastry between 2 sheets of floured (with rice flour) parchment paper into a 14-inch round. Fit into the tart pan and trim the edge. Bake for 12 minutes. Cool.

Heat the oil in a medium skillet with a lid. Add the onion, carrot, celery, and garlic and sauté until tender. Add the tomatoes and cook slowly, covered for 30 minutes. Remove the lid and cook until the mixture is slightly thick and most of the moisture has evaporated. Let cool for 15 minutes. Transfer to a food processor and process until smooth. Stir in the basil, parsley, and cheese. Season with the salt and pepper. Lightly beat the eggs and stir in.

Pour into the pastry shell and bake on the middle rack for 20 to 25 minutes or until the filling is firm.

WILD MUSHROOM TART *Makes 1 (9-inch) tart*

Another inspiration from chef Bugialli. This tart is best if made in a tart pan with a removable bottom. I usually serve it warm or at room temperature. The filling can be made ahead and frozen.

1 single-crust recipe Flaky Pastry (page 183), flavored with ⅛ teaspoon nutmeg
2 tablespoons extra virgin olive oil
1 red onion, finely chopped
2 cloves garlic, chopped
½ pound assorted wild mushrooms, cleaned and sliced
½ pound white mushrooms, cleaned and sliced
¼ teaspoon salt
24 grinds black pepper
5 eggs, lightly beaten
½ cup grated Parmesan cheese
¼ cup chopped fresh parsley

Preheat the oven to 375°F. Lightly grease a 9-inch tart pan, preferably one with a removable bottom.

Roll out the pastry between 2 sheets of floured (with rice flour) parchment paper and fit into the tart pan. Bake the tart shell for 12 minutes. Cool.

Heat the oil in a medium skillet. Add the onion and garlic and sauté until tender and translucent. Toss in the mushrooms. Raise the heat. Sprinkle with the salt and pepper. Cook until all the juices have evaporated. Remove the skillet from the heat and let it cool slightly. Stir in the eggs, cheese, and parsley. Pour the filling into the prebaked shell. Bake for 20 minutes or until the filling feels firm.

GINGER BRIE QUICHE *Makes 1 (9-inch) quiche*

We were surprised and pleased when my restaurant, the Madd Apple, was mentioned in an article in *Bon Appétit.* The author loved our Ginger Brie Quiche!

- 1 single-crust recipe Flaky Pastry (page 183)
- 4 eggs
- ¼ teaspoon salt
- ¼ teaspoon ginger
- Freshly ground black pepper to taste
- 3 cups heavy cream
- ¼ pound Brie, rind removed, sliced
- 2 tablespoons chopped fresh parsley
- Salmon caviar, for garnish

Preheat the oven to 400°F. Lightly grease a 9-inch quiche dish.

Roll out the pastry between 2 sheets of floured (with rice flour) parchment paper. Fit the pastry into the quiche dish. Flute the edge. Refrigerate while preparing the filling.

Whisk together the eggs, the salt, ginger, and pepper. Whisk in the cream. Lay the slices of Brie over the bottom of the pastry. Strain the egg mixture over the cheese. Sprinkle the parsley on top.

Bake on the next to the lowest rack for 15 minutes. Transfer the dish to the middle rack and lower the oven temperature to 375°F. Bake for another 30 minutes or until the custard is set. Let cool 10 minutes before serving. Serve with a teaspoon of salmon caviar on top of each slice.

MAINE CRABMEAT QUICHE *Makes 1 (8-inch) quiche or pie*

Maine crabmeat has a very delicate flavor and texture, so the seasonings in this quiche do not overpower the crab. Serve a nice crisp green salad with a vinaigrette dressing.

- 1 single-crust recipe Flaky Pastry (page 183)
- 1 tablespoon Madeira or dry sherry
- 6 ounces fresh crabmeat, picked over to remove any cartilage
- 3 eggs, lightly beaten
- 2 cups heavy cream, heated
- 1 teaspoon chopped fresh tarragon or 2 teaspoons dried
- ¼ teaspoon salt
- Freshly ground black pepper

Preheat the oven to 400°F. Lightly grease an 8-inch quiche dish or pie plate.

Roll out the pastry between 2 sheets of lightly floured (with rice flour) parchment paper. Fit the pastry into the greased dish.

Mix the Madeira or sherry into the crab. Evenly distribute the crab over the bottom of the pie shell. Whisk together the remaining ingredients and pour over the crab.

Bake on the bottom shelf for 15 minutes. Transfer the quiche to the middle rack and lower the oven temperature to 375°F. Bake for another 30 minutes or until the custard is set. Cool slightly before serving.

NEW ENGLAND SALMON PIE *Makes 1 (8-inch) pie*

Susan Phillips's grandmother used to make this when she cooked at logging camps in the backwoods of Maine. I bet just knowing that this pie was waiting for them helped the loggers fell those tall pines even faster. I serve the pie with an egg sauce and a fresh spinach salad.

- 1 single-crust recipe Flaky Pastry (page 183)
- 1 tablespoon unsalted butter
- 1 medium onion, finely chopped
- 1 bunch scallions, minced
- 3 potatoes, peeled, cooked, and mashed
- 1 (14-ounce) can salmon, skin and bones removed
- ¼ to ½ teaspoon salt
- Freshly ground black pepper to taste
- 1 egg, lightly beaten
- Egg Sauce (recipe follows)

Preheat the oven to 375°F. Lightly grease an 8-inch pie plate.

Roll out the pastry between 2 sheets of floured (with rice flour) parchment paper. Line the pie plate with the pastry. Flute the edge.

Melt the butter in a medium skillet. Add the onion and scallions and sauté until the onion is translucent. Transfer to a large bowl, add the mashed potatoes and salmon, and mix together. Taste the mixture. Overseason a bit with the salt and pepper. Stir in the egg. Spoon the mixture into the pie shell.

Bake for 25 to 30 minutes or until the pastry and filling brown slightly. Serve with warm Egg Sauce.

VARIATION Use sweet potatoes and add a pinch of allspice.

EGG SAUCE

4 eggs
2 cups milk
¼ cup cornstarch
¼ to ½ teaspoon salt
Freshly ground black pepper
Generous pinch of nutmeg
1 tablespoon chopped fresh parsley

Put the eggs in a saucepan and cover with cold water. Slowly bring the water to a boil. Lower the heat so that the water barely simmers. Cook for 10 minutes. Take 1 egg out, peel it, and then cut it in half to see if it is properly hard-cooked. If not, continue cooking the other eggs for another minute or two (you'll need to cook another egg to replace the undercooked test egg). If the test egg is cooked properly, run ice-cold water over the remaining 3 eggs. Crack the shells, then peel them all. Put all 4 eggs back into the cold water until you are ready to chop them for the sauce.

In a heatproof bowl, whisk ½ cup of the milk with the cornstarch until smooth. Heat the remaining 1½ cups of milk. Whisk the hot milk into the cornstarch mixture. Return to the pan. Over medium heat, whisking constantly, cook until the sauce is thickened. Season with the salt, pepper, and nutmeg. Finely chop the eggs and fold them into the sauce along with the parsley.

CRUSTS

FLAKY PASTRY *Makes 1 single or double crust for an 8- or 9-inch pie*

When I studied with Madeleine Kamman at Modern Gourmet, pastries came easily to me, and I did a great job teaching others how to make the best pie crusts. Once I started on the gluten-free path, I not only had to use what I knew but at the same time unlearn what I had previously learned. This pie crust recipe is easy to make and roll out.

SINGLE CRUST:

- 1 cup Basic Gluten-Free Mix (page 16)
- 2 tablespoons sweet rice flour
- 1½ teaspoons sugar (omit if using crust for savory foods)
- ¼ teaspoon salt
- 6 tablespoons cold unsalted butter
- 1 egg
- 1 tablespoon cider vinegar or lemon juice

DOUBLE CRUST:

- 1½ cups Basic Gluten-Free Mix
- 3 tablespoons sweet rice flour
- 2 teaspoons sugar (omit if using crust for savory foods)
- ¼ teaspoon salt
- 9 tablespoons cold unsalted butter
- 1 jumbo egg
- 1½ tablespoons cider vinegar or lemon juice

Mix together the gluten-free mix, sweet rice flour, sugar, and salt. Cut the butter into chunks and, using your fingertips, work the butter into the dry ingredients to form a coarse meal. Make a well. Break the egg into the well. Add the vinegar or lemon juice. Use a fork to stir from the center, working the flour into the egg to form a soft dough. Shape into a flat cake. Cover and refrigerate if too soft to roll out.

To prebake a pie shell, preheat the oven to 400°F. Use the single-crust recipe and roll the pastry into a round 10 to 12 inches in diameter (depending on the size of the pan). Grease the pie pan, springform pan, tart pan, or quiche dish and fit the pastry into it. Flute the edges and bake for 12 to 15 minutes or until golden brown. Generally, pie weights are not needed for gluten-free pastry.

VARIATIONS For the single-crust recipe:

- Add ¼ teaspoon nutmeg, cinnamon, cardamom, or allspice to the dry ingredients.
- Replace 2 tablespoons of the butter with 4 tablespoons cream cheese.
- Replace 2 tablespoons of the gluten-free mix with 2 tablespoons unsweetened cocoa powder.

CORNMEAL CRUST *Makes 1 (8- or 9-inch) pie shell*

I like this crust so much that sometimes I bake it as cookies and sprinkle the cooled cookies with confectioners' sugar.

This dough is easier to press into the pan or roll out for cookies when first made. If you refrigerate, let the dough sit out on the counter until soft enough to work.

⅔ cup rice flour
⅓ cup cornstarch
3 tablespoons stone-ground cornmeal
1 tablespoon sweet rice flour
⅛ teaspoon salt
1 stick cold unsalted butter
¼ cup sugar
1 egg yolk

Mix together the rice flour, cornstarch, cornmeal, sweet rice flour, and salt. Cut the butter into chunks and, using your fingertips, work the butter into the dry ingredients until you have pea-size pieces. Make a well and put the sugar and egg yolk in the well. Using a fork, stir from the center to incorporate these into the flour mixture and form a dough.

To prebake a shell, see instructions on page 157.

PASTA FROLLA *Makes enough for bottom crust and lattice for 1 (8- or 9-inch) pie*

There are many wonderful pastries you can make using this crust. It will require refrigeration because the dough can be sticky. If the dough sits in the refrigerator too long, however, it will be difficult to roll out. If this happens, allow the dough to sit on the counter for a bit until it softens slightly and rolls out without too much effort on your part. This pastry will puff up more than the Flaky Pastry does.

¾ cup plus 2 tablespoons bean flour or brown rice flour
¾ cup rice flour
½ cup sugar
3 tablespoons sweet rice flour
2 teaspoons gluten-free baking powder
⅛ teaspoon salt
1 stick cold unsalted butter
2 egg yolks, lightly beaten
1 tablespoon lemon juice

Put the bean flour, rice flour, sugar, sweet rice flour, baking powder, and salt in a food processor. Pulse to mix everything. Cut the butter into chunks and add. Pulse, breaking the pieces into smaller pieces about the size of hazelnuts. Continue pulsing as you add the eggs and the lemon juice. Once everything is incorporated, stop. Put the dough on the counter and gather it into a cake. Do not overwork or the result will be a wet, sticky paste. Wrap and refrigerate until ready to use.

To prebake a shell, see instructions on page 157.

GRAHAM CRACKER CRUST *Makes 1 (8-inch) pie shell*

Use our recipe for Graham Crackers and discover a new world of gluten-free desserts that the entire family will love!

1½ cups finely ground Graham Crackers (page 69)
¼ cup confectioners' sugar
6 tablespoons melted unsalted butter or oil

Preheat the oven to 350°F.

Mix all the ingredients together until well blended. Pat into an 8-inch pie pan. Bake for 10 to 12 minutes. Cool completely before filling.

VARIATION

CHOCOLATE GRAHAM CRACKER CRUST

Add 1 tablespoon unsweetened cocoa powder to the crust ingredients.

MERINGUE CRUST *Makes 1 (9-inch) pie shell or 6 to 8 individual shells*

4 egg whites
¼ teaspoon cider vinegar or lemon juice
1 cup sifted confectioners' sugar
1 teaspoon gluten-free vanilla
½ cup coarsely chopped lightly toasted nuts (optional)

Preheat the oven to 225°F. Lightly grease a cookie sheet or 9-inch pie pan and then dust with rice flour or cornstarch, or line the lightly greased sheet with parchment paper. Draw an outline of the size and shape you want for your meringue shells.

Beat the egg whites until they are foamy. Add the vinegar or lemon juice and beat until white and almost stiff. Begin adding the sugar, 1 tablespoon at a time. Beat until the whites are stiff and glossy. Add the vanilla. If using nuts, fold them in now.

Fit a pastry bag with a fluted nozzle. Fill the bag with the meringue. Pipe onto the prepared cookie sheet. You can shape individual nests or pipe the meringue into a greased and floured pie pan. You can also spoon the meringue onto the sheet or into the pie pan. Bake for 1 hour. Leave the oven door ajar and let the meringue cool in the oven. Or leave in the closed oven overnight with the oven turned off.

Store meringues in airtight containers and do not refrigerate. Meringues are best made when the day is cool and dry.

OIL CRUST *Makes enough for 1 (9-inch) pie shell*

Not a flaky pastry but it does make a tasty crust, and there's no rolling necessary. You can also double the recipe for a double-crust pie. I recommend this for sweet pies or tarts.

- 1¼ cups Basic Gluten-Free Mix (page 16)
- ¼ cup sweet rice flour
- 2 tablespoons sugar
- 2 tablespoons finely ground almonds, walnuts, or hazelnuts
- ½ teaspoon salt
- ½ cup oil

Mix together the gluten-free mix, sweet rice flour, sugar, nuts, and salt. Pour the oil into the dry ingredients and mix together using a fork.

To prebake, preheat the oven to 375°F. Pat the dough into a 9-inch pie pan and bake for 12 minutes.

RICH PASTRY *Makes enough for 2 (8-inch) pie shells*

I love this tender pastry because you can pat it into the pie plate. You can also double the recipe for a double-crust pie.

- ½ cup cornstarch
- ½ cup brown rice flour
- 2 tablespoons sweet rice flour
- 1 tablespoon sugar
- ⅛ teaspoon salt
- 1 stick cold butter, cut into cubes
- ½ cup farmers' cheese or dry cottage cheese
- 1 teaspoon lemon juice

Mix together the cornstarch, brown rice flour, sweet rice flour, sugar, and salt. Using your fingers, pinch the butter into the dry ingredients until you have coarse meal. Mix in the farmers' cheese or cottage cheese and the lemon juice. Gather into a dough. If the dough is too soft, to work with, cover and refrigerate for several hours, but not so long that it becomes too firm to pat into the pie plate.

To prebake, preheat the oven to 400°F. Pat the pastry into 2 lightly greased 8-inch pie plates. Prick the sides and bottom with a fork. Bake for 12 to 15 minutes or until golden brown.

PECAN BUTTER CRUST *Makes 1 (8-inch) tart shell*

I remember making a crust like this at Rosalie's Restaurant in Marblehead, Massachusetts, when I cooked there in the mid-1970s. We used to fill it with vanilla pudding and whipped cream, then arrange seasonal fresh fruit artfully on top. The customers loved it. Sometimes I will pat this dough out and simply bake it to use for crumbs for the Lemon Icebox Cake (page 133) or for the crusts for any of the cheesecakes. You can also make tartlets with this crust and present them with an assortment of fillings.

¼ cup pecans, toasted
¼ cup plus 1 tablespoon granulated sugar
1 cup Basic Gluten-Free Mix (page 16)
1 tablespoon sweet rice flour
⅛ teaspoon salt
6 tablespoons cold unsalted butter, cut into cubes

Preheat the oven to 375°F. Lightly grease an 8-inch tart or quiche pan with a removable bottom.

Finely grind the toasted pecans and 1 tablespoon sugar in a food processor.

Mix together the ground nuts, gluten-free mix, ¼ cup sugar, sweet rice flour, and salt. Blend well. Using your fingertips or a pastry cutter, work the butter into the dry ingredients until you have coarse meal. You may find it necessary to use your hands to work this into a dough, but resist working it so much that it becomes a ball of dough. Press the dough into the prepared pan. Bake for 15 to 20 minutes or until lightly golden.

Fill with cooked fruit, sweetened whipped cream topped with fresh fruit, ice cream (keep frozen), pudding topped with whipped cream or fresh fruit, or ganache topped with whipped cream and strawberries.

VARIATIONS Replace the toasted pecans with toasted hazelnuts or almonds.

CEREAL CRUST *Makes 1 (8- or 9-inch) pie shell*

4 cups gluten-free rice flakes, cornflakes, puffed rice, or Rice Krispies
2 tablespoons sugar
⅓ cup melted unsalted butter or oil

Preheat the oven to 350°F.

Put the cereal and sugar into a food processor fitted with the metal blade and process until coarsely ground. Drizzle in the melted butter or oil. Do not overprocess. Pat into an 8- or 9-inch pie plate and bake for 10 minutes.

SUGGESTED FILLINGS FOR PREBAKED CRUSTS

- chilled cooked fruit
- sweetened whipped cream topped with fresh fruit
- vanilla pudding topped with whipped cream or fresh fruit
- zabaglione mousse covered with lightly sweetened whipped cream, served with a raspberry sauce
- lemon curd covered with meringue and then baked, or just covered with lightly sweetened whipped cream
- lemon mousse covered with lightly sweetened whipped cream
- nondairy chocolate pudding covered with nondairy whipped cream
- ganache topped with whipped cream and strawberries

PUDDINGS, CRISPS, AND COBBLERS

SWEET

Rich Vanilla Pudding
Vanilla Pudding
Chocolate Pudding
Crème Anglaise
White Chocolate Zabaglione Mousse
Zabaglione Mousse
Lemon Curd
Pots de Crème Caramel
Traditional New England Indian Pudding
Blueberry Pudding Cake
Mississippi Mud Pie
Chocolate Pudding Cake
Fruit Cobbler
Blueberry Buckle
Almond Crisp Topping
Nondairy Crisp Topping
Crisp Topping with Cornflakes
Apple Crisp
Peach Blueberry Crisp
Strawberry Rhubarb Crisp
Rhubarb Brown Betty
Apricot Bread Pudding
Chocolate Bread Pudding
Shaker Fresh Berry Pudding

SAVORY

Roasted Colored Peppers Bread Pudding
Corn Bread and Lobster Bread Pudding
Curried Vegetable Bread Pudding

Puddings, crisps, and cobblers are in a dessert category all their own. Often overlooked as pedestrian, they are ignored in favor of more glamorous offerings. But for a soothing and sweet ending to meal, there is nothing like a cool bowl of pudding, a warm fruit crisp smothered in cream, or a warm bread pudding just pulled from the oven. And best of all, they are quite simple to make gluten-free.

The creamy texture of homemade puddings bears little resemblance to the boxed versions which try to pass for pudding today. Puddings can be sweet or savory and enjoyed alone or as an elegant filling or sauce for your favorite pastry or fruit.

To create a basic pudding, mix cornstarch with a cold liquid. If there is sugar in the recipe, mix the cornstarch and sugar together first, then add the liquid. A heavy pan should be used to ensure even temperature while the pudding is cooking. Stir the mixture over medium heat for 10 minutes to prevent lumps. (Stirred custards, such as crème anglaise, should never be boiled or they will turn to scrambled eggs, though puddings can be cooked to a higher temperature thanks to the presence of starch.) When the temperature of the hot mixture reaches 185°F, slowly add some of it to the lightly beaten eggs that are going into the pudding; this "tempers" the eggs so they do not scramble when added to the hot mixture. Then whisk the tempered eggs into the hot mixture and cook for another minute, until the entire mixture is thickened. Strain the mixture. At this point, you may want to enrich the pudding with a tablespoon of unsalted butter and/or the addition of vanilla or other flavorings. Pour the pudding into a serving bowl or individual serving bowls and cool. Cover the pudding with plastic wrap laid directly on the surface of the pudding and refrigerate.

Baked puddings, such as bread puddings, should be baked in a heavy pottery baking dish. If you desire a creamy texture for your pudding, make a water bath by setting the pudding dish in a roasting pan and filling the pan with boiling water to come halfway up the sides of the pudding dish. During baking, the water in the water bath must be boiling hot (but not boiling) so that the custard will bake in the minimum amount of time. The pudding itself should not boil, or it will develop air pockets and a watery texture. To avoid overboiling, try this trick I learned from my cooking instructor, the famed Madeleine Kamman: line the bottom of the roasting pan with a kitchen towel. Cover the pudding dish with buttered parchment paper or foil. The pudding is done when a sharp knife inserted into it comes out clean and hot to the touch. Egg yolk custards are done when they are not liquid but shake slightly when tapped. Jasper White, chef, restaurateur, and cookbook author, calls these puddings "jigglers." Remember that the custard will continue to cook as it cools. Avoid overcooking.

In early America, thrifty New England homemakers didn't waste anything. They used stale bread, cornmeal, milk, and eggs to make boiled or steamed puddings. While we often think of puddings as sweet, I've included a number of delicious savory puddings in this chapter to serve as wonderful main courses or side dishes.

The family of desserts once known as grunts, slumps, or pandowdies are today called cobblers, buckles, and crisps—fruit combined with a biscuit or crumb mixture. Try mixing fruits for a delicious variety, remembering that pitted fruits tend to work best.

SWEET

RICH VANILLA PUDDING *Makes about 5½ cups*

This is a very good basic all-purpose pudding. Use it to fill cream puffs, prebaked pie shells, cakes, and crêpes, or serve it plain with fresh fruit.

⅔ cup sugar
⅓ cup cornstarch
⅛ teaspoon salt
3¾ cups half-and-half, whole milk, or light cream
5 egg yolks
1 teaspoon gluten-free vanilla

Put the sugar, cornstarch, and salt into a saucepan. Whisk until blended. Gradually whisk in the half-and-half. Cook over medium heat, whisking constantly, until the mixture thickens and comes to a boil. Boil for 1 minute.

In a small bowl, whisk the egg yolks together. Slowly whisk in some of the hot mixture, then whisk the warmed yolks into the rest of the hot mixture. Return to the stove and cook over low heat, stirring, for about 2 minutes. The pudding will be thick. Remove the pudding from the heat and stir in the vanilla. Strain into a small bowl. Cover the surface with a piece of plastic wrap. Refrigerate until ready to use.

VANILLA PUDDING *Makes about 2 cups*

This is what I always use to fill my Boston Cream Pie (page 125). You can also use it to fill a cream puff, crêpes, or a prebaked pie shell. I especially like to serve it with fresh berries.

2½ tablespoons cornstarch
1⅓ cups light cream
1 egg yolk
⅓ cup sugar
Pinch of salt
1 teaspoon gluten-free vanilla

Dissolve the cornstarch in ⅓ cup of the cream. Whisk in the egg yolk.

Mix the sugar, salt, and remaining 1 cup cream in a saucepan. Scald. Whisk some of the hot cream into the egg yolk mixture. Pour this into the hot cream. Whisk over medium heat until the pudding thickens. Remove the pudding from the heat and stir in the vanilla. Strain into a clean bowl. Cool slightly and then cover the surface with plastic wrap. Refrigerate until ready to use.

CHOCOLATE PUDDING *Makes 2½ cups*

One of my all-time favorite desserts as a child was what my mother called "Spring Thaw." It was hot homemade chocolate pudding with a scoop or two of French vanilla ice cream. The contrast between the hot pudding and the cold ice cream was amazing.

⅓ cup sugar
2½ tablespoons cornstarch
⅛ teaspoon salt
1¾ cups plus 2 tablespoons milk
3 egg yolks
1 teaspoon gluten-free vanilla
1½ ounces unsweetened chocolate, melted
1 tablespoon unsalted butter

Put the sugar, cornstarch, and salt in a saucepan. Whisk until blended. Gradually whisk in the milk. Cook over medium heat, whisking constantly, until the mixture thickens and comes to a boil. Boil for 1 minute.

In a small bowl, whisk the egg yolks together. Slowly whisk in some of the hot milk mixture, then whisk the warmed yolks into the rest of the hot milk mixture. Return to the stove and cook over low heat, stirring, for about 2 minutes. The pudding will be thick.

Remove the pan from the heat. Stir in the vanilla, the melted chocolate, and the butter. Strain the pudding into a small bowl. Cover the surface with plastic wrap. Refrigerate until ready to use.

CRÈME ANGLAISE *Makes 1¾ cups*

This is an extremely rich sauce for cakes, fresh fruit, meringues, and soufflés. The trick to making it is not to beat in too much air when mixing the egg yolks and sugar together. Air will create a layer of foam on the surface, making it difficult for you to see when the custard is done.

1 cup light cream or whole milk
4 egg yolks
7 tablespoons sugar
1 teaspoon gluten-free vanilla

In a saucepan over medium beat, bring the cream almost to a boil. In a bowl, whisk together the egg yolks and sugar without ribboning. Whisk in some of the hot cream. Pour the heated egg yolk mixture into the remaining hot cream. Over medium heat, stirring in figure eights with a wooden spoon, cook until the custard begins to thicken and coat the back of the spoon. *Do not allow the custard to boil.* Any foam that was on the surface will disappear. Strain into a clean bowl and whisk in the vanilla. Cool, then cover and refrigerate.

VARIATIONS

LEMON CRÈME ANGLAISE

Heat the cream and add 1 teaspoon grated lemon zest. Let this infuse for 1 hour. Reheat and proceed with recipe.

LIQUEUR-FLAVORED CRÈME ANGLAISE

Stir in 1 tablespoon liqueur of your choice once the custard cools.

WHITE CHOCOLATE ZABAGLIONE MOUSSE *Makes 4 to 6 servings*

Zabaglione all by itself is heavenly. Add melted white chocolate and whipped cream, and the result is without words to describe.

Serve with fresh raspberries and a raspberry sauce, or use to fill a prebaked tart shell, crêpes, or cream puffs.

5 ounces excellent-quality white chocolate, such as Lindt
4 egg yolks
½ cup sugar
⅓ cup Marsala
¼ cup heavy cream

Chop the chocolate and melt over hot water. Keep warm while you make the zabaglione.

Whisk together the egg yolks and sugar in the top of a double boiler. Pour in the Marsala. Whisk constantly over the hot water until the mixture is thick, foamy, and hot to the touch. Whisk in the melted chocolate. Cool.

Whip the cream and then fold into the cooled zabaglione. Refrigerate for at least 1 hour.

ZABAGLIONE MOUSSE *Makes 4 to 6 servings*

Many years ago, when I first started my cooking school and catering business in Portland, Maine, I made this mousse often. Then we all became cholesterol conscious. Now I make it every once in a while for clients who, like me, believe in having all good things in moderation.

4 egg yolks
½ cup sugar
⅓ cup Marsala
¾ cup heavy cream

Whisk the egg yolks and sugar together in the top of a double boiler. Do not let the water boil or touch the bottom of the pan. Pour in the Marsala. Whisk constantly over the hot water until the mixture is thick, foamy, and hot to the touch. Cool.

Whip the cream and then fold into the cooled zabaglione. Refrigerate for at least 1 hour.

LEMON CURD *Makes 2½ cups*

One Christmas while I was living in Florence, Italy, I made my dear friend Margo Spitz a mason jar full of lemon curd for her Christmas present. She told me she would sit in her favorite reading chair with her silver spoon and eat lemon curd all by herself, never sharing. I will always carry that memory with me. Use this to fill cakes or prebaked tart shells, to spread on muffins or scones, to flavor buttercream, or as a base for a mousse.

8 egg yolks
¾ cup sugar
Juice and grated zest of 3 lemons
¾ stick unsalted butter

Whisk together the egg yolks and sugar in a saucepan. Do not ribbon this because you do not want to incorporate too much air. Whisk in the lemon juice and zest. Cut the butter into small chunks and add. Over medium heat, stirring constantly, cook until the custard thickens but does not boil. The thin layer of foam will disappear at the point that the lemon curd is done. Strain into a clean bowl. Cool. Cover and refrigerate until ready to use.

POTS DE CRÈME CARAMEL *Makes 6 individual pots de crème*

This will send you into ecstasy. Remember that the caramel will end up like a sauce. Make sure that the dish is large enough and has a lip so that the caramel sauce does not spill over.

CARAMEL:
½ cup sugar
Few drops of lemon juice
3 tablespoons water

CUSTARD:
2 cups light cream
6 egg yolks
½ cup sugar
1 teaspoon gluten-free vanilla

Preheat the oven to 350°F. Have 6 ½-cup ramekins ready. Custard cups work just fine.

To make the caramel, mix the sugar with the lemon juice and water in a saucepan. Cook the sugar until it reaches a caramel color. Be careful not to let the sugar brown too much because it will continue cooking after you fill the ramekins, and if sugar cooks too much, it will have a bitter, burned taste. If that happens, start over. Once the sugar is golden brown, coat the bottoms of the ramekins. Set aside while you prepare the custard.

To make the custard, bring the cream almost to a boil in a saucepan over medium heat. In a bowl, lightly whisk the egg yolks and sugar. Whisk in some of the hot cream. Then pour the warmed yolks into the remaining hot cream. Whisk to blend well. Add the vanilla. Strain the custard into the ramekins, filling them three-quarters full. Cover each ramekin with foil, dull side out.

Place the ramekins in a roasting pan large enough to hold all six. Put the pan in the oven. Add boiling water to come halfway up the sides of the ramekins. Bake for 20 minutes. Check halfway through the cooking time to make sure that the water is not boiling. The pots de crème will be done when a knife inserted two-thirds of the way to the center comes out clean. The center should "jiggle" slightly. Remove the ramekins from the water bath and cool. Refrigerate for at least 4 hours before serving.

To serve, run a sharp paring knife around the sides of each custard. Place a dessert plate on top. Holding the plate and ramekin together, carefully invert and shake. The custard should slip out of the ramekin. You may have to shake a few times. Lift off the ramekin.

TRADITIONAL NEW ENGLAND INDIAN PUDDING

Makes 6 to 8 servings

New England has some unforgettable desserts. Indian pudding, in my estimation, is one of those. The "Indian" in the title refers to the corn in the pudding. This pudding is especially satisfying during the cold winter months. A mother can feel good about her children eating such a wholesome dessert. It reheats well in a microwave.

- 4½ cups milk
- ½ cup cornmeal
- ¾ cup molasses
- ½ stick unsalted butter
- 1 teaspoon ginger
- ½ teaspoon salt
- 1 egg or 2 tablespoons cornstarch or bean flour

Scald 3 cups of the milk. Moisten the cornmeal with 1 cup of the remaining cold milk. Whisk the moistened cornmeal into the hot milk. Cook in a double boiler for 15 minutes. Whisk in the molasses, butter, ginger, salt, and the egg or cornstarch. Cook for another 5 minutes, stirring.

Preheat the oven to 300°F. Butter an 8-cup baking pan.

Pour the pudding into the buttered baking pan. Bake for 1 hour. Pour the remaining ½ cup cold milk over the pudding. Do not stir. Bake for another 1½ hours. Check for doneness. It should be slightly firm and set. The pudding may need to bake for another 30 minutes. Serve hot with hard sauce, ice cream, heavy cream, or whipped cream.

BLUEBERRY PUDDING CAKE *Makes 6 servings*

The first time I was served this pudding cake, Mary Verenis made it with the wild blueberries her daughter, Barbic, and I had picked. She was kind enough to write down the recipe for me. I like it with either wild Maine blueberries or the cultivated ones. Sometimes I will have a craving for it in the middle of the winter, so I use frozen Maine blueberries.

This is best served hot.

- 1½ cups Basic Gluten-Free Mix (page 16)
- 1¼ cups sugar
- 1½ teaspoons Egg Replacer
- 1½ teaspoons gluten-free baking powder
- ¼ teaspoon xanthan gum
- ⅛ teaspoon salt
- 3 tablespoons oil
- ⅔ cup warm milk
- 2 cups blueberries
- 1 tablespoon cornstarch or arrowroot
- 1 cup boiling water

Preheat the oven to 350°F.

Mix together the gluten-free mix, ½ cup of the sugar, the Egg Replacer, baking powder, xanthan gum, and salt. Stir in the oil and warm milk.

Put the blueberries in the bottom of an 8-inch square baking pan. Spread the batter over the berries.

Mix together the arrowroot or cornstarch and the remaining ¾ cup sugar. Sprinkle over the batter. Slowly pour the boiling water over everything. Bake for 40 to 45 minutes.

MISSISSIPPI MUD PIE *Makes 6 servings*

When my sister, Stefanie, heard that my son was on a very strict diet (no eggs, no gluten, no dairy, no soy, and no peanuts), she sent me her recipe for Mississippi mud pie. My mother and I began working on it to change it into gluten-free. For a year this was a weekly treat, my son's birthday cake, and the cake he would take when he went to his friends' birthday parties.

This cake makes its own sauce on the bottom of the pan.

- ¾ cup granulated sugar
- ½ cup chopped walnuts (optional)
- ½ cup chickpea flour or Garfava
- ½ cup rice flour
- 2 tablespoons plus ¼ cup unsweetened cocoa powder
- 2 teaspoons gluten-free baking powder
- ¼ teaspoon xanthan gum
- ⅛ teaspoon cinnamon
- Pinch of salt
- ½ cup milk
- ¼ cup vegetable oil
- ¾ cup packed light brown sugar
- 1½ cups boiling water

Preheat the oven to 350°F. Lightly grease an 8-inch square baking pan.

Mix together the granulated sugar, nuts, chickpea flour, rice flour, 2 tablespoons of the cocoa, the baking powder, xanthan gum, cinnamon, and salt. Stir in the milk and oil. Spoon the mixture into the prepared pan.

Mix the brown sugar and remaining ¼ cup cocoa together and sprinkle over the batter. Pour the boiling water over the top. Bake on the middle rack for 30 to 35 minutes. The cake part should feel somewhat firm. Serve hot or cold or reheat in the microwave.

CHOCOLATE PUDDING CAKE *Makes 8 servings*

I have great childhood memories of this dessert, which my mother made with a box mix. One day while driving to work, I had a flash: Why couldn't I combine the Blueberry Pudding Cake recipe and the Mississippi Mud Pie recipe to make Chocolate Pudding Cake? That night I did just that. As the cake came out of the oven, my son was waiting, mouth wide open, for a taste. That night when my mother spooned out the dessert, I think I was eight years old again and very happy.

This is best served warm and reheats nicely in the microwave.

1½ cups Basic Gluten-Free Mix (page 16)
½ cup granulated sugar
1½ teaspoons Egg Replacer
1½ teaspoons gluten-free baking powder
¼ teaspoon xanthan gum
⅛ teaspoon salt
3 tablespoons vegetable oil
⅔ cup warm milk
1 teaspoon gluten-free vanilla
1 cup packed light brown sugar
6 tablespoons unsweetened cocoa powder
2¼ cups boiling water

Preheat the oven to 350°F.

Mix together the gluten-free mix, sugar, Egg Replacer, baking powder, xanthan gum, and salt. Stir in the oil, milk, and vanilla. Pour the batter into an 11 × 7-inch nonstick baking pan.

Combine the brown sugar and cocoa. Whisk in the boiling water. Pour the mixture over the cake batter. Bake for 20 to 25 minutes.

FRUIT COBBLER *Makes 6 to 8 servings*

Cobblers belong to the family of slumps, grunts, buckles, crisps, and pandowdies. Slumps, grunts, and buckles are cobblers cooked with sugar and water on top of the stove. Crisps have a crumb topping over the fruit and are baked in the oven. Cobblers have biscuit dough over the fruit and are baked. Cobblers get their name from the biscuits on top, which look like cobblestone streets. You can be creative and cut shapes out of the biscuit dough, such as stars. Always leave space between the biscuits to allow the juices to bubble up.

FILLING:

3 cups cut-up fruit (nectarine, cherry, plum, apple, blackberry, cranberry, peach, apricot, or raspberry)
2 teaspoons lemon juice
¾ to 1 cup sugar

BISCUIT DOUGH:

1½ cups Basic Gluten-Free Mix (page 16)
2 tablespoons sugar
2 teaspoons gluten-free baking powder
1 teaspoon Egg Replacer
½ teaspoon xanthan gum
⅛ teaspoon salt
½ stick unsalted butter, cut into pieces
½ cup milk or cream
Cinnamon sugar for sprinkling

Preheat the oven to 400°F.

To make the filling, toss the fruit with the lemon juice and sugar. Spoon the mixture into an 8- or 9-inch square baking dish.

To make the dough, mix together the gluten-free mix, sugar, baking powder, Egg Replacer, xanthan gum, and salt. Using your fingertips, work the butter into the dry ingredients to form a coarse meal. Make a well in the center and pour in some of the milk. Use a spoon or fork to incorporate the milk. Add more milk as needed to make a soft dough. If you want to roll the dough out and cut it into biscuits or other shapes to place on top of the fruit, the dough needs to be drier.

Place cut-out shapes or spoonfuls of the dough over the fruit, leaving some spaces for the juices to bubble up. Sprinkle the dough with cinnamon sugar. Bake for 20 minutes or until the juices bubble up and the biscuits are golden brown.

BLUEBERRY BUCKLE *Makes 6 servings*

Another one of those great New England desserts with a funny name.

TOPPING:
¼ cup sugar
1 tablespoon brown rice flour
¼ teaspoon cinnamon
1 tablespoon butter

FILLING:
1 cup Basic Gluten-Free Mix (page 16)
½ cup sugar
1 teaspoon baking powder
¼ teaspoon xanthan gum
Pinch of salt
2 tablespoons butter
1 egg
½ cup milk
½ teaspoon gluten-free vanilla
⅔ cup frozen blueberries

Preheat the oven to 350°F. Lightly grease an 8-inch square baking pan.

To make the topping, mix sugar, brown rice flour, and cinnamon. Using your fingertips, pinch in the butter until you have a coarse, crumbly texture. Set aside.

To make the filling, mix together the gluten-free mix, sugar, baking powder, xanthan gum, and salt. Pinch in the butter until you have a sandy texture.

Lightly beat the egg with the milk and vanilla. Gently stir into the dry ingredients. Fold in the frozen blueberries.

Spoon the filling into the prepared pan. Sprinkle the topping over and bake for 20 to 25 minutes.

ALMOND CRISP TOPPING *Makes enough for 1 large crisp*

Use this topping on any crisp or as a crumb topping for a pie.

1½ cups Basic Gluten-Free Mix (page 16)
¾ cup ground almonds
¼ cup sugar
¼ teaspoon cinnamon
⅛ teaspoon xanthan gum
Pinch of salt
1 stick unsalted butter, melted

Combine the gluten-free mix, ground almonds, sugar, cinnamon, xanthan gum, and salt in a bowl. Stir in the melted butter. Set aside until ready to use. The mixture will be a bit firm and chunky. Break it into ½-inch pieces.

NONDAIRY CRISP TOPPING *Makes enough for 1 large crisp*

Use this topping when you are baking for those who avoid dairy products.

½ cup Basic Gluten-Free Mix (page 16)
½ cup packed light brown sugar
½ teaspoon cinnamon
¼ cup vegetable oil

Mix together the gluten-free mix, brown sugar, and cinnamon. Blend the oil into the dry ingredients. Do not overmix. The topping needs to be crumbly, not oily.

CRISP TOPPING WITH CORNFLAKES *Makes enough for 1 large crisp*

⅔ cup gluten-free cornflakes
½ cup packed brown sugar
6 tablespoons brown rice or bean flour
¾ teaspoon cinnamon
Unsalted butter

Put the cornflakes, brown sugar, brown rice flour, and cinnamon in a food processor and process until finely ground. Add the butter and pulse.

VARIATION Decrease the amount of cinnamon to ¼ teaspoon and add ¼ teaspoon ginger and 2 tablespoons sliced almonds.

APPLE CRISP *Makes 4 to 6 servings*

An apple crisp is such a fall season dessert. Serve it warm with a scoop of French vanilla ice cream or some heavy cream. I have been known to enjoy a dish of it for breakfast, if there is any left over from the night before.

- 4 cups sliced peeled Granny Smith apples (about ¼ inch thick)
- 2 teaspoons lemon juice
- Crisp topping of your choice (page 205)

Preheat the oven to 350°F. Lightly butter an 8- or 9-inch pie plate or baking dish.

Toss the apples with the lemon juice. Put them in the buttered dish. Sprinkle the topping over the apples. Bake for 25 to 30 minutes or until the apples begin to juice and are soft when pierced with a sharp paring knife. Serve hot or cold with heavy cream, whipped cream, or any gluten-free vanilla ice cream or frozen yogurt.

VARIATIONS

PEAR CRISP

- 4 to 5 pears, peeled, cored, and thinly sliced
- Juice and grated zest rind of 1 orange
- Crisp topping of your choice

Toss the pears with the orange juice and zest. Proceed with the recipe.

PEAR APPLE CRANBERRY CRISP

- 2 cups sliced peeled apples (about ¼ inch thick)
- 2 cups sliced peeled pears (about ¼ inch thick)
- 1 cup dried cranberries
- 2 teaspoons lemon juice
- Crisp topping of your choice

Toss the apples, pears, and cranberries together with the juice. Proceed with the recipe.

APPLE RHUBARB CRISP

- 2 cups diced peeled Granny Smith apples
- 2 cups diced rhubarb
- 2 teaspoons lemon juice
- ½ cup granulated sugar
- Crisp topping of your choice, made with ½ teaspoon ginger instead of cinnamon

Toss the apples and rhubarb together with the juice, and then add sugar. Proceed with the recipe.

PEACH BLUEBERRY CRISP *Makes 4 to 6 servings*

Use ripe peaches or nectarines. Peeling is easier if you blanch the fruit; the skins will slip right off.

- 2 cups blueberries
- 2 cups peeled and sliced peaches or nectarines
- 2 teaspoons orange juice
- 2 tablespoons sugar
- Crisp Topping with Cornflakes (page 205), made with 2 tablespoons sliced almonds, ¼ teaspoon cinnamon, and ¼ teaspoon ginger

Preheat the oven to 350°F. Lightly butter a shallow 8- or 9-inch square baking pan.

Toss the fruit with the orange juice and sugar and spoon into the baking dish. Sprinkle the crisp topping over the fruit. Bake for 25 to 30 minutes. Serve warm or cold.

STRAWBERRY RHUBARB CRISP *Makes 4 to 6 servings*

During the few weeks in June when strawberries are in season in Maine, I use them in every way possible. Remember that strawberries need a little acid, such as lemon juice or orange juice, to keep their bright red color when they are cooked.

- ½ pound strawberries, hulled and quartered
- ½ pound rhubarb, cut into small chunks
- ¼ teaspoon cinnamon
- Pinch of ginger
- Grated zest of 1 orange
- 2 tablespoons orange juice
- ¼ cup orange flower honey or 2 tablespoons sugar
- Crisp topping of your choice (page 205)

Preheat the oven to 350°F. Lightly grease an 8-inch square baking pan.

Mix the fruit with cinnamon, ginger, orange zest, orange juice, and honey or sugar. Spoon into the prepared baking pan. Sprinkle the crisp topping over and bake for 35 minutes.

RHUBARB BROWN BETTY *Makes 6 servings*

Brown Betties are very similar to crisps, except the crumb mixture is layered with the fruit instead of being sprinkled on top.

Serve with gluten-free French vanilla yogurt, whipped cream, or French vanilla ice cream.

- 1½ pounds rhubarb, cut into 1-inch pieces
- 1 cup packed dark brown sugar
- 2 tablespoons chopped candied ginger or 1 teaspoon ground ginger
- ¼ cup orange juice
- 6 tablespoons unsalted butter, melted
- 2 cups fresh gluten-free bread crumbs or gluten-free cookie crumbs
- ¼ cup chopped walnuts

Preheat the oven to 350°F.

Combine the rhubarb, brown sugar, ginger, and orange juice.

Mix together the butter, bread crumbs or cookie crumbs, and nuts. Sprinkle one-third of the crumb mixture over the bottom of a 6-cup (1½-quart) baking dish. Cover with half of the rhubarb. Repeat the layers, finishing with the crumb mixture on top. Cover loosely with foil and bake for 25 minutes. Uncover and bake for another 25 minutes.

APRICOT BREAD PUDDING *Makes 6 servings*

Bread puddings are very comforting desserts. This one is elegant enough to serve at a dinner party.

- 4 gluten-free dinner rolls
- ½ stick unsalted butter, melted
- 6 tablespoons sugar
- 5 eggs
- 2¾ cups hot cream
- ½ cup apricot preserves, melted and strained
- Confectioners' sugar for dusting

Preheat the oven to 300°F. Lightly butter a 6-cup baking dish.

Cut the rolls into ¼-inch-thick slices. Arrange the slices on the bottom of the baking dish. Drizzle the melted butter over the slices.

Whisk together the sugar and eggs. Slowly whisk in the hot cream. Strain this over the buttered slices.

Place a roasting pan in the oven. Put the pudding dish into this pan. Pour boiling water into the larger pan until it comes halfway up the sides of the pudding dish. If you like your bread pudding to have a soft top, cover the dish with buttered parchment paper or buttered foil. Bake for 25 to 30 minutes.

Remove the pudding from the hot water bath. Brush the preserves over the top of the bread pudding. Serve warm with a dusting of confectioners' sugar.

CHOCOLATE BREAD PUDDING *Makes 6 servings*

My mother remembers how she and her brothers loved to eat this when they were young, and I grew up on this dessert. As children, my sisters, cousins, and I loved this bread pudding best when my mother or Gran-mère would serve it warm with cold heavy cream poured over it.

- 3 cups evaporated milk
- 1 cup water
- 1½ cups sugar
- 2 cups cubed gluten-free bread, crusts removed
- 4 ounces semisweet chocolate, chopped
- 2 eggs
- ½ teaspoon salt
- 1 teaspoon gluten-free vanilla
- 1 teaspoon unsalted butter, melted

Preheat the oven to 300°F. Lightly butter a 2½-quart baking dish.

Scald the milk and water in a large saucepan. Add ¾ cup of the sugar and stir until it is dissolved. Add the bread cubes to the scalded milk. Stir in the chopped chocolate. Once the chocolate has melted, remove the pot from the heat. Let the mixture sit for 30 minutes.

In a separate bowl, whisk together the eggs, remaining ¾ cup sugar, salt, vanilla, and melted butter. Fold into the chocolate mixture. Pour the pudding into the buttered baking dish. Bake for 1 hour, covered with buttered parchment paper, in a hot water bath if you want a creamy bread pudding (see technique in Apricot Bread Pudding, page 208). If you prefer the pudding with a crunchy top, bake it uncovered, not in a water bath, for 1 hour.

SHAKER FRESH BERRY PUDDING *Makes 6 servings*

Use a traditional New England pudding bowl for this delicious pudding, or substitute any slope-sided bowl. Also known as summer berry pudding, this dessert is inspired by the thrifty Shakers, whose last working village is located in New Gloucester, Maine. Stale leftover bread works best.

Serve with a pitcher of heavy or lightly whipped cream.

- ¾ cup cranberries
- ¼ cup water
- ⅓ cup plus 2 tablespoons sugar
- Drop of lemon juice
- About ¼ cup cranberry juice
- 1 loaf day-old sliced gluten-free bread
- 1½ pounds mixed fresh berries, such as blueberries, raspberries, and blackberries
- 2 tablespoons sugar
- 2 tablespoons orange juice

Put the cranberries into a nonaluminum saucepan with the water, ⅓ cup of the sugar, and the lemon juice. Cook the cranberries until they begin to pop. Puree them and then force them through a sieve. Thin the puree out with some cranberry juice to the consistency of a medium-thick sauce. If the sauce is too tart, stir in more sugar.

Trim the crusts off the slices of bread. Using a biscuit cutter, cut out a round to fit the bottom of the pudding bowl. Dip the round into the cranberry puree and fit it into the bottom of the bowl. Then dip all the bread slices into the cranberry puree. Line the sides of the bowl, overlapping the slices.

Mix the berries with the remaining 2 tablespoons of sugar and the orange juice. Carefully pour the berries into the lined pudding bowl. Cover with bread slices dipped in the cranberry puree. Cover this with a piece of plastic wrap and then put a plate on top as a weight. Refrigerate overnight. Remove the plastic wrap and unmold onto a serving platter.

SAVORY

ROASTED COLORED PEPPERS BREAD PUDDING

Makes 4 to 6 servings

I can never resist colored peppers. They are visually appealing, and their flavors are so sweet. During the holidays this makes a very festive side dish for any roast. Try making it with leftover corn bread or muffins.

- 1 each red, green, yellow, and orange bell peppers, quartered and seeded
- Olive oil for brushing on the peppers
- 3 cups stale gluten-free bread, crusts removed and cubed
- 3 cups evaporated milk or half-and-half, heated
- 1 tablespoon chopped fresh parsley
- 1 teaspoon oregano
- ½ to ¾ teaspoon salt
- 12 grinds black pepper
- 3 eggs, lightly beaten
- ½ cup grated Parmesan or Asiago cheese

Preheat the oven to 450°F. Line a cookie sheet with parchment paper.

Lightly brush the pepper quarters with olive oil. Place the peppers on the cookie sheet. Roast for 15 to 20 minutes or until the skins are charred. Put the peppers in a bowl and cover with a towel. When the peppers are cool enough to handle, peel the charred skin off. Cut the peppers into julienne strips.

Lower the oven temperature to 325°F. Butter a 2½-quart baking pan.

Spread the bread cubes in the baking pan. Mix the hot milk with parsley, oregano, salt, and pepper. Taste for seasoning. Whisk in the eggs. Mix half of the peppers with the bread. Pour the milk over the bread and peppers. Arrange the remaining peppers and the cheese on top. Cover with a buttered piece of foil or parchment paper. For a creamy, soft bread pudding, bake in a hot water bath (see technique in Apricot Bread Pudding, page 208). Otherwise, place the pan directly in the oven. Bake for 45 minutes or until done. The pudding will feel firm.

CORN BREAD AND LOBSTER BREAD PUDDING *Makes 6 servings*

This is a wonderful savory pudding. Use leftover lobster meat after a lobster feast. My mother is a great one for taking everyone's lobster bodies and picking out the meat they left because getting it was too tedious to bother with. We are always glad that she is not one to waste anything.

- 4 cups milk or evaporated milk, scalded
- 2 cups cubed corn bread or Cornmeal Scones (page 45)
- 3 eggs, lightly beaten
- ½ teaspoon salt
- Freshly ground white pepper
- 2 cups cooked lobster meat
- 2 tablespoons butter, melted

SAUCE:

- 3 red bell peppers
- Extra virgin olive oil
- Salt and pepper to taste

Preheat the oven to 300°F. Lightly butter a 2½-quart baking pan.

Pour the scalded milk over the bread. Let sit for 30 minutes.

Whisk the eggs, salt, and pepper together and gently stir into the milk and bread. Pour into the buttered baking pan. Arrange the lobster meat over the pudding. Press into the pudding. Drizzle the melted butter over the top. Bake for 1 hour. For a creamier pudding, cover with buttered foil or parchment paper and bake for 1 hour in a hot water bath (see technique in Apricot Bread Pudding, page 208).

To make the sauce, preheat the oven to 450°F. Rub the peppers with extra virgin olive oil. Place the peppers on a jelly roll pan lined with parchment paper. Roast in the oven for 20 minutes or until the skins are charred. Put the peppers in a bowl and cover with a towel. When the peppers are cool enough to handle, peel the charred skin off. Remove the stem and seeds. Put the peppers in a food processor or blender and puree. Season with salt and pepper.

CURRIED VEGETABLE BREAD PUDDING *Makes 4 to 6 servings*

My mother, grandmother, and godmother were brilliant when it came to using leftovers. They taught me how to create masterpieces from odds and ends. Savory bread puddings are a great way to use up stale bread or scones and any leftovers cluttering up your refrigerator. This curried vegetable bread pudding is an excellent example. When I prepared it for a cooking demonstration for a local celiac support group in Dewitt, New York, it was a big hit.

2 cups milk
6 slices gluten-free bread, cubed
3 tablespoons oil of your choice
1 cup broccoli florets, blanched
1 cup chopped mushrooms
1 onion, chopped
1 red bell pepper, diced
2 cloves garlic, chopped
2 teaspoons curry powder, commercial or homemade (page 19)
2 tablespoons pale dry sherry
¼ to ½ teaspoon salt
12 grinds black pepper
6 eggs
½ cup grated mozzarella cheese

Preheat the oven to 325°F. Butter a 6-cup soufflé dish or 1½-quart baking pan.

Heat the milk and pour over the bread cubes. Let sit 20 minutes.

Heat the oil in a skillet. Add the broccoli, mushrooms, onion, bell pepper, and garlic and sauté until the mushrooms have given off their juices. Add the curry powder and continue cooking for 1 minute. Pour in the sherry. Stir in the salt and pepper. Fold the vegetables into the bread mixture. Taste for seasoning. Correct if necessary.

Lightly beat the eggs. Gently fold into the bread mixture. Spoon the mixture into the prepared pan, sprinkle the cheese on top, and bake for 40 minutes. No hot-water bath is necessary.

CREAM PUFFS, FILO PASTRIES, AND CRÊPES

Cream Puff Paste
Gâteau Saint-Honoré
Saint Joseph's Cream Puffs
Hazelnut Bongo Bongo
Filo Dough
Baklava
Pita
Apple Strudel
Crêpes
Chocolate Fettuccine
Dairy-Free Chocolate Blintzes

What is it about tender pastry wrapped around a delicious filling that intrigues us so? Perhaps it is the mouth feel or the mystery of what lies beyond the dough. But every culture, it seems, lays claim to pastry specialties. While the origins of crêpes and filo are indisputable, Italy and France vie for discovery of the cream puff. Food history gives the Italians credit for their creation, but acknowledges the French for popularizing the dough that goes "pouf."

Once you master the technique, creating wonderful gluten-free cream puffs is easy. And like the other pastries featured in this chapter, you will find them very versatile and easy to freeze. Fill them with chicken, shrimp, or ham salad; make them small for hors d'oeuvres; deep-fry them; or fill them with ice cream, whipped cream, pudding, or mousse.

Using a pastry bag makes shaping the puffs easier, especially if you are interested in creating swans or other shapes, but they are just as easily shaped using two spoons. The small and round shape is, technically speaking, considered a cream puff, while the longer oval shape is an eclair.

Be certain to add the eggs slowly to the hot choux paste mixture. If you add it too quickly, the pâte à choux paste will be impossible to mix. The more egg you can incorporate into the paste, the lighter the cream puffs will be. Bake cream puffs in the lower third of a 400°F oven. If you put them on the lowest rack, the bottoms of the puffs will, literally, blow out from the heat. The puffs are done if they sound hollow when you tap them. Do not underbake them or they will be too moist and will collapse—no pouf in your puff!

Whether you call them pancakes, blintzes, blini, blinchicki, or pannequets—crêpes, or French pancakes, should become a staple in your gluten-free repertoire. They are easily made ahead and frozen unfilled, to be pulled out of the freezer on a moment's notice to give glamour to leftovers or turn ordinary fruit into an elegant dessert. And the technique of making them is easy to master. Make a "well" in the flour and add the eggs; whisk the mixture slowly to incorporate the milk, then add the butter or oil. The final batter will be the consistency of heavy cream. Invest in a crêpe pan—a nonstick one works best. If the first crêpe does not turn out, throw it away and try again. The pancakes should be very thin and light, with a golden brown color on the outside.

Creating the gluten-free filo dough featured in this chapter was quite satisfying for me. I am very fond of using the flaky pastry dough for a number of Middle Eastern and Greek specialties and was delighted when I perfected a gluten-free recipe and technique. This dough rolls and stretches quite easily and is not as finicky as regular filo—it won't dry out or get "papery," as gluten filo is known to do. Although it is not as crisp and flaky, you will be able to enjoy delicious Middle Eastern favorites again, such as baklava and spanakopita.

CREAM PUFF PASTE (PÂTE À CHOUX) *Makes 12 (3-inch) puffs*

Everyone loves cream puffs. They are so versatile. You can fill them with whipped cream, ice cream, pastry cream, or chicken salad. Using a fluted or plain nozzle, you make them bite-size, round, or long.

½ cup water
½ stick unsalted butter, diced
½ tablespoon sugar
⅛ teaspoon salt
½ cup Basic Gluten-Free Mix (page 16)
2 or 3 eggs
½ teaspoon gluten-free vanilla
1 egg yolk mixed with 2 tablespoons cream or milk

Preheat the oven to 400°F. Lightly butter a cookie sheet.

Put the water, butter, sugar, and salt in a saucepan and bring to a boil. As soon as the butter melts, stir in the gluten-free mix. Over medium heat, stir until the mixture becomes oily-looking and a crust develops on the bottom of the pot. Remove from the heat.

Lightly beat 2 eggs in a bowl. Slowly mix the eggs, a little at a time, into the hot paste. Make sure that the egg is well blended before adding more. After the 2 eggs have been incorporated, check the texture. It should be smooth and shiny yet not runny. If it isn't, stir in a little of the third egg until the mixture looks right. Add the vanilla.

Fit a pastry bag with a plain nozzle. Fill with the cream puff paste. Pipe puffs or éclairs onto the cookie sheet. Remember that the paste will puff up and out 2 to 3 times its size. Brush with the egg yolk mixture and put the cookie sheet in the lower third of the oven. Bake for 20 to 30 minutes. The puffs are done when they sound hollow when tapped. They should be very golden brown. If underbaked, they will collapse. Cool on a rack.

TO MAKE SWANS

Fit a pastry bag with a plain nozzle. Fill with the cream puff paste. Pipe puffs as you would for any cream puff. The swans' heads are made using a smaller plain nozzle. Pipe out into question marks. Remember that the paste will puff up and out 2 to 3 times its size. Brush with the egg yolk mixture and put the cookie sheet in the lower third of the oven. Bake for 15 to 25 minutes. The heads bake faster than the "bodies."

Cut the tops off the puffs and set aside. Fill the bottom with ice cream, chocolate mousse, or flavored whipped cream. To make the wings, cut the tops in half. Place half of a top on either side of a filled puff, cut side down. Place the head and neck between the wings. Put the swan on a pool of chocolate sauce! Serve.

GÂTEAU SAINT-HONORÉ *Makes 12 servings*

This may seem like an overwhelming recipe to follow. There are three parts to this recipe: pie crust, pudding, and cream puffs. Once you have made each one of these recipes separately, this dessert will no longer be intimidating.

This dessert is best made on a dry, cool day. Serve soon after assembly.

1 single-crust recipe Flaky Pastry (page 183)
1 recipe Cream Puff Paste (page 217)

FILLING:

1 cup light cream
½ cup sugar
Pinch of salt
¼ cup cornstarch
2 eggs
3 egg yolks
1 teaspoon gluten-free vanilla

CARAMELIZED SUGAR TOPPING:

1 cup sugar
¼ cup water
⅛ teaspoon lemon juice

2 to 3 cups fresh fruit, such as strawberries, raspberries, blueberries, sliced peeled peaches, or a combination of these

Preheat the oven to 350°F. Lightly grease a cookie sheet and line with parchment paper.

Roll the pastry out between 2 sheets of floured (with rice flour) parchment paper to a 9-inch round. Place the pastry on the prepared cookie sheet. Bake for 15 to 20 minutes or until golden brown. Transfer to a rack.

Increase the oven temperature to 400°F. Lightly grease 2 cookie sheets and line with parchment paper.

Fit a pastry bag with a large plain nozzle and fill with the cream puff paste. Put the baked pastry round on one of the cookie sheets lined with parchment. Pipe a ring of the cream puff paste about 1 inch in from the edge of the baked pastry's edge. Pipe 8 to 10 cream puffs on the second cookie sheet. Bake each sheet for 20 minutes or until the puffs are done. Cool on a rack.

To make the filling, heat the cream, sugar, and salt in a saucepan. In a bowl, whisk the cornstarch, whole eggs, and egg yolks together. Slowly whisk in some of the hot cream, being careful not to scramble the eggs. Pour the warmed egg mixture into the saucepan. Cook over medium heat, stirring with a wooden spoon, until the custard thickens enough to coat the back of the spoon. Remove from the heat, strain into a clean bowl, and whisk in the vanilla. Cover the surface with plastic wrap and refrigerate.

To assemble, put the pastry round on a plate. Cut off three-quarters of the puff tops and remove any wet dough inside. Fill each puff with the cooled filling. Place the tops back on. Arrange the filled puffs on top of the baked cream puff ring.

To make the caramelized topping, put the sugar, water, and lemon juice in a saucepan and bring to a rapid boil. Without stirring, boil until the sugar begins to turn golden brown. Watch very carefully because it can burn very quickly.

Pour most of the caramelized sugar over the filled puffs. This will hold the puffs in place. Arrange the fresh fruit in the center of the ring. With the remaining caramelized sugar, use the back of 2 spoons to spin sugar over the puffs and the fruit. You do this by dipping both spoons into the sugar and pressing the backs together and then pulling them apart. The more you do this, the more spun sugar you will have. Work quickly because the sugar hardens fast.

SAINT JOSEPH'S CREAM PUFFS *Makes 12 (3-inch) puff*

When I taught this in a gluten-free baking class, one of the students said, "If this is what I can have to eat, then I am glad I am a celiac!"

FILLING:

1 cup gluten-free ricotta cheese
3 tablespoons confectioners' sugar

Enough vegetable oil to fill a saucepan to a depth of 2 to 3 inches
1 recipe Cream Puff Paste (page 217)
Confectioners' sugar for dusting

The day before you plan to make this dessert, place the ricotta in a fine sieve and set it over a bowl. Refrigerate overnight.

To make the filling, put the ricotta in a food processor and blend until smooth. Transfer to a bowl. Add the confectioners' sugar and beat with an electric mixer until fluffy. Refrigerate until ready to fill the puffs.

Preheat the oven to 250°F.

In a saucepan or a deep-fryer, heat 2 to 3 inches of oil to 350°F. Drop the cream puff paste, a teaspoon at a time, into the hot oil. Do not overload the pan or you will have heavy, greasy puffs instead of crisp, light ones. Fry for about 3 minutes, turning the puffs over. Drain on paper towels or a brown paper bag. Keep warm in the oven.

Fit a pastry bag with a small plain nozzle. Fill the bag with the sweetened ricotta. Make a small hole in the bottom of each puff and fill with the ricotta. Dust with confectioners' sugar and serve immediately.

HAZELNUT BONGO BONGO *Makes 12 (3-inch) puffs*

One of the favorite desserts I had while living in Florence, Italy, was Bongo Bongo. Very simply, it is a pile of cream puffs filled with cream or pudding and literally swimming in a thick chocolate sauce.

- 1 double recipe Cream Puff Paste (page 217), made with ¼ cup finely ground lightly toasted hazelnuts added to the batter with the vanilla
- 3 cups heavy cream
- 2 to 3 tablespoon confectioners' sugar
- 3 teaspoons Jell-O white chocolate instant pudding mix
- ⅓ cup lightly toasted finely ground hazelnuts
- Elegant Hot Fudge Sauce (page 151)

Bake the cream puffs as instructed on page 217 and cool.

Whip the cream until it begins to thicken. Sprinkle in the confectioners' sugar and instant pudding. Continue beating until the cream is stiff. Stir in the hazelnuts.

Fit a pastry bag with a medium plain nozzle and fill with the cream. Making a small slit in the bottom of each cream puff, push the nozzle gently into the slit and pipe in some whipped cream. Pile the filled puffs in a large shallow bowl. Pour the fudge sauce over the pile. Serve.

VARIATION Substitute almonds for the hazelnuts in both the cream puffs and the filling.

FILO DOUGH *Makes enough for 2 (8-inch) squares of baklava*

I never thought I would be able to make any of the Middle Eastern foods that use filo dough. One day it dawned on me that filo dough was similar to pasta dough. That is when I began working on creating a dough that would allow me to make baklava, strudel, and other great dishes.

1¾ cups rice flour
¼ cup sweet rice flour
4 teaspoons xanthan gum
1 teaspoon unflavored gelatin
1 egg
¼ to ½ cup milk
1 stick unsalted butter, melted
1 tablespoon honey

Mix together the rice flour, sweet rice flour, xanthan gum, and gelatin. Make a well in the dry ingredients large enough to hold the liquids.

Lightly beat the egg with ¼ cup of the milk, the butter, and the honey. Pour this into the well. Mix everything together until you have a soft dough. Depending upon which brand of rice flour you are using, you may need to stir in more of the milk. Wrap the dough in plastic wrap until you are ready to use it. Store in the refrigerator if not using immediately.

BAKLAVA *Makes 2 (8-inch) square pans of baklava*

Baklava is a Middle Eastern pastry I would not like to live without. Once I figured out how to make a gluten-free filo pastry, I no longer had to worry about never enjoying a piece of baklava again. My Middle Eastern friends were very impressed with my creation. In fact, the consensus was that it was lighter, and it was easy to eat more than one piece at a time. You can halve the recipe or freeze one pan. It also makes a great gift.

This is best made a day ahead. It can be stored at room temperature.

FILLING:

4 cups ground walnuts, almonds, or pistachios
1 cup sugar
1 tablespoon cinnamon

1 recipe Filo Dough (above)
¼ cup light vegetable oil

SYRUP:

1½ cups sugar
¾ cup water
1 tablespoon lemon juice
1 (3-inch) piece cinnamon stick
1 tablespoon honey
1 teaspoon orange flower water

Preheat the oven to 350°F. Lightly grease two 8-inch square baking pans.

Put the nuts, sugar, and cinnamon in a food processor. Pulse until the nuts are ground somewhat fine but still have a little texture.

Cut the filo dough into 6 equal pieces. Keep the pieces not being rolled out covered in plastic wrap. Roll out one piece at a time between 2 sheets of plastic wrap about 16 inches long. Roll the filo as thinly as possible. Remove the top piece of plastic wrap. Carefully fit the dough into one of the pans. The piece should be large enough so that it fits up the sides and hangs over a bit. Roll out a second piece of dough the same way and fit it into the other pan. Sprinkle 1 cup of the ground nuts over the dough in each pan. Roll out 2 more pieces of filo and carefully lay over the filling. Sprinkle another cup of filling over the second layer of each pan. Roll out the last 2 pieces of filo and carefully cover the layer of nuts. Trim the edges that are hanging over the sides of the pan. Leave enough to roll under to form an edge.

Using a sharp paring knife, score the top of the baklava. Cut into 1½-inch-wide strips. Then, starting from one of the corners, cut diagonally to the opposite corner, spacing the cuts 1½ inches apart. This will create a diamond shape, which is a traditional baklava shape. Drizzle 2 tablespoons of oil over the scoring of each baklava. Bake for 30 minutes or until the baklava is golden.

While the baklava is baking, make the syrup. Put the sugar, water, lemon juice, and cinnamon stick in a saucepan and bring to a boil. Simmer for 5 minutes.

Whisk in the honey and the orange flower water. Set aside until the baklava is finished baking.

Once the baklava is baked, slice the scores again, cutting all the way through to the bottom. Use a spoon to drizzle the syrup into the cuts. Cool completely before serving.

PITA *Makes 1 (11 × 7-inch) pan*

Another Greek treat. I love cream of rice and I love baklava. This is a way for me to get both in one bite.

FILLING:

3 cups milk
2 whole eggs
2 egg yolks
½ cup sugar
½ cup cream of rice
1½ teaspoons cinnamon
1 teaspoon gluten-free vanilla
2 tablespoons lemon or orange juice

½ cup coarsely chopped nuts
2 tablespoons sugar
⅛ teaspoon cinnamon

SYRUP:

2 cups sugar
1½ cups water
Juice of ½ lemon
1 small cinnamon stick

3 tablespoons oil
3 tablespoons unsalted butter, melted
½ recipe Filo Dough (page 221)

To make the filling, heat the milk to the scalding point.

Whisk together the eggs, egg yolks, and sugar without producing too much foam. Slowly whisk in some of the hot milk to warm the eggs. Then whisk the warmed eggs into the remaining hot milk in the pan. Over medium heat, using a wooden spoon, stir in figure eights until the foam on top disappears and the mixture thickens slightly. *Do not boil!* Gradually whisk in the cream of rice. Stir and cook over low heat for 4 to 5 minutes. Cover the surface with a piece of buttered plastic wrap. Cool. After the filling has cooled, whisk in the cinnamon, vanilla, and lemon or orange juice.

Mix together the nuts, sugar, and cinnamon. Set aside.

To make the syrup, put the sugar, water, lemon juice, and cinnamon stick in a saucepan and boil for 10 minutes. Cool.

Preheat the oven to 350°F. Lightly grease an 11 × 7-inch baking pan.

To assemble, mix together the oil and melted butter. Roll out half of the filo dough between 2 large pieces of plastic wrap. Make sure it is larger than the pan. Roll the filo as thinly as possible. Remove the top piece of plastic wrap. Carefully fit the dough into the pan. The piece should be large enough so that it fits up the sides and hangs over a bit. Brush the dough with some of the oil and melted butter. Spoon the filling into the pan. Sprinkle the chopped nuts over the filling. Roll out the remaining piece of dough and lay it on top of the nuts. Trim the edges of dough that hang over the sides of the pan. Brush the top of the dough with oil and melted butter. Roll the edges in.

Using a sharp paring knife, score the top of the pita. Cut into 1½-inch-wide strips. Then, starting from one of the corners, cut diagonally to the opposite corner, spacing the cuts 1½ inches apart. This will create a diamond shape. Drizzle the oil and butter over the scoring. Bake for 30 minutes or until the top is golden. Pour the cool syrup over the hot pita.

APPLE STRUDEL *Makes 8 to 10 servings*

I used to love teaching my students how to make strudel using homemade filo dough. We needed at least three students plus myself; it was always an exercise in patience and trust around my oak table as we pulled and stretched that dough until it was as thin as we could get it without tearing it. Never in my wildest dreams did I ever imagine that I would one day figure out how to make a gluten-free filo dough and be able to roll out thin sheets all alone.

FILLING:
- 6 Granny Smith apples, peeled and cut into ½-inch slices
- ⅔ cup sugar
- ¾ teaspoon cinnamon
- 2 teaspoons grated lemon zest

- 1 recipe Filo Dough (page 221)
- ½ stick unsalted butter, melted
- ½ cup ground nuts of your choice
- Cinnamon sugar for dusting

Preheat the oven to 400°F. Place a lightly greased piece of parchment on a jelly roll pan.

Mix all the filling ingredients together in a large bowl and set aside while you roll out the dough.

Roll out half of the filo dough as thin as possible between 2 long pieces of plastic wrap. Remove the top piece of plastic. Brush the dough with some of the melted butter and sprinkle with half of the ground nuts. Roll out the second piece of dough between 2 more pieces of plastic wrap. Remove the plastic and lay the filo on top of the first piece. Brush the dough with melted butter and sprinkle with the remaining ground nuts. Place the apple filling along the edge nearest you. Make a 3-inch-wide strip of filling with a 2-inch edge at both ends. Using the bottom piece of plastic wrap, begin rolling up like a jelly roll. Tuck the ends under. Carefully place the strudel on the prepared jelly roll pan. Brush the top with more melted butter and sprinkle with cinnamon sugar. Bake on the middle rack for 20 minutes or until golden and crisp.

Helpful hint: Once the filo is rolled out, place it and the plastic wrap on the prepared jelly roll pan. Then fill and roll.

VARIATIONS

CHERRY STRUDEL

FILLING:

2 cups dried sour cherries
Juice of 2 navel oranges
3 cups peeled and diced Granny Smith or Mutsu apples
1 cup chopped toasted almonds, pecans, or walnuts
1 cup sugar

NUT MIXTURE:

¼ to ⅓ cup (approximately) ground nuts
1 tablespoon sugar
¼ teaspoon cinnamon
¼ teaspoon ground nutmeg

3 tablespoons melted butter
3 tablespoons oil
Cinnamon sugar for dusting

To make the filling, soak the cherries in the orange juice for 15 minutes. Drain the cherries and then toss them with the diced apples, chopped nuts, and sugar.

To make the nut mixture, mix together the ground nuts, sugar, cinnamon, and nutmeg.

Mix together the melted butter and oil. Have that ready to brush over the filo dough as soon as it is rolled out.

Proceed as for the Apple Strudel.

RHUBARB STRUDEL

FILLING:

1 pound rhubarb, cut into ½-inch pieces
1 cup chopped lightly toasted walnuts
¾ cup sugar
¼ teaspoon cinnamon
Grated zest of 1 orange

3 tablespoons unsalted butter, melted
3 tablespoons vegetable oil
⅓ cup ground gluten-free ginger snaps

To make the filling, mix together the rhubarb, walnuts, sugar, cinnamon, and orange zest.

Mix together the melted butter and oil. Have that ready to brush over the filo dough as soon as it is rolled out. Sprinkle the dough with the ground ginger snaps (instead of cinnamon sugar). Proceed as for the Apple Strudel.

CHEESE STRUDEL

FILLING:

1 pound farmers' cheese
½ pound cream cheese
2 tablespoons sugar
2 teaspoons grated lemon zest
2 egg yolks
1 cup dried cranberries, rinsed in hot water and drained

3 tablespoons unsalted butter, melted
3 tablespoons oil
Gluten-free bread crumbs

To make the filling, by hand, mix together the farmers' cheese, cream cheese, sugar, lemon zest, egg yolks, and cranberries. Do not cream the cheeses.

Mix together the melted butter and oil. Have that ready to brush over the filo dough as soon as it is rolled out. Sprinkle the dough with the gluten-free bread crumbs (instead of cinnamon sugar). Proceed as for the Apple Strudel.

CRÊPES *Makes 16 to 20 crêpes*

When I was a little girl, my mother used to make me crêpes filled with her homemade strawberry jam for breakfast. Crêpes are also a great way to dress up leftovers. Fill them with scrambled eggs and asparagus or sautéed wild mushrooms and grated Gruyère cheese. I remember an elegant dessert served at Lutèce in New York: crêpes filled with a raspberry soufflé and served with crème anglaise and chocolate sauce.

Crêpes can also be flavored with herbs and cut up like fettuccine to go in a clear chicken broth.

3 eggs
1 cup milk
½ cup potato starch
Pinch of salt
2 tablespoons vegetable oil or melted butter

Put the eggs and the milk in a blender or food processor. Blend. Add the potato starch and salt. Blend again. Strain and refrigerate for 20 minutes. When you are ready to make the crêpes, whisk in the oil or melted butter.

Heat a crêpe pan or skillet and lightly spray with cooking oil. Pour a small amount of batter, about 1½ tablespoons, into the pan and swirl it around to coat the bottom of the pan. The amount of batter will depend upon the size of the pan. What is important is to make thin crêpes. Cook over medium heat for about 1 minute. The surface will look dry. Slide a thin flexible spatula under the crêpe and flip it over. Cook the other side for 30 seconds. Slide the crêpe onto a plate and continue until all the batter is used. Before cooking each crêpe, you may need to wipe more oil over the pan bottom.

VARIATION

CHOCOLATE CRÊPES

2 tablespoons unsweetened cocoa powder
½ cup potato starch
½ cup soy flour
3 tablespoons sugar
Pinch of salt
3 eggs
1⅓ cups milk
3 tablespoons vegetable oil or melted unsalted butter

Mix the dry ingredients together. Put the eggs and milk in a blender or food processor. Blend. Add the dry ingredients and blend again. Strain and refrigerate for 20 minutes. When ready to make crêpes, whisk in the oil or melted butter.

CHOCOLATE FETTUCCINE *Makes 6 to 8 servings*

We served this trompe l'oeil dessert at my restaurant, the Madd Apple Café. It is quite simple to make and always delights the diner.

1 recipe Chocolate Crêpes (above)
1 recipe Chocolate Sauce (page 152)
Sweetened softly whipped cream
1 recipe Raspberry Sauce (page 152)
Fresh raspberries

After the crêpes are made and cooled, roll up each crêpe and slice into ¼-inch-wide strips. To assemble the dessert, make a pool of chocolate sauce in the middle of the plate. Place a pile of the chocolate "fettuccine" on top of the sauce. Drizzle more chocolate sauce over the "fettuccine." Nap the pile with some whipped cream. Using a squirt bottle filled with the raspberry sauce, make a design around the plate. You can do the same with some chocolate sauce and then garnish with a few fresh raspberries.

DAIRY-FREE CHOCOLATE BLINTZES *Makes 24 blintzes*

I used to teach a series called "The Joy of Soy." It was always a challenge to win students over to thinking of soy and joy together. This recipe certainly helped.

CHEESE FILLING:

1½ pounds soy cream cheese
½ cup sugar
1 teaspoon gluten-free vanilla
½ teaspoon grated orange zest

24 Chocolate Crêpes (page 227)
3 tablespoons soy margarine, melted
Sliced strawberries
½ cup lightly toasted slivered almonds

To make the cheese filling, blend together the soy cream cheese, sugar, vanilla, and orange zest.

To assemble the blintzes, preheat the oven to 325°F. Line a jelly roll pan with parchment paper. Lightly butter the parchment paper.

Lay the crêpes out on the counter. Fill each crêpe with 2 tablespoons of the filling. Resist overfilling the crêpes; they will puff while baking. Fold the opposite edges to the middle of the filling to create a pillow. Make sure that the filling is closed in tightly. Arrange the blintzes on the jelly roll pan, not touching but close together. Brush the tops with the melted margarine. Bake for 15 minutes or until puffy. Serve 2 per person with some strawberries and a sprinkling of the almonds.

METRIC EQUIVALENCIES 

LIQUID AND DRY MEASURE EQUIVALENCIES

CUSTOMARY	METRIC
¼ teaspoon	1.25 milliliters
½ teaspoon	2.5 milliliters
1 teaspoon	5 milliliters
1 tablespoon	15 milliliters
1 fluid ounce	30 milliliters
¼ cup	60 milliliters
⅓ cup	80 milliliters
½ cup	120 milliliters
1 cup	240 milliliters
1 pint *(2 cups)*	480 milliliters
1 quart *(4 cups, 32 ounces)*	960 milliliters *(.96 liter)*
1 gallon *(4 quarts)*	3.84 liters
1 ounce *(by weight)*	28 grams
¼ pound *(4 ounces)*	114 grams
1 pound *(16 ounces)*	454 grams
2.2 pounds	1 kilogram *(1,000 grams)*

INDEX